THE WAYS WOMEN AGE

CONTENTS

ACKNOWLEDGMENTS

First and foremost, I would like to express my deepest appreciation and gratitude to the women who courageously and generously shared their stories with me. It is these women, their insights, perspectives, experiences, thoughts, and feelings—that inspired and created this book.

My adored and admired grandmothers, Polly Schoyer Brooks and Priscilla Brock Baker, ignited my passion for the subject matter that is this book. My mother, Pebble Baker Brooks, my dear friend, my guide, and my mentor, inspired and sustained me in infinite ways, and in all stages, throughout the writing of this book. I cannot begin to express in words my love and gratitude for my husband and life partner, John E. Rogers, for his boundless love, support, and nurturance for me throughout this years-long process. Both of our children, Cora Rosemary and Thomas Lee Benjamin, were born during different stages of the research and writing of this book and the love, cheer, and refreshment they bring offered just the right balance of grounding and buoying to get me through.

Without John's infinitely generous and loving care of our children, and without being able to continuously depend on the love and caretaking of their amazing grandmothers, it would have been impossible for me to write this book. Thank you to John, and to Mom, and to my lovely mother-in-law, Ailene Rogers, for taking such wonderful care of Cora and Thomas over these many months and years—I am beyond lucky, as they are too.

My father, Turner Brooks, has been unwavering in his love, and instrumental and enthusiastic in his support, throughout the entirety of this project. My sister and brother, Rosie and Ben Brooks, provided constant support, and showered me with love, humor, and compassion from beginning to end.

I am incredibly grateful to Ilene Kalish, Executive Editor at New York University Press, for her steadfast belief in, enthusiasm for, and commitment to this book, and for her invaluable editorial feedback, wisdom, and guidance throughout. I am most appreciative of the excellent feedback I received from my anonymous reviewers. Caelyn Cobb, Assistant Editor at NYU Press, was instrumental in shepherding this book to completion, and generously shared vital expertise and assistance from beginning to end. Managing Editor of Production and Design at NYU Press, Dorothea Stillman Halliday, and her outstanding team, provided exceptional guidance and oversight in the final stages.

I treasure my friendships with Ann Woodruff and Laney Nielson, who tirelessly shared with me their love, insights, confidence, support, and perspectives throughout this long process. My wonderful friend, Leah Schmalzbauer, was incredibly generous with her love, support, and mentorship every step of the way. My friendships with Meika Loe and Deborah Piatelli were instrumental, and much-relied-upon, sources of support, guidance, nurturance, and humor over the course of this long journey. I am also grateful to Kelly Joyce, Patricia Arend, and Aimee Vanwagenen for their encouragement and helpful feedback at various stages of this project. Thanks go, too, to Liz Barragato and Erma Vizenor for their fundamental belief in me, for their nurturance and skilled guidance, and for their clear-eyed vision that proved essential to my moving forward.

Stephen Pfohl, I thank you for believing in this project from the beginning to end, for your inspiring and brilliant teaching and scholarship, for your unwavering support, invaluable feedback, and guidance, and for your friendship. Juliet Schor, I thank you for the instrumental insights, advice, and wisdom you provided me in crucial stages of this project, for teaching me to be a better writer, and for your continuing and most generous mentorship. David Karp, I thank you for being an inspiration to me as a teacher, way back when I was a TA for your Introduction to Sociology class, for your invaluable feedback and support, and for your scholarship, the epitome of exemplary qualitative research. I would also like to thank Diane Vaughan and Arthur Kroker, who provided pivotal encouragement in the very early stages of this project, and Sharlene Hesse-Biber, who provided excellent feedback at various stages, as well. I am grateful, too, to Margaret Morganroth Gullette, for her interest in my work, for her insights and feedback, and for her own inspiring and path-breaking work as a feminist age studies scholar.

I am very lucky to call Providence College my institutional home, and I am grateful for my wonderful colleagues and friends in the Sociology Department, and in the Women's Studies Program, here. Maureen Outlaw and Charlotte O'Kelly, of the Sociology Department and the Women's Studies Program, and Eric Hirsch and Cedric de Leon, of the Sociology Department, have been especially supportive. My heartfelt thanks to the first and founding members of the Providence College Women's Studies Program whom I have had the honor of working with: Jane Lunin Perel, Mary Anne Sedney, Deborah Johnson, Wendy Oliver, Carmen Rolon, and again, Charlotte O'Kelly—to each of you, I remain infinitively appreciative of your support, wisdom, guidance, and friendship.

I thank the Director of the Black Studies Program, and my colleague in women's studies, Julia Jordan-Zachery, for her invaluable advice and encouragement. I am also indebted to my colleague in women's studies, Gloria-Jean Masciarotte, for her inspiration, much-relied-upon knowledge and expertise, and for her friendship. Enthusiastic thanks also go to women's studies faculty Mary Bellhouse, Elizabeth Bridgham, Jennifer Illuzzi, Jessica Mulligan, and Tuire Valkeakari; to Professor Emerita, Jo-Anne Ruggiero; and to Tuba Agartan and Deborah Levine. Cindy Walker of the Women's Studies Program remains a treasured and essential source of expertise, assistance, support, and friendship. I thank Marcia Battle, of the Sociology Department, for her compassion, humor, and friendship. I am grateful to Beth Macleer, of O'Neill Library at Boston College, and Julie de Cesare and Mark Caprio, of Phillips Memorial Library at Providence College, for their research support and assistance. I am an incredibly appreciative recipient of the Providence College pretenure, one-semester, research leave.

Last but not least, I would like to thank my students in both sociology and women's studies—first, at Boston College, and now, at Providence College—for their inspiration, enthusiasm, and invigorating relationships of mutual learning and critical thinking. I never cease to be energized by my students—both inside and outside of the classroom—and my relationships with current students, and with former students well after graduation and into their rich, varied, and important post-college pursuits, provide me an endless source of joy and inspiration.

My sister, brother, and I would push ourselves, walking speedily along the hilly dirt road that led to our house, after being dropped off by the school bus onto another, more major, dirt road in the valley below. If we were lucky, we would make it home in time to watch the last few minutes of *Guiding Light*, a soap opera that offered us a riveting story line about a young woman, her evil stepfather, and the young man who would ultimately rescue her after disentangling himself from another woman's grasp. Growing up in rural Vermont offered many more charms for us than watching soap operas. In fact, for years we had no television at all, until we started borrowing a small black-and-white TV each winter from some friends who "summered" nearby. Even then, our parents strictly limited our television viewing to a handful of evening shows per week. And yet, on those wintery afternoons, huddled around the television and hoping our mother didn't return home from work soon enough to make us turn it off, my long-enduring fascination with soap operas began.

Many years later, I was in graduate school and found myself, for the first time in a long time, spending time at home in the middle of the day. It was too tempting for me not to turn on the television (only as a reward and a break from my studies, of course!) to get reacquainted with my favorite soaps after all these years. The year was 2002, and, while twenty years had passed, many of the story lines and actors remained the same. Most eerie of all, for me, however, was the fact that many of the faces of the female actors appeared unchanged and unmarked by the passing of time and years lived. Actresses who had played the roles of young women twenty years earlier were now embodying characters who were mothers, and even grandmothers. Life evolved and changed over time for these actresses and the characters they played, but their faces did not evolve and change to reflect their accumulated life experience. I found it difficult to decipher, on the grounds of physical appearance alone, who was the mother and who was the daughter, or who was the grandmother and who was the mother. Most grandmothers, mothers, and daughters had smooth skin and few wrinkles and nearly no other indicators of aging: actresses all appeared to be of a similar age, despite empirically real chronological age differences between them.

I also was viscerally disturbed by the lack of movement in the faces of many of the actresses I remembered from my childhood. The range of facial movements, both subtle and dramatic, and the complexity of expression of thoughts and feelings that can play out on the face—these capacities appeared reduced among the middle-aged and older actresses who clearly subscribed to cosmetic anti-aging procedures. I found myself listening harder for sounds and language that would communicate their thoughts and feelings, and watching for tears, a telltale sign of emotion, to fill in the gaps left by faces less capable of expression. Perhaps my own close relationship with my grandmothers, each of whom were beautiful inside and out to me—and whose faces were lovely medium for communicating past and present experiences and emotions—was at the heart of my distress at these ageless faces. My mother, too, my dearest friend and mentor, and my frame of reference for most things, provided me a model for growing older I hoped to emulate, and one largely absent from the soap opera landscape.

Yet, beyond my personal responses to these ageless faces, my mind filled with questions about the social and political implications for women and aging and, even more broadly, for gender equality in contemporary American culture. In the early 2000s, soap operas still held sway as one of the most popular genres of television programming in the United States. Soap opera viewership was impressive in its representation of everyday American women—inclusive of racial and class diversity—many of whom tuned in to watch their favorite soaps.[1] Soap operas were a touchstone of popular culture, with soap opera characters and story lines often offering a familiar conversation starter or shared knowledge source for many.[2] What did it mean, I wondered, that so many American women were continuously exposed to these female actors and characters—actors and characters they had come to know and care about over the years—most of whom showed very few visible signs of aging on their faces over time?

What began, initially, as a guilty indulgence and a distraction from my graduate work soon became the focus of my research. I investigated common representations of older women in soap operas and other popular media. I analyzed mainstream media coverage and advertising of cosmetic surgeries and technologies designed to reduce visible signs of aging, nearly all of which targeted women. I discovered that direct-to-consumer advertising of cosmetic procedures had just begun, and that more Americans than ever before were having them. And then, I started to talk to women themselves about aging and identity, and to listen to what they had to say about growing older in a youth-focused culture saturated with cosmetic anti-aging products. It is the voices of these women that inspired this book.

Throughout the course of my research, and with the passage of time, I have witnessed and experienced cultural and personal changes connected to the subject of women and aging. The genre of the traditional daytime soap opera has not disappeared entirely, but its dominance has been eclipsed by reality TV.[3] Television viewing habits and styles are changing. Watching weekly and daily episodes of shows at predetermined times is less common in light of "on demand" technologies, like streaming via Netflix, Apple TV, and Amazon. Traditional mainstream networks are losing some of their popularity due to the explosion of new cable stations and programming. Televisions—flat screen or no—are now just one of many viewing medium as Americans turn to their laptops, iPads, and even their phones, to watch their favorite shows.

Some shared cultural experiences and reference points may be eroding as a result of these changes in media technologies. Yet, as the women in this book make clear, the common cultural expectation of a youthful appearance for women, and the media as a prime site of transmission for this expectation, is stronger than ever. In fact, many Americans now live lives of near-to-constant interaction with media—social media, entertainment media, or otherwise—via cell phone, laptop, or television screen.

When I first started this research, I was young enough not to have encountered many changes in my physical appearance. I set out to talk to women who were significantly older than myself, and I learned a great deal from what women had to say, both about why they were choosing to have and use cosmetic surgeries and technologies to combat changes in their appearance due to aging, and why they were choosing to grow older without them. As I continued interviewing women, and as I began transcribing and analyzing the interview material, and, ultimately, writing this book, I had grown old enough to witness age-driven changes in my own physical appearance, and to experience changes in how others responded to me as a result. Now in my forties, I am able to more personally connect to the feelings of alienation and frustration expressed by most women in this book as they confront age-driven changes in their faces and bodies. I can directly empathize with the pain in invisibility that many shared with me in light of no longer being perceived as sexually desirable, and no longer attracting and holding the admiring gaze of others. Like many of the women in this book, I am struggling to define and redefine myself, working out who I was and who I am, as I witness signs of aging on the surface of my body. But I am also enjoying this process of renegotiating the relationship between my body and my sense of self. I am enjoying the freedom I feel from worrying too much about how I look, and the freedom from that uncomfortable, self-conscious feeling I would get sometimes when I was being "checked out" by others. I am experiencing and enjoying an age-driven freedom from some of the pressures, expectations, and unfair stereotypes that confront young women in our culture whom various others deem physically attractive.

As I myself grow older, I continue to find wisdom, knowledge, and inspiration from the women in this book. They offer rich and varied perspectives, not only on the personal experience of aging for women, but also on the connection between personal experience and the larger social, cultural, and economic landscape in which we all live. It is my hope that you, the readers of this book, will find these women's stories as compelling, insightful, and useful as I do.

Introduction

Older Women in Cosmetic Culture

"Once you get it, you really get it." A woman—it is hard to tell just how old she is, but that is part of the point—smiles out at us from a face remarkably free of frown and laugh lines, a convincing example of "why millions of women have experienced Botox Cosmetic."[1] This Botox advertising slogan offers a window into rapidly changing cultural attitudes and expectations of females aging in the United States. Over the past several decades, profit-based medicine has merged with technological innovation to produce a dizzying array of cosmetic anti-aging products. Direct-to-consumer pharmaceutical advertising, combined with the fast-track approval process for new pharmaceutical drugs, means that older women's faces and bodies are increasingly targeted as profitable sites for surgical and technological intervention. Images and words—in print and digital media and advertising, in the waiting rooms of primary care physicians and gynecologists, and in shopping malls—saturate women with new opportunities to mold their aging faces and bodies in compliance with the cultural imperative of a youthful appearance. Not all women partake of cosmetic anti-aging products and procedures, yet their exposure to them is almost inevitable. What is it like to be a woman growing older in a culture where you cannot go to the doctor's, open a magazine, watch television, or go online without being confronted with information about the latest cosmetic anti-aging surgeries and technologies?

"Once you get it, you really get it." Enlightened women, rational women, women with common sense, or so the increasingly prevalent cultural narrative goes, are those who battle age-driven changes in their physical appearance with technology. Women are the overwhelming consumers of cosmetic anti-aging products and procedures in the United States today. Since 1997, when the American Society for Aesthetic

1

Plastic Surgery first began keeping statistics on cosmetic procedures, women's consumption of cosmetic surgeries and technologies has consistently surpassed men's at a rate of approximately 10 to 1. In 2015, a typical year, women had more than 11.5 million, or just over 90%, of the more than 12 million surgical and nonsurgical cosmetic procedures performed, and procedures specifically designed to reduce and minimize aesthetic signs of aging on the face and body toped the charts.[2]

The Normalization of Cosmetic Intervention

Cosmetic surgeries and technologies are on the rise around the globe. Mostly women, but men too, are having cosmetic procedures in growing numbers in countries in Latin America, Asia, Europe, and the Middle East. Brazil actually beats out the United States by a hair as the nation with the highest numbers of plastic surgeries performed.[3] Nation-state histories, economic and political structures, and cultural contexts—including social mores and hierarchies, and material inequalities along race, class, and gender lines—inform what procedures are most popular where and why. Cosmetic surgery scholars call attention to the ways in which popular cosmetic procedures in different nation-states connote social status and consumer power complicated by racism, sexism, and classism.[4] The rapidly expanding transnational market for skin whitening technologies in parts of the United States, and in different nation states in Asia, Africa, and Latin America, is but one example of how specific cosmetic technologies can reflect and (re)produce the desire to accentuate and celebrate features associated with a particular ethnicity or to minimize and erase characteristics read as ethnic markers of inferiority.[5] The cosmetic surgery tourism industry, wherein consumers traverse nation-state boundaries to seek anonymity and cheaper procedures, is booming.[6]

The current practice of cosmetic intervention in the United States reflects its own unique history, economy, and culture of classism, sexism, racism, and ageism. To learn about the evolution of rhinoplasty in the United States, for instance, is to confront racist ideologies head-on.[7] Today, the cosmetic surgery industry in the United States continues to be dominated by white consumers.[8] Cosmetic surgery scholars call attention to troubling trends among non-white cosmetic

surgery patients, and their doctors, to consume and promote procedures that create Caucasian-looking faces and bodies. On the other
hand, women of diverse racial and ethnic backgrounds also point to
their cosmetic procedures as celebrations of their unique racial and
ethnic identities and heritage.[9] Recent research centered on personal
narratives of Asian American and African American women who have
had procedures that can be read as making their features look more
Caucasian—like double eyelid surgeries, nose-bridge surgeries, and
nose-thinning surgeries—reveal personal expressions of individual
freedom, autonomy, and empowerment in light of the decision to have
these procedures.[10]

Women provide the lion's share of profit for the American cosmetic
surgery industry today. Current statistics also suggest, however, that
white women, ages thirty-five and older, are particularly lucrative consumers.[11] This book centers on these women and their intersecting stories about aging, gender, and the cosmetic-anti-aging explosion. The
women whose stories are showcased throughout this book are nearly
all white, though their material resources, biographical histories, and
current life circumstances vary widely (single, married, divorced, working, retired, unemployed, economically secure, economically struggling). Before I deepen and sharpen the gender and aging lens that is
this book, however, I must finish setting the stage for what has become
an increasingly popular and normalized practice in the United States
today.

More than half of Americans (51%) now approve of cosmetic plastic
surgery, regardless of income, and 67% of Americans say that they would
not be embarrassed if their family or friends knew they had cosmetic
surgery.[12] The rise of cosmetic intervention in the United States today
reflects long-entrenched and newly evolving inequalities tied to race,
class, gender, and aging. This rise also has historical roots, however, in
the transformative structural processes of industrialization and urban-
ization in late nineteenth- and early twentieth-century America and,
more recently, in the deregulation of American medicine. The latter, initiated in the late 1970s, and expanded throughout the 1980s and 1990s,
culminated in the commercialized system of medicine in place in the
United States today. Finally, the skyrocketing acceptance and approval
of cosmetic intervention in the United States in recent years reflects new

and changing perspectives on health and illness, body and identity, and builds on the emergence of mass media throughout the twentieth century, and the fast-paced evolution of new visual technologies today.[13]

Commercialized Medicine and Medical Marketing

When I was watching too much TV in the early 2000s, and beginning to notice that the faces of my favorite female soap opera stars appeared untouched by signs of aging despite their increasing chronological ages, I was disturbed, too, by something else. For the first time, it seemed to me, I was watching advertisements, often long in duration and filled with compelling first person narratives and visuals, that encouraged me, with authoritative and commanding tone and language, to seek medical treatment for symptoms, conditions, and syndromes that I often did not recognize, nor had heard of, before. These advertisements *were* new, I came to realize a short time later, and, as part of the new paradigm of commercialized medicine in the United States, they were not entirely unrelated to those ageless soap opera faces, either.

Many of us have already forgotten that we weren't always bombarded with advertisements for new pharmaceutical drugs and medical products and procedures. In fact, the commercialization of medicine in the United States is a recent phenomenon. A series of Federal Trade Commission mandates from the late 1970s until the late 1990s, and upheld by the Supreme Court, resulted in the de-regulation and privatization of American medicine and the American pharmaceutical industry. The regulatory power of the American Medical Association, including its ban on direct-to-consumer advertising, was eclipsed and the resources, funding, and regulatory capacity of the Food and Drug Administration were similarly eroded. A new fast-track approval process for pharmaceutical drugs was approved by congress in the early 1990s, and direct-to-consumer advertising of pharmaceuticals began in 1997.[14]

Today, we encounter a market-based model of American medicine. Profit clearly and significantly informs medical practice. Media coverage, advertisements, and marketing for medical and pharmaceutical products and procedures often devote as much, or more, language, imagery, and air time to introducing and naming symptoms, disorders, conditions, and illnesses as to the products themselves. "Medical marketing" is the new catch phrase in American medicine, with a plethora of consulting firms and print and online journals—including the *Journal of Medical Marketing* and *Medical Marketing and Media*—dedicated to the subject. As Americans we are constantly confronted with advertisements for new drugs to treat and improve a multitude of symptoms and conditions, mental and physical, some of which we may not have even known existed. Take, for example, a sampling of only six recent issues of *People* magazine. By perusing the pages—and it is not uncommon for one issue of *People* to have four, five, even six pharmaceutical advertisements—I am exposed to a multitude of medical conditions and the drugs and products to treat them. I learn about Juvaderm to treat lost "volume and sag" in the face that comes with age, Linzess to treat "irritable bowl syndrome with constipation," Stelara to treat "plaque psoriasis," Pristiq and Abilify for "depression" and Latuda for "bipolar depression," Vysera-CLS to "reshape your body," Botox for "moderate to severe frown lines between the brows and moderate to severe crows feet in adults," Belviq for "weight-loss," Premarin for "hot flashes," Estring for "pain during intercourse after menopause," Lyrica for "over-active nerves," hormone growth therapy for "getting rid of wrinkles and tightening saggy skin," and plenty of other conditions and their corresponding treatments.[15] The benefits of many of these new drugs and treatments coming to market not withstanding, the new commercialized paradigm of American medicine also introduces troubling questions. As pharmaceutical companies and other private industries increasingly determine medical research agendas, design and fund medical research and clinical drug trials, and become a primary source of education about health and illness for physicians and for the general public, we find too many examples of drugs and treatments coming to market prematurely, without adequate testing and thorough review, and at potential cost to human health and even to human lives.[16] Today, nearly three in five Americans take prescription drugs.[17] Some of these drugs may be developed to treat unarguably serious medical conditions, like heart disease, while others may be proscribed to "treat" phenomena not previously understood as medical conditions at all. Addiction to pharmaceutical drugs, accidental deaths from pharmaceutical drug overdoses, or from a lethal combination of pharmaceutical drugs, is on the rise.[18] Forty-four Americans die everyday from an overdose of prescription painkillers.[19] The Centers for Disease Control and Prevention now classifies pharmaceutical drug abuse in the United States as an epidemic.[20]

The Medicalization of Aging and Aesthetics

In our new commercialized paradigm of American medicine, pharmaceutical drugs designed to treat normal bodily phenomena flood the medical marketplace, even as many Americans struggle to afford the drugs they need to treat serious and life-threatening medical conditions. We need more research and resources to be channeled into the treatment of serious illnesses, and to make those treatments affordable. But, as critic Ray Moynihan and others have pointed out, transforming routine bodily processes into conditions in need of medical treatment is a profitable practice.[21] Take common aspects of aging, for instance. Everybody ages, and, therefore, everyone becomes a prospective consumer of new medical drugs, products, and procedures to "treat" age-related "symptoms." Menopause—a normal component of aging for almost all women—offers a powerful example. Women's attitudes, interpretations, and emotional and physical experiences of menopause vary in concert with diverse racial and cultural identities, sexual orientations, and nation state settings.[22] Still, many women experience menopause as a largely unremarkable experience—15% of women barely notice it— and, if women do encounter challenging physical manifestations, they often go away on their own over time.[23] In the United States, however, menopause continues to be aggressively marketed and advertised as a "deficiency disease" with "symptoms" that require medical intervention.[24] In the late 1990s and early 2000s, and on the recommendation of their primary care doctors, thousands of American women began taking synthetic estrogen, progestin, or a combination of the two, commonly known as hormone replacement therapy (HRT). Branded by several different pharmaceutical companies, hormone replacement therapy remains highly profitable, aggressively marketed, and commonly prescribed for menopausal women in the United States today. Savvy advertising campaigns for drugs like Osphena, Premarin, Estring, and Duavee proliferate even as evidence of the risks of adverse health effects—including heart disease and breast cancer—accumulates.[25] The overwhelming popularity of the pharmaceutical drug Viagra offers another successful case study in the transformation of what was largely perceived as a natural, everyday aspect of aging into a "dysfunctional" condition in need of medical treatment. Men, as they grow older, commonly experience a less firm penis with arousal, and longer time spans between arousal and ejaculation. Yet, in the late 1990s and early 2000s, this normal component of aging for many men was reconceptualized and redefined as a medical condition in need of repair. Erectile dysfunction, or "ED," and several pharmaceutical drugs to treat it, including Viagra, Levitra, and Cialis, continue to be widely advertised, marketed, and prescribed today.[26]

The American cosmetic surgery industry, a prime beneficiary of commercialized medicine, is a leader in medical marketing. Nearly every aspect of physical appearance has been re-conceptualized into a flaw or defect in need of cosmetic intervention. Everything from age-related changes like wrinkles and balding, to normal size and shape diversity in noses, eyes, breasts, and vaginas, have been redefined as flaws or abnormalities in need of repair and placed within a framework of medical language and expertise alongside the treatments and procedures designed to "improve" and "fix" them.[27] We learn about our aesthetic flaws and abnormalities, and their needed treatments, through prevalent and savvy advertising and marketing campaigns on television, online, in magazines and newspapers, and in our own doctors' offices.

Cosmetic intervention is quickly becoming one of the most lucrative areas of medicine in the United States today, not just for cosmetic surgeons and dermatologists, but for gynecologists and primary care physicians, as well.[28] The medicalization of normal and natural diversity in physical appearance brings with it not only an exponential increase in the numbers of prospective consumers in "need" of cosmetic procedures, but also increased authority, legitimacy, and weight to the practice of cosmetic intervention.[29] When cosmetic procedures are marketed and advertised by institutions and practitioners of medicine, and as women learn about new cosmetic options from their gynecologists and primary care physicians, the concept of cosmetic intervention itself gains broader cultural acceptance and approval. In fact, as more of our physical characteristics are incorporated into a medical paradigm of defects and deviations from the norm, it becomes increasingly *healthful* to do something to fix them.[30] Cosmetic intervention itself—as the recommended treatment for these deviations—increasingly signifies mental and physical health and wellness. The language and imagery of health, fitness, and self-care permeates marketing and advertising campaigns for cosmetic procedures. In brochures and posters in the waiting rooms and exam rooms at doctor's offices, and in television, in print, and online, we are confronted with medical professionals in white coats accompanied by slogans like "Call 1–800-Botox-MD." Cosmetic intervention is frequently touted as a healthful approach to life in women's fashion magazines. Features in *Vogue* and *Harper's Bazaar* describe new procedures that "get your skin in shape, just like going to the gym does for your body" and equate new technologies with "a cardio for your face." Micro-lipo is recommended for people who have been working out for a year but "still cannot lose the fat": "The solution is modest lipo, true body sculpting used as an add-on to a healthy lifestyle." Dermaplaning treatments produce a "rosy glow." As one woman exclaims: "Nothing has made my skin glow quite like this!"[31]

Me, Myself, and I: American Individualism, Pragmatism, and Consumerism

In historian Elizabeth Haiken's account of the rise of cosmetic surgery in the United States throughout the twentieth century, American individualism repeatedly surfaces as an ideology most receptive to cosmetic intervention.[32] The "self-made," "pull yourself up by your bootstraps," mentality, the expectation of individual problem solving, personal responsibility, and practical action in the face of adversity, and finally, the celebration of self-esteem, self-confidence, self-expression and the uniqueness of the self—each of these aspects of American individualism compliment the practice of cosmetic intervention as a means to "reinvent" the self in multiple ways. In the early twentieth century, and throughout the World War I and depression years, plastic surgeons couched their work in terms of improving individuals' chances for societal acceptance and economic survival. They repaired and fixed war-caused physical "deformities" to improve veterans' chances of reintegration into society, and they made individuals more "physically attractive" to improve their chances of finding and keeping a job. In the 1930s, when the practice of psychology was growing in popularity in the

United States, plastic surgeons began to frame cosmetic intervention as a positive tool for improving self-confidence and self-esteem. Austrian psychologist Alfred Adler's concept of the "inferiority complex," particularly influential here in America, proved useful for plastic and cosmetic surgeons as they touted cosmetic intervention as means to overcome it.[33] In each of these eras, improving the self through cosmetic intervention meant bettering one's life chances of happiness, economic success, and social acceptance. According to Elizabeth Haiken, to study the history of cosmetic surgery in the United States is also to study the unwavering American tendency to "individualize social problems of inequality," and to be reminded of Americans' overwhelming "belief that the only practical solution is the individual one."[34]

Today, cosmetic intervention continues to be framed as means to improve self-confidence, self-esteem, social acceptance, and to achieve economic success, and even economic survival. This individualized formula for success and fulfillment—cosmetic intervention equals improved physical appearance, equals improved self, equals improved life—features prominently in current marketing and advertising campaigns for cosmetic surgeries and technologies, and in first person narrative accounts of cosmetic intervention in print and online media. Phrases and headlines that communicate individual responsibility and practical action, a can-do, problem-solving approach to life, and increased confidence and self-esteem are common. For example: "Some people never do anything about it—and some people go for it," or "I'm an independent type—no one tells me what to do," or "I feel like I can do anything—I took control."[35] Advertisements for the new injectable, Dysport, command women to stand up to wrinkles—"Take charge of your frown lines"—and warn that failing to do so risks losing the real you: "Don't surrender to a look that's not you."[36] This theme of authentic self-expression, as well as more playful equations between cosmetic intervention, and individual freedom and creativity, populate advertisements for Botox, too. "It's all about freedom of expression . . . Ask your doctor about Botox Cosmetic. Don't hold back! Express yourself by asking your doctor about Botox Cosmetic. Millions of women already have," proclaims one recent ad.[37] Another challenges women to reinvent themselves by taking Botox: "REIMAGINE: It's time to take a closer look."[38]

Portrayals of cosmetic intervention as an unnecessary, but welcome, self-indulgence or treat also permeate current media coverage and advertising campaigns for cosmetic surgery. Historians and sociologists have traced the origins of this positive spin on consuming for the self to the post–World War II economic boom years. The post-war years, which marked the demise of industrial capitalism in the United States in the mid-twentieth century, and the rise of consumer culture that continues today, offered a welcome atmosphere for plastic surgeons to promote cosmetic surgery as luxury item beyond absolute need. New technologies and surgical techniques, and the advent of antibiotics, known as the "wonder drugs," also helped to demystify cosmetic procedures and made it easier for surgeons to sell cosmetic intervention as a modern amenity for purchase. Today, in our era of celebrity culture, social media, and reality television, consuming for the self and showing it off to everyone—conspicuous consumption—is cooler than ever. And new, ever more user-friendly cosmetic technologies and procedures like injectables and fillers—much less painful, less expensive, and less time-intensive than surgery—make "treating" yourself a whole lot easier.

Celebrating Science, Technology, and Medicine

The recent commercialization of American medicine, combined with American individualist ideology, and a culture of conspicuous consumption, produce a friendly social and economic landscape for the expansion of cosmetic surgeries and technologies in the United States today. Americans' reverence for technology—part and parcel of our pride in our nation's contributions to the fields of science and medicine—also contributes to the increasing normalization of cosmetic intervention. The language of science, medicine, and technology commonly converges in current media coverage and marketing and advertising campaigns for cosmetic procedures. In my own investigation into early and mid-2000s media coverage and advertising of cosmetic surgery in *Vogue*, *Harper's Bazaar*, *People*, and *US Weekly*, cosmetic procedures were consistently placed within a positive narrative frame of new technology. Cosmetic procedures were favorably equated with feats in scientific discovery and technological innovation and doctors were described as using "wand-like devices." Articles with titles like "Artificial Intelligence" and "Face

Forward" featured ebullient patients proclaiming things like "I saw my chins disappear! The fat dissolved in front of my eyes!" and "As it turns out you *can* fool Mother Nature! She's not that bright." Botox advertising slogans proclaimed: "It's Not Magic, It's Botox Cosmetic."[39] Consumers of cosmetic intervention were celebrated for their boldness, risk-taking, and experimentation ("When people ask, 'Aren't you afraid of having a foreign substance injected into your body?,' I invariably answer, 'Which one?'") and for their fearless embrace of the future ("The future is here!").[40]

On the one hand, media and advertising commonly present cosmetic intervention as uncharted and new terrain traversed by courageous risk takers; on the other hand, new technology means less invasive and more accessible cosmetic procedures. Technological, scientific, and pharmaceutical innovation produces cosmetic procedures that are increasingly less painful, less time-consuming, and, in some cases, less of a risk to physical health and safety, and even less expensive. These technology-driven, friendly attributes of new cosmetic procedures are also a common and positive refrain in media coverage and advertising for cosmetic anti-aging intervention. "It took forty years to get it. And ten minutes to do something about it," a Botox advertisement entices.[41] "I injected freshness and life into my face with less time and effort than a visit to the hairdresser!" proclaims the writer of a *Harper's Bazaar* feature, referring to her Perlane injections.[42] "Rush Hour: Laser Facials, Light Therapy— and even Botox—in a Flash" boasts a *Vogue* feature about the newest "in-and-out" beauty trend: speed spas. At speed spa "Skin Laundry," for instance, you can get ten-minute laser facials and enjoy a full range of injectables, including Restylane and Sculptra, at the "Botox Bar."[43] Whether the procedure is risky and experimental, or more accessible and user-friendly, understanding cosmetic intervention as new technology means understanding cosmetic intervention as evidence of scientific progress and technological innovation, two touchstones of American cultural pride and identity.

It's All about the Body

SOCIAL FRAGMENTATION AND THE BODY

Pervasive individualism and consumerism, combined with a cultural reverence for new advancements in technology and medicine, create a welcome environment for the growth of the cosmetic surgery industry in the United States. Implicit, or perhaps better put, explicit, in each of these interrelated currents is an overwhelming focus on the body. According to historians, literary critics, and social theorists alike, we are living in a somatic society wherein the body is increasingly conflated with the self.[44] This "growing tightening of the relationship between body and self-identity," as sociologist Chris Shilling puts it, has been traced back to the late nineteenth-century and early twentieth-century processes of industrialization in the United States and Europe, and is attributed to resultant and prevalent trends of geographic transience and social fragmentation throughout the twentieth century and into present day.[45] As people disperse and become more geographically mobile, and as they move from agrarian communities into more densely populated urban settings, identity formation becomes increasingly privatized and individualized, and less rooted in shared systems of meaning outside the self. Historian Elizabeth Haiken sums up the first American wave of this transformation from communal to individual identity as follows:

> Early in the twentieth century, the interrelated processes of industrialization, urbanization, and immigration and migration transformed the United States from a predominantly rural culture, in which identity was firmly grounded in family and locale, to a predominantly urban culture, in which identity derives from 'personality' or self-presentation.[46]

With this shift in the roots and ingredients of identity formation from the community to the individual, the body achieves greater prominence as a marker of identity and as a vehicle for self-expression. Or, as sociologists of the body explain, when meaning becomes more privatized, people seek meaning at the individual (private) level: through their bodies.

THE MALLEABLE BODY

Social theorist Anthony Giddens, among others, argues that the tightening bond between the body and self-identity in the industrialized West throughout the twentieth century and into the twenty-first is accompanied by an increasing perception of the body itself as malleable and transformable. As individuals invest more in the body as constitutive of self-identity, they also become more responsible for the design of their bodies: their bodies become their own "identity projects."[47] Advancements in technological, surgical, and pharmaceutical products and procedures—directly advertised and marketed to consumers—offer new means to change and reshape the body and fuel Americans' propensity for bodily intervention. These advancements—ever more accessible and available—can also contribute to the expectation that individuals *use* these advancements to "manage" their own bodies effectively.

VISUAL TECHNOLOGIES AND THE TWO-DIMENSIONAL BODY

Living in an increasingly somatic society has come to mean that the body provides a primary marker for the self and self-identity, and that we understand our bodies as our own malleable identity projects. Even further, we are experiencing a notable strengthening of the relationship between identity, self-worth, and the *exterior of the body*. According to cosmetic surgery scholar, Virginia Blum, we are living in an era wherein we "cannot help but locate who we are on the surface of our bodies."[48] Many argue that this preoccupation with the exterior of our bodies—or what Blum calls the "lure of the two-dimensional"—directly reflects our increasingly media and screen-saturated culture. Beginning with the advent and explosion of mass media throughout the twentieth century— film, billboards, and television—and continuing into our near-constant interaction with digital screens today, Americans' daily social realities are increasingly lived out in a two-dimensional realm. As we confront and communicate with two-dimensional images via mobile phone, tablet, laptop, and television, we may be more likely to understand ourselves through a two-dimensional lens and to conflate ourselves with our bodily exteriors. The current celebrity-inspired "selfie" explosion, wherein Americans spend lots of time taking, posting, and looking at pictures of themselves and others on social media via phones, tablets, and laptops, bespeaks a culture that privileges the two-dimensional image as a tool for self-expression and for evaluating the self and others. The rise of cosmetic intervention in the United States today offers more evidence of the growing importance of the exterior of the body—of how the body looks—as a route for achieving self worth and social value.

A Gendered Tale

Heath, fitness, and self-care . . . self-confidence, self-esteem, self-assurance, self-expression . . . rationality, practicality, and common sense . . . bravery and courage . . . future-embracing, forward-looking, risk-taking . . . This is by no means an exhaustive list of the positive characteristics equated with cosmetic surgeries and technologies and attributed to those who have and use them. The overwhelmingly positive framing of cosmetic intervention in American media and advertising, and the growing popularity of cosmetic procedures, must be understood within new and more established trends in American culture, ideology, society, and economy. Commercialized medicine, consumerism, social fragmentation and individualism, science and technology, television, the internet, social media, personal electronic devices, an overwhelming focus on the body—each of these commonly intertwined phenomena contribute to the rise of cosmetic intervention. Yet, it is impossible to achieve a comprehensive explanation of the rising popularity of cosmetic intervention in the United States today without talking about women and the gendered expectations, norms, and narratives that continue to inform women's roles and value in contemporary American society. Women are the overwhelming consumers of cosmetic products and procedures in the United States today. Without women, the cosmetic surgery industry would lose its foundation. Gone would be its consumer- and profit-base and gone would be the cultural assumptions, expectations, and rationales upon which the vast majority of marketing and advertising campaigns for cosmetic intervention are built.

Women have made great strides towards social, economic, and political equality with men in the United States, particularly in the eras of first- and second-wave feminism, in the early and later years of the twentieth century, respectively. Most recent legislative gains have addressed the ongoing realities of sexual harassment, violence against women, and gendered inequality in the workplace. Women continue to outnumber men as applicants and students, and to outperform male students academically, at most colleges in the United States. Female applicants and students are nearing parity with, and even outpacing and outnumbering, their male counterparts in graduate schools for traditionally male-dominated professions including law and medicine.[49] Elite colleges like Brown, Harvard, Princeton, the University of Pennsylvania, and the University of Virginia now have, or have recently had, female presidents. In the United States, Loretta Lynch is the first African American woman to hold the position of Attorney General; Susan E. Rice is National Security Advisor to the President; and Janet Yellen serves as the first chairwoman of the Federal Reserve. The U.S. recently had its first female Speaker of the House of Representatives in Nancy Pelosi and, in the last nine years, the country has seen two female Secretary of States, Condoleezza Rice and Hillary Clinton, respectively. Sarah Palin served as running mate to Republican nominee John McCain in the 2008 presidential race. Carly Fiorina was in the pool of presidential contenders at the 2016 Republican Convention. Hillary Clinton, now the official Democratic nominee for president, is poised to potentially become the first woman ever elected to the American presidency on November 8, 2016.

The rising representation of women in key arenas of power and decision-making in the United States today—and the prospect of our first female president ever—brings exciting and hopeful implications for greater gender justice and equality. And yet, despite this encouraging progress, the majority of women in the United States today work in low pay, low-status jobs.[50] The United States offers women no federal guarantee of paid maternity leave, nor affordable, quality childcare.[51] The gendered pay gap stubbornly persists, and, even as most women work outside the home, they continue to perform the majority of labor inside the home, like cooking, housework, and childcare.[52] Women's increasing representation and outstanding performance in higher education has not, for the most part, translated into equal gender representation and power distribution in high-status, high-pay fields like business, law and medicine.[53] More women than men are graduating from professional schools of journalism. Yet, men make up the vast majority of news content and continue to dominate producing, directing, hosting, and reporting roles in print, television, and online news media. Striking gender role disparities persist in film and television, and in the numbers of female-to-male producers and directors.[54] The percentage of women in the United States Congress reached nearly 20% for the first time ever in the 2012 elections, yet the U.S. ranks ninety-eighth in the world for percentage of women in national legislature.[55] The horrifying reality of rape and sexual assault in the United States military and on college campuses—reflective of a widespread culture of sexual violence against women—bespeaks a broad pattern of gender inequality in the United States today.[56]

Real structural change is required to effectively confront and overcome the gender inequalities that persist in the United States today. We need new social and economic policies to address everything from women's low wage work, to the gendered pay gap, to the lack of paid parental leaves and affordable, quality childcare, to inadequate legal recourse and protections against gender discrimination, sexual harassment, and sexual violence. But gender inequality in the United States today also illustrates the persistence of limited social and cultural attitudes about women. The question of how successfully a woman conforms to traditional norms of heterosexual femininity continues to provide key means for her individual and social evaluation: Is she physically attractive? Sexually desirable? Reproductively viable? Evidence of this stubborn cultural residue—or what feminist philosopher Susan Bordo calls the "unbearable weight" of the female body—is everywhere.[57] Jennifer Siebel Newsom's critically acclaimed documentary, *Miss Representation*, calls attention not only to the glaring underrepresentation of women in American media, politics, and other high-paying professions, but also to the over-representation of women as two-dimensional images and as sex objects. Current research on top grossing films in the United States shows not just that females are strikingly underrepresented (2.51 males to every 1 female on screen) but that females are more than three times more likely to be shown in sexy, tight, alluring attire or partially naked.[58] The Victoria Secret fashion show, broadcast live on television and on-line and an annual leader in ratings, along with the ubiquitous advertisements via billboards, television, print, and the internet for the multi-billion dollar lingerie and swimsuit company, often feature women in attire, imagery, and poses that connote pornography. Covers and photo shoots in men's mainstream magazines like *Maxim* and *GQ*, and in popular celebrity-centered magazines like *W* and *Paper*, commonly feature actresses and other female celebrities scantily clothed, posed provocatively, or naked (see, for instance, the famous *Paper* cover of naked reality TV star Kim Kardashian from 2014) and accompanied by sexualized headlines. The annual *Sports Illustrated* swimsuit issue features woman after woman with breasts and buttocks exposed. According to sociologist Gail Dines, we live in a culture wherein pornography itself has lost much of its stigma, and is becoming increasingly mainstream and normalized, even cool.[59] Take the popularity of *The Howard Stern Show*, for example. Stern, himself a friend to many celebrities, speaks publicly about his own porn use and regularly interrogates women—including porn stars and other well known actresses in reality television and in Hollywood film—about their body parts and sexual practices on his talk radio and television show.

Not only women, but girls too, are being incorporated into what journalist Ariel Levy calls "raunch culture."[60] Communications scholar M. Gigi Durham illuminates and analyzes a growing "Lolita effect," or hyper-sexualization of girls, in American and global media.[61] Educational researchers Diane E. Levin and Jean Kilbourne link the deregulation of American media over the past several decades to rising violence, and to the increased sexual objectification of girls, in children's television programming, in advertising, and in children's clothing, toys, video games, and other consumer products for purchase.[62] In top-grossing G-rated family films in the United States today, male characters outnumber female characters 3 to 1. Female characters commonly show noticeably more skin than their male counterparts, have exaggerated physical characteristics that invoke sexuality, and embody sexually provocative movements, expressions, and gestures. The fact that female characters account for only 28.3% of the speaking parts in family films, and 30.8% of the speaking parts in children's television shows, offers more troubling evidence of gender imbalance and the objectification of women and girls in children's media.[63]

Several recent alternative princess narratives—like in the Disney movies *Frozen* and *Brave*—that focus on sisterly love over romantic heterosexual love, or on being the best archer in the land and finding fulfillment without heterosexual marriage, are encouraging and refreshing. Yet, the stark underrepresentation of women and girls in American media overall continues to be punctuated not only by sex object roles, but also by traditional conceptions of femininity in other respects: namely the role of heterosexual wife and mother. In *Cinderella Ate My Daughter: Dispatches from the Frontlines of the New Girlie-Girl Culture*, journalist Peggy Orenstein gets us thinking about how and in what ways the current Disney princess craze—via movies, television, and consumer projects for purchase—is impacting American girls' identity formation and aspirations for the future.[64] Diane Levin and Jean Kilbourne's research on media and consumption calls attention to a surprising re-gendering of children's toys and television programming along traditional lines in recent years. How can it be that in today's films designed for an audience of American children, 80.5% of all characters that engage in paid and meaningful employment outside of the home are male?[65] The deafening silence of women's voices in movies for grownups—in 2012, only 28.4% of speaking parts in the top one hundred films went to women—is also accompanied by an overwhelming underrepresentation of women who are leaders, and/or have meaningful occupations, missions, and goals outside of the home. In movies and on television, female characters are more likely to be married, and to have children, than their male counterparts.[66]

In a recent public conversation, feminist writer and *Ms. Magazine* founder Gloria Steinem and actress Jennifer Aniston agreed—with a combination of humor and chagrin—that women in the United States today still live in a reality wherein, as Aniston put it, "our value and worth is dependent on our marital status and/or if we've procreated."[67] Television and movies are not the only sources that teach us to value women based on their physical characteristics, and on whether and how they embody the roles of heterosexual wife and mother. Contemporary female figures in American politics provide more examples of how sexual desirability, motherly and wifely roles and duties, emotionality, nurturance, and sensitivity—all elements associated with traditional heterosexual femininity—continue to impact a women's path towards achieving her professional goals. Recent democratic candidate for governor of Texas, Wendy Davis, faced continued questions and critique in the press, and from her opposing party, regarding her mothering skills.[68] Former Secretary of State and Senator of New York, and Democratic nominee for the 2016 presidential election, Hillary Clinton, endured a range of contradictory critiques while campaigning for the Democratic nomination for presidency in 2008. Clinton's failure to meet criteria of youthful beauty, fashionable dress, and intensive mothering were a liability in one moment—any facial blemishes or wrinkles, her hair style, her body weight and clothing choices, her approach to mothering and her capacity for traditional wifely skills such as baking cookies, were regular media talking points of evaluation, critique, and ridicule—yet, her expression of emotion revealed weakness and sensitivity, qualities not deemed "presidential," in the next.[69] Sarah Palin, the former governor of Alaska and Republican vice presidential candidate in the 2008 presidential race, arguably conformed quite successfully to traditional feminine norms of youth-beauty, fashionable and sexy dress, and intensive mothering. Yet, this conformity garnered not only media praise, but also ridicule, as Palin was deemed merely a "hot woman in a skirt," unworthy of the brainpower and rational thinking required of a vice-president.[70]

The Gendered Double Standard of Aging

It was over forty years ago when literary critic Susan Sontag first proclaimed that in American society men were valued more for "what they do than how they look" whereas for women the reverse was true: physical appearance trumped women's achievements and actions as a measure of their social worth.[71] Sontag's proclamation can be read as exaggerated and over-generalized, and, in the intervening decades, women in the United States have continued to achieve and to be recognized for achievements that reflect their multiple skills and knowledge sets outside of the realm of physical appearance alone. There is also some compelling evidence and analysis to suggest that men are becoming increasingly concerned with physical appearance and body image, and are spending more time and money on activities designed to "improve" how their bodies look.[72] The male body currently circulating in American media and popular culture is one that is increasingly bulked up in muscle and trimmed down in fat—a body type that is difficult, and even nearly impossible, to attain without working out and potentially using additional pharmaceutical, chemical, or technological means of intervention.[73] It is still women, however, and not men, who are starkly underrepresented in key professional fields in the United States today, including journalism, law, and politics, and in complex and leading roles in film and television. Women, and their body parts—not men's—overwhelmingly saturate the airwaves in the name of selling products. American men are spending more than ever before—just over $5 billion in 2012—on face and body grooming and beautification products.[74] Yet, this number pales in comparison to what women in the United States spend annually.[75] Sontag's claim that physical appearance trumps all as the evaluative means of a woman's worth may well be overblown, but we still live in a society wherein a woman's physical appearance (whether or not she is considered physically attractive or sexy) continues to matter more for women than for men.

What happens to this gendered discrepancy when aging begins? Certainly, all aging individuals in the United States, both male and female, confront ageism one way or another, sooner or later. In our youth and fitness obsessed culture, women and men are increasingly encouraged to subscribe to what scholars and researchers on aging call the "successful aging" paradigm. Aging "well" is understood as an individual responsibility and within individual control, and individuals are expected to adopt a lifestyle of conscious diet and exercise to achieve a healthy, active, "successful" old age.[76] Men and women can experience greater social status and occupational and economic success with age. But they are also likely to encounter invisibility and negative stereotypes, both in their own lived realities, and in the media and popular culture, as their faces and body betray signs of aging.[77]

Despite the shared benefits and drawbacks associated with aging that both men and women in the United States encounter, however, women are penalized to a greater degree than men are when visible signs of aging appear on their faces and bodies. This greater penalty is about looks mattering more for women than for men in contemporary American society. But it is also about the fact that women are held to a narrower and more stringent standard of physical attractiveness than men are. Susan Sontag calls this two-tiered gendered inconsistency the "double standard of aging."[78]

When it comes to looks, Sontag argues, men are more likely than women to be considered physically attractive and sexually desirable at older ages. On a woman, gray hair and wrinkles are commonly perceived as an impediment to her perceived physical attractiveness. For a man, on the other hand, these same age-based characteristics can be "judged quite positively." The lines in a man's face "are taken to be signs of 'character.' They indicate emotional strength, maturity . . . (They show he has 'lived')." A woman's face, on the other hand, "is prized so far as it remains unchanged (or conceals the traces of) her emotions, her physical risk taking. Ideally, it is supposed to be a mask—immutable, unmarked."[79]

A woman's physical attractiveness—her value, her desirability, and her visibility—decline when her face and body communicate what Sontag calls "the product of her experience, her years, her actions." A man's value, desirability, and visibility, on the other hand, is more likely to grow with age and in conjunction with the evidence of accumulating life experience and achievements born out on his face and body. That a beautiful face for a woman is "unmarked," and that her value, to a greater extent than a man's, stems from that unmarked face, brings us straight back to the troubling question of female objectification. What of her mind? What of her unique thoughts and actions? If a woman's worth is equated with an exterior unblemished by lived experiences, and unanimated by thoughts and emotions, is that really so different from equating her with stone, or plastic, or other non-living matter?

The marks of aging on a woman's face and body also signal the waning of her reproductive capacity and, as such, give new and sobering meaning to that "unbearable weight" of the female body that Susan Bordo illuminates. If we accept that a woman's value continues to be—at least to an extent—equated with the hetero-normative expectations of sexual desirability and reproductive viability (and the accompanying, traditional "feminine" roles of sex object, wife, and mother) then, as her body loses its capacity to adequately perform these roles and characteristics, her value declines. New reproductive technologies not withstanding, aging brings an end to a woman's ability to have and bear children, while men can continue reproducing at any age.

Concrete evidence of the double standard of aging—wherein women are penalized more than men are for age-driven changes in their biology and physical appearance—is ubiquitous enough to be taken for granted. Current research shows that heterosexual women in middle age and older who have lost a spouse either through divorce or death are just as eager as men are to engage in new sexual and romantic relationships, yet they are less successful than men are in finding interested partners.[80] Single heterosexual men who are in their forties and older, when compared to heterosexual women who are in their forties and older, are more likely to seek out and engage in sexual/romantic relationships with partners who are younger than they are. Older women seeking relationships are at a disadvantage as men their age and older pursue relationships with younger women, and as younger men are less open to relationships with older women than younger women are to relationships with older men.[81] Ageism is widespread in the workforce overall, yet older women confront age-based discrimination earlier than men do, and are less economically secure than older men.[82]

In Hollywood, women generally enjoy a shorter "screen life" than men do. It is common for female actors to find offers for roles declining once they reach age forty. Yet, male actors in their forties and older are widely represented as leads in popular film.[83] In any given film, it is more common for female actors to be younger than their male counterparts than the other way around. As male actors age, and continue to play leading roles in films, their female co-leads do not age along with them. Instead, the reverse is true: the age gap actually increases between male lead actors and their female co-leads over time. Male movie stars like Johnny Depp, George Clooney, Tom Cruise, Richard Gere, Denzel Washington, Harrison Ford, and Colin Firth—who represent a fifties through seventies age range—typically share the screen with female actresses who are significantly younger than they are.[84] Colin Firth was fifty-four, and Emma Stone was only twenty-six, in the 2014 film, *Magic in the Moonlight*. Olga Kurylenko was eighteen years younger than Tom Cruise in *Oblivion* (2013). The age gap between Johnny Depp and Amber Heard in the 2011 film *The Rum Diary* was twenty-three years, and the list goes on.[85]

Film roles for women in their forties and older are more likely to be stereotyped in unflattering ways than roles for men of equivalent ages, and women in middle age and older are less likely to occupy leadership roles and wield occupational power than male characters of the same age.[86] American television offers more roles for women than film does, and there are some encouraging new examples of strong female leads and rich and complex central characters in contemporary television programs who are in their forties and older. Some examples include *Empire*, co-starring Taraji P. Henson; *The Good Wife*, starring Julianna Margulies; *Veep*, starring Julia Louis-Dreyfus; *Madam Secretary*, starring Téa Leoni; *How to Get Away with Murder*, starring Viola Davis; and *Sensitive Skin*, starring Kim Cattrall. And yet, like in film, older women are not only vastly underrepresented, but also more likely to be negatively stereotyped and portrayed as having unappealing personality traits compared to older men.[87] The roles of Glenn Close in *Damages*, and Jane

Lynch in *Glee*, speak to the still common tendency to stereotype and pathologize female characters who wield power. And, recent shows like *Cougar Town* with Courtney Cox, *Desperate Housewives*, and all of the many *New Housewives* reality series, while offering examples of women who have power in some respects, also reinforce negative stereotypes regarding women, race, age, power, and sexuality.[88]

American politics is a world not only of overwhelming gender imbalance overall, but also one wherein examples of gendered ageism are easy to find. The physical appearance of Congresswoman and former Speaker of the House Nancy Pelosi, who is in her seventies, frequently surfaces as a subject of critique and ridicule, particularly among Republicans and in the right wing media. Pelosi, who sports a smooth face with very few wrinkles and no gray hair, cannot win as she receives endless barbs about her plastic surgeries. If we return to the example of Hillary Clinton, and her 2016 presidential campaign, her age and her appearance—as I write this she is sixty-eight—is a common theme in the media.[89] In an interview published in *Glamour* in September 2014, Clinton shared, with a combination of humor and honesty, that she is held to higher standards when it comes to physical appearance, beauty work, and attire than her male colleagues are: "I've often laughed with my male colleagues like, 'What did you do?' You took a shower, you combed your hair, you put your clothes on. I couldn't do that."[90] Overwhelmingly framed as a liability, Clinton's age is negatively contextualized in multiple respects, from her wrinkles and her weight, to concerns about her health and stamina, to worries about her role as a grandmother keeping her away from political duties and responsibilities. The ages of Clinton's male competitors, like Democrat Bernie Sanders (now seventy-five) or Republican Donald Trump (who is seventy) appear to be of little interest to the press. The media storm around Clinton, the grandmother, betrays a particularly glaring example of the double standard of aging. Many male politicians are grandfathers without mention. Donald Trump, for instance. Or 2012 GOP presidential candidate, Mitt Romney, who, as journalist Aliyah Frumin points out, "proudly touted his eighteen grandchildren on the campaign trail."[91]

There are certainly female politicians, television and film actors, and other celebrities, entertainers, and public figures in the United States today who achieve power, status, economic success, and popularity in their forties and older. Yet, many of these women, Nancy Pelosi and Hillary Clinton among them, continue to embody a more youthful aesthetic than the men of equivalent ages in their fields. The media and entertainment industry offers some striking examples. Not all, but many, heterosexual male actors in their forties and older in Hollywood are coupled with women who are younger than they are both on and off screen. I have already mentioned actor Johnny Depp and actress Amber Heard who co-starred together in 2011. When they married in 2015, he was fifty-one; she was twenty-eight. Then there's George Clooney who is married to Amal Alamuddin (he's fifty-five; she's thirty-eight), and Brad Pitt and Angelina Jolie (he's fifty-two, she's forty-one) . . . the examples, it seems, are endless.[92] But let's now compare the looks of female and male actors who are approximately the same age. How does the physical appearance of Nicole Kidman compare to actor Daniel Craig (they are both in their mid-to-late forties)? Demi Moore to George Clooney (they are both in their early-to-mid-fifties)? Jane Fonda to Harrison Ford (both in their seventies)? Barbara Walters to Clint Eastwood (both in their early-to-mid-eighties)? Each of these women have few, if any, wrinkles and no gray hair, while each of these men have plenty of both. Take female television news anchors, journalists, and talk show hosts. Most, regardless of their biological age, have little in the way of gray hair, wrinkles, and other visible signs of aging on their faces and bodies. Among their male peers in the business, however, these age markers are more commonly displayed. Compare, for example, Yahoo newscaster and former television talk show host Katie Couric to Wolf Blitzer of CNN: both in their sixties, she has scarcely a gray hair or wrinkle, while he has plenty of both.

Female Aging and Cosmetic Intervention

Women generally, and older women in particular, are overwhelmingly underrepresented in the worlds of film, television, politics, journalism, and other high-status, high-pay fields in America today. Older women who *do* achieve success and recognition in the public eye commonly bear few traces of normal aging on their physical appearance. American women's use of cosmetic procedures at a rate of 10 to 1 over men makes clear that, regardless of what an older woman has accomplished or achieved in any number of arenas, she continues to confront pressure and expectations about her physical appearance, namely: to keep looking young. Images and narratives of older women in popular culture and media are scarce. Yet, older women are bombarded with products and treatments to "repair" and "fix" evidence of aging on their physical exteriors. Their faces and bodies are the lucrative targets of advertising and marketing campaigns for surgical and pharmaceutical treatments and interventions, and provide the bread and butter for many a dermatologist, gynecologist, and plastic surgeon.

"Maintenance"—ongoing treatment and repair over time—is the buzzword in the world of cosmetic anti-aging intervention. Maintenance is a savvy and profitable strategy for the cosmetic anti-aging industry: all women grow older and all will require some corrective tweaks sooner or later—it is not a question of *if*, but a question of *when*. And the younger you start, the better. "Slow Anti-Aging: The New Secret to Looking Your Best" is the title of a recent *More* magazine feature wherein readers are introduced to this "latest approach to beauty," one that enables us to "keep (or recreate) a contoured, nearly lineless face through a series of steady, tiny tweaks that leave you looking natural and unaltered."[93] Readers are encouraged to go in "two or three times a year" for "derm visits" that can include glycolic acid peels, muscle-relaxing toxins (or injectables like Botox), hyaluronic acid fillers (or injectables like Juvaderm), light treatments (like Clear and Brilliant or Fraxel Dual), and skin tightening (like Ultherapy/Thermage). Starting at age thirty-five as opposed to fifty-five is recommended: "A key tenet of slow anti-aging is starting sooner and keeping yourself in a good place," says Dr. Ranella Hirsch, a dermatologist in Boston.[94]

Subscribing to the maintenance method—otherwise known as the "new secret to looking your best"—is incredibly expensive. If *More* magazine's estimates are on target, maintaining a youthful appearance costs anywhere between $8,000 and $20,500 for the first year, and between $4,500 and $13,700 for each year after that. The earlier you start, the more money you spend. And yet, women—from writers and journalists to actresses and other celebrities—increasingly use the language of maintenance as an acceptable, common sense, and even "no-brainer" justification for having cosmetic procedures. Memoirist and movie producer/director Nora Ephron wrote openly about her maintenance routine inclusive of Botox shots, Restylane, and fat injections.[95] Actresses like Scarlett Johansson and Liv Tyler speak about their intention to maintain their youthful looks with cosmetic intervention. Indie actress Virginia Madsen has been featured in advertising campaigns for Botox and Juvederm.

The decision to have cosmetic procedures designed to more dramatically change a physical feature or characteristic—say, for example, a nose job or breast implants—may still be greeted by some as vain, superficial, obsessive, or unnecessary. The decision to have cosmetic anti-aging procedures over time, on the other hand, is increasingly read as a rational, practical, and even necessary one. Journalist Alex Kuczynski openly catalogues her own cosmetic anti-aging maintenance regimen, including an eyelift, liposuction, and ongoing rounds of Botox shots and collagen injections. Kuczynski explains that she is not "obsessed" with the way she looks, nor is she "anorexic or bulimic." She does, however, believe in maintenance: "I am not preoccupied beyond therapeutic reach or common sense; I maintain."[96]

Maintenance invokes the ease and accessibility of new and less invasive cosmetic technologies and the legitimacy that comes with the medical language of treatment and repair. It also calls up, however, the gendered expectation of disciplined beauty-body work and the cultural equation between a woman's worth and her physical appearance. A woman makes the "right" decision when she asks her doctor about Botox: "Ask your doctor about Botox Cosmetic. Millions of women already have." A woman makes the "right" decision when she chooses to have the Botox injections: "It's really up to you. You can choose to live with wrinkles. Or you can choose to live without them." A woman who chooses cosmetic anti-aging intervention accepts the long-standing reality that her value is fundamentally intertwined with how youthful she looks: "Once you get it, you really get it." This is the woman who bows down to what Laura Hurd Clarke calls the "moral imperative to modify the aging face."[97] This is the woman we commend in our culture because she refuses to "let herself go."

Overview of the Book

We have heard from women in the public eye—journalists, actresses, and other celebrities—but less from real, everyday women. How do everyday women feel about growing older in a world where they are increasingly targeted by cosmetic procedures and products designed to make them look younger?[98] Does the growing availability of cosmetic anti-aging surgeries and technologies make women feel better about aging? Or worse? What leads a woman to say "yes" to cosmetic anti-aging interventions? And, alternatively, what leads a woman to choose to grow older without them? The voices and stories of everyday women populate the pages of this book and inspired me to write it.

I use in-depth interview methods informed by a feminist epistemo-logical framework to uncover what everyday women have to say about growing older in an increasingly normalized climate of cosmetic anti-aging intervention.[99] Sociologist C. Wright Mills's call for the need to investigate the reflexive interrelationship between "private trou-bles" and "public issues"—to exercise what he terms the "sociological imagination"—sharpened my commitment to articulate the meanings women ascribe to aging, and to explore the impact and implications of the anti-aging explosion on women themselves. This book joins a rich field of contemporary sociological research that applies qualitative methods to explore social, economic, and cultural trends from the per-spective of everyday individuals. Centered on forty-four in-depth inter-views with women between the ages of forty-seven and seventy-six who use, refuse, and are currently undecided about whether or not to use cosmetic anti-aging surgeries and technologies in the future, this book aims to offer a fresh gendered reading of the landscape of commercial-ized medicine in the United States today.

The women who share their lives and perspectives in this book hail from a range of socioeconomic backgrounds and life circumstances.[100] They are working, retired, and unemployed. All but one, who is Latina, are white. Most, but not all, live in New England. Some live in cities, oth-ers in towns near urban centers, and some in small towns in rural areas. All identify as heterosexual. Some are married, some are divorced and single, and some are single and have never been married. Because the women in this book are heterosexual and almost all white, by and large they see women who look like them reflected in the images in cosmetic anti-aging advertising and media coverage. Mainstream cultural depictions of femininity and beauty—namely sexual desirability and reproductive viability embodied in the heterosexual, white woman—mirror their own race and sexual identity. New and emergent research explicitly and comparatively explores the ways in which women's experiences of aging, and the meanings they attach to it, are differently mediated by race and sexual identity and orientation.[101] It is my hope that this research continues, and that the women's stories in this book will contribute to urgently needed discussion and dialogue among women of diverse sexualities, races, and ethnicities on what it means to be an aging woman in the United States today.

The book's organization and analytic framework reflects a multilayered approach. Women's stories of aging are simultaneously individual and social, cultural and economic. The lens of analysis shifts throughout the book, expanding, contracting, and intersecting among different entry points of analysis as women share their experiences. The themes of self-concept, self-perception, and identity—including questions pertaining to femininity, physical attractiveness, and sexuality desirability—populate the first half of the book. In chapter 1, women who have and use cosmetic anti-aging procedures are introduced. In chapters 2 and 3, women who refuse cosmetic anti-aging intervention take center stage. The second half of the book expands the lens, moving out from the individual to incorporate social, cultural, and economic layers of analysis. Here the full spectrum of women I interviewed—women who have and use, refuse, and who are currently undecided about whether or not they will have and use cosmetic anti-aging interventions in the future—share their experiences and perspectives. Chapter 4 opens with interplay between women's views on aging and the youth-centered, cosmetic anti-aging-product-saturated culture in which they live. Chapters 5 and 6 illuminate women's views and experiences of aging through the web of social interactions that populate their everyday lives. I save the conclusion to assess some of the wider implications gleaned from the women's stories in the book, and to offer some final reflections on gender, aging, and cosmetic intervention in the United States today.

1

"I Wanted to Look Like Me Again"

Aging, Identity, and Cosmetic Intervention

Age-driven changes in appearance can challenge a woman's fundamental understanding of herself, of *who she is*. The question of identity
permeates each of the women's stories in this chapter. They draw from
a language of the self—self-expression, self-esteem, self-confidence,
and self-awareness—to express their feelings about the changes in their
physical exteriors, and to speak about their decisions to have and use
cosmetic anti-aging procedures. To hear these women's stories is to be
confronted, head-on, with the "growing tightening of the relationship
between body and self-identity" in our late-modern era of consumer
capitalism.[1] However, embedded in these women's narratives is not
only an inextricable link between body and self, but, more specifically,
between the self and *how the body looks*. When the women in this chapter articulate their shared desire to re-create the familiar self through
cosmetic anti-aging intervention—"I wanted to look like *me* again"—
and when they frequently and anxiously describe their aging faces and
bodies as alien—"That is *not me*"—they betray a privileging of the exterior of the body as a primary marker for the self. To listen to the women
in this chapter talk about their motivations for having cosmetic anti-
aging procedures is to begin to understand, firsthand, what it means
to live in a culture wherein, to repeat Virginia Blum's summation, "we
cannot help but locate who we are on the surface of our bodies."[2]

As the women in this chapter talk about the age-driven changes in
their physical appearance, and recount their decisions to have cosmetic
anti-aging procedures, a dynamic relationship between body and self
emerges. On the one hand, these women experience the changes in their
physical appearance as an uncomfortable and alienating loss of self. On
the other hand, they identify their bodies as moldable, malleable, and,
at least to some extent, controllable. Women's faces and bodies become

their "identity projects" as they shape and mold them to better match up with their conceptions of an authentic self, or to more accurately reflect the new and improved person they feel they have become. For the women in this chapter, cosmetic anti-aging intervention is itself transformative. As women talk about how their cosmetic anti-aging procedures engender new selves, it is hard not to be "convinced that internal feelings and even character can be transformed by interventions on the surface."[3]

To take the perspectives and experiences of these women seriously is to confront the reality of a looks-based culture. For some, it is seeing a two-dimensional image of themselves, or considering the prospect of being captured in a two-dimensional image, that inspires the decision to have cosmetic anti-aging intervention. For others, the decision to have the surgery or use the technology reflects a positive age-induced ability for self-awareness and self-knowledge—and for honest admission that looking physically attractive (read: youthful) really matters to them and to society at large. For others, the decision to have cosmetic anti-aging intervention can be inspired by the ageist treatment of others. Looking older means that people are not as interested in interacting with you, and getting to know you, as an individual. Having cosmetic anti-aging intervention means looking less old, suffering less invisibility, and, therefore, successfully reclaiming and expressing individual identity.

The women's rich and varied stories in this chapter capture a complex and porous relationship between body, self, *and* the social category "woman." Individual identity intertwines with sexual desirability and physical attractiveness as women couch the age-driven changes in their physical appearance in a language of invisibility and loss, and as they use narratives of losing and regaining the self to explain their decision to reduce evidence of aging on their faces and bodies via cosmetic intervention. For each of these women, losing and reclaiming the self also means losing and reclaiming the traits that prove her heterosexual femininity, and that continue, at least to some extent, to determine her self and social value. Frequent talk of a fierce commitment to "keeping myself up"—or maintaining a youthful, attractive appearance—and commonly voiced critiques of aging women who "let themselves go" also betray a deeply embedded conflation between a woman's individual value, self-esteem, and self-respect and her capacity to look physically attractive and pleasing to others.

Aging and Identity Struggles

Invisibility

"I AM SOMEBODY WHO, IN MY PAST, WOULD WALK INTO A ROOM AND BE NOTICED."—CLAIRE

Claire is a personal trainer who is forty-nine years old. She has had several rounds of Botox shots in her forehead and around her eyes and openly discusses the likelihood of facial plastic surgery in the near future. Claire tells me about how she cultivated her physical appearance as a means of positive reinforcement from a young age. Having an attractive physical appearance "has been with me my whole life," and is "a big part of my life and my identity," she says. Claire uses words like "avenue," and "tool," as she recounts how her physical appearance has helped her with everything from having interesting conversations, to getting jobs, to eliciting much-needed attention she wasn't receiving from her mother. When I asked Claire about how she feels about growing older, she says:

> It's something I've been thinking about a lot lately. . . . Mostly I'm talking about my face changing right now. And there has been a gradual change over the last year, but there's been a remarkable change in the last three to four months. And so it's something I've been fairly obsessive about, let's say, mostly between me and my mirror. But I'm going to say that the biggest thing that's coming up for me is a sense of loss. And I am somebody who, in my past, would walk into a room and be noticed.

Claire's identity—what makes her *who she is*—is enmeshed in being a woman whom others notice and find physically attractive. Yet, the evidence of aging on Claire's face brings a diminishing of attention from others and painfully disrupts this identity. As she explains:

> Like from walking into a room, knowing that, you know, eyes would at least glance at me, to walking into a room and I'm another middle-aged

woman. I'd say that's the main thing I'm dealing with right now. I know this may sound like a strong word, but there may be, for me, a little bit of a grieving period.

Claire experiences the age-driven changes in her face as a loss of self—a loss of her individuality, what made her, *her*. At the same time, however, Claire's fear of becoming just "another middle-aged woman" betrays her awareness of the invisibility and de-valuing she will inevitably encounter when she no longer conforms to the youthful aesthetic that dominates mainstream conceptualizations of heterosexual femininity and female beauty. Claire endures an age-induced "identity stripping" that is at once individual and cultural—her value, as a woman, in her own eyes, and in the eyes of others, erodes.[4] She mourns the shift, as she puts it, from "the way I was viewed in the world to now how I will be viewed in the world."

"NOBODY WANTS TO THINK THAT THEY'RE BEING CAST ASIDE."—CAROLINE

Caroline is a radio producer who is forty-seven years old. Caroline has ongoing Botox shots and collagen injections, and is open to having more invasive surgical procedures in the future. Caroline equates the age-driven changes in her physical appearance with painful feelings and experiences of invisibility and with losing a fundamental part of herself. Like Claire, Caroline's sense of self-worth and self-value has been caught up in her own understanding of herself as a physically attractive and sexually desirable woman, and in the attention and positive affirmation she has received from others for how she looks. As Caroline deftly articulates, along with the accumulating evidence of aging on her face, she is losing that part of herself by which society measures and values women:

> Nobody wants to think that they're being cast aside. You know, especially if you've been an attractive person and you've gotten so much. I'm not even saying if it's important to the woman or not. I think it's the feedback you're getting from the outside. That's always been something that other people have valued. I'm not looked at the same way that somebody half my age is. You realize, you know, you're losing that whole piece of you. I don't know if it's sexuality, desirability, just whatever. There's just the loss in that, that I think you have to come to grips with.

Caroline's language of invisibility and loss communicates a tightly bound conflation between a woman's self-worth, her physical appearance, and how society responds to it. When Caroline and Claire lose their "capacity to draw admiring glances from others," they also lose what feminist philosopher Sandra Bartky calls "a chief marker of femininity in our culture."[5] Bartky's description of aging from the female perspective offers a clear explanation of what Claire and Caroline are experiencing: "The loss of an admiring gaze falls disproportionately on women. . . . A woman's worth, not only in the eyes of others, but in her own eyes as well, depends, to a significant degree, on her appearance."[6]

"PEOPLE DIDN'T WANT TO TALK TO ME."—JANET

Janet is a retired airline ticket agent who is sixty-eight years old. Janet has had upper and lower eyelift surgeries and is open to having more cosmetic anti-aging surgeries in the future. Janet told me about how she noticed a decline in attention and interest from others when she started to look older. Janet clearly attributes this lack of attention and interest from others to her older-looking appearance: "People didn't want to talk to me because I was starting to look old." At work, Janet explained to me, customers saw her as "just a grandmother"—they paid less attention to her, and sought out her expertise less often, compared to her younger co-workers. Like Claire and Caroline, Janet equates the evidence of aging on her face with invisibility in the eyes of others. And yet, Janet's experience is less about diminished attention and positive feedback for how she looks, and more about a diminished capacity to be respected, recognized, and listened to as an individual and a professional with unique skills and expertise. Janet's story illustrates not only the necessary criterion of youthfulness for a woman to draw recognition and attention for having a physically attractive appearance, but also the reality that, for a woman, not looking young (i.e., physically attractive) can mean that she is scarcely recognized as a person with any value at all. In Janet's experience, looking old discouraged people from interacting with her and getting to know her as an individual. More bluntly put, for Janet, not being perceived as a young and attractive woman meant that people did not see her at all.

Janet's story, like the stories of Claire and Caroline, offers sobering evidence of Sandra Bartky's assertion that a physically attractive (read:

youthful) appearance continues to serve as a key measure of a woman's self and social value in the United States today. However, Janet's encounters with intersecting ageism and sexism also lend new weight to aging as a story of "identity stripping" and "losing what we had."[7] Similar to Claire and Caroline, Janet equates the age-driven changes in her physical appearance with losing her identity as a physically attractive woman. Yet, for Janet, these same age-driven changes also lessened her capacity to be recognized, and to express herself, as a unique individual in ways *outside* of the realm of physical appearance. Janet's wisdom, experience, and professional expertise are not recognized or valued—she is made invisible at worst, and, at best, she is perceived as a grandmotherly figure who may be sweet, kind, and nurturing, but who does not possess the skills needed to do her professional job well.

Alien Faces and Bodies

As we've seen thus far in this chapter, the evidence of aging on a woman's face and body can provoke feelings and experiences of invisibility and loss. Age-driven changes in physical appearance—and the subsequent lessening of attention and interest from others—can challenge a woman's understanding of herself and her identity as a physically attractive woman. These changes, and the likely reality that others will be less inclined to interact with her and take the time to get to know her because of them, can also limit a woman's opportunities to express herself, and to be known and recognized, as an individual. One way or another, age-driven changes in appearance mean losing defining aspects of one's sense of self *and* social worth. Anne, who appears later in this chapter, sums up the experience of many women when she says, simply, that looking older means being "dismissed."

Changes in physical appearance and the accompanying shift in self-perception, and in the perception and treatment of others, can be unsettling. Women can feel alienated and disconnected from their faces and bodies as the evidence of aging appears. These feelings are well-captured by what aging studies scholars call the "mask of aging," or a gap between "Look-Age" and "Feel-Age."[8] My interviewees frequently spoke about aging in terms of a widening gap (or mask) between the exterior of their bodies and their inner selves, between how they looked on the outside and felt on the inside. Age-driven changes in physical appearance are encountered as distortions of "my true self," or as barriers that stifle the expression of the "real me." Evidence of aging can provoke uncomfortable unfamiliarity with the "face I've always known" and even prevent the communication of inner feelings. Women's feelings of disconnection from their age-marked faces and bodies reflect a complex and deeply intertwined relationship between the body and the self, and offer a stark reminder of the instrumental role that the physical exterior plays in their understanding of themselves as individuals.

"I DON'T WANT TO LOOK TIRED IF I'M NOT FEELING TIRED."—CAROLINE

We have already learned that Caroline, who is forty-seven, is struggling with what she perceives and experiences as an age-driven loss of physical attractiveness and the resulting loss of attention from others. For Caroline, losing her youthful physical appearance—"losing that whole piece of you," she says—is about losing her identity as a sexually desirable woman. Yet, Caroline's aging face betrays her sense of who she is fundamentally, as a person, in other ways too. She says about her aging face: "It feels like it's not me. All of a sudden, my face is really hollow, and that isn't me." Caroline explains to me, with frustration, how the age-driven changes in her face can misrepresent her inner feelings and can send false signals about her physical energy level:

> I think some of the aging that we get makes us look tired. . . . Because I don't want to look tired if I'm not feeling tired. . . . I look tired and I don't feel tired. Or I look tense and I'm not feeling tense at this moment.

Caroline is distraught about the fact that the age-driven changes in her face, like its increasing hollowness or its tendency to look tense or tired, literally engender a miscommunication of her inner feelings. Lisa's experience of her aging face also raises troubling questions of misrepresentation.

"THAT IS *NOT* ME."—LISA

Lisa is a retired financial planner who is fifty-eight years old. Her cosmetic anti-aging procedures include under and upper eyelift surgeries, a neck lift, and ongoing Botox shots. Lisa explained to me that, prior to having her cosmetic procedures, her face had changed dramatically due to aging. Like Caroline, Lisa was unsettled by the age-driven changes in her face because they meant that her face didn't look like "me" anymore. For Lisa, these changes in her physical appearance inhibited her ability to recognize herself and to be recognized by others:

> I really think my face had changed. It had changed a lot. Starting in my late forties and early fifties, a lot of people used to say to me, people I hadn't seen for a while, 'I didn't recognize you.' And I would look at this [*pointing to her face*] and go, "This *can't* be me." I would look and say, "That is *not me*."

The feelings of disconnection that Lisa articulates can also signify a lack of control. As we'll learn from Julia, age-driven changes in physical appearance can be alienating not only because you no longer look like you used to, but also because you have no control over them.

"WHO INVITED *THAT*?"—JULIA

Julia is a stay-at-home mom, who is forty-seven years old. Julia has had varicose veins and age-spots removed via laser treatment, and she is enthusiastic about having Botox, collagen, and more invasive cosmetic procedures, "like an eyelift," in the future. Julia expresses shock and discomfort in response to the age-driven changes in her physical appearance. With each of these changes, her body feels less familiar to her and less her own:

> It's doing different things that are very surprising. Things are popping up uninvited and it's a little shocking, because we all live in our skin and we know ourselves so well. And then you look one day and all of a sudden I have this wrinkle, or I have these wrinkles, and you're like, who invited *that*?

Julia has started to "feel differently" about her body because it is "changing rapidly." She encounters the age-driven changes in her physical appearance like unwelcome thieves of the face and body she has always known. As Julia confronts her changing body, she feels disconnected from it and a jarring lack of control over it: "It's all of a sudden not who you're used to, and not who you used to know, and not who you asked for."

When once familiar faces and bodies become alien, women can feel like they are no longer at the helm of their own faces and bodies. Julia's depiction of the age-driven changes in her physical appearance is echoed by many of the women I spoke to. Women frequently described these changes as something that "just happened" as a result of growing older. Most implicitly attributed these changes to nature and biology—that is, the natural aging process. However, a few women pointed to specific aspects of their biographies and lived experiences, like smoking, alcoholism, or a difficult marriage, as the culprit of their changed appearance. Wendy is one of them.

"THERE WAS A SADNESS IN MY FACE THAT ADDED TO MY AGING."—WENDY

Wendy is a retired nurse who is fifty-three years old. Wendy has had two eyelift surgeries. She also has ongoing Botox shots and is open to having more cosmetic surgery in the future. Wendy described to me how the experiences of her mother's death and her own unhappy marriage imprinted signs of aging on her face:

> As I started to age, I really was doing fine physically I think until I hit forty. I lost my mother at forty and I realized then when I would look in the mirror that I was beginning to look aged. I was also in a very unhappy marriage. And I really felt that added to my aging. There was a sadness in my face that added to my aging. I think that became part of me. You know, you cry a lot, and you end up with bags under your eyes.

In contrast to Caroline, Lisa, and Julia, who describe their aging faces as inauthentic representations of themselves, Wendy portrays her aging face as an authentic reflection of the sadness that she had experienced at a certain time in her life. That sadness became "a part of [her]" and the literal evidence of that sadness—evidence of all that crying—was deposited on her face. But after Wendy got herself out of the unhappy marriage, and came to terms with her mother's death, she no longer felt that same sadness. The bags under her eyes meant having to confront a previous version of herself that didn't exist anymore, and that she would rather forget. The face that she saw in the mirror no longer accurately represented who she was, the *new* self she had become.

Identities (Re)born through Intervention

"THIS IS HOW I REMEMBER YOU."—ANNE

As women talked to me about their cosmetic procedures, they repeatedly shared stories of reconnection: cosmetic intervention was a means to *reattach* the face/body to the self by *undoing* age-related changes in the face/body. Barbara, who appears later in this chapter, speaks for many when, she describes her motivation for her first facelift and her likely second one this way: "I want what's in my head to match up better with what people see."

We have already learned from Lisa about how she struggled with feelings of alienation from her aging face before her cosmetic anti-aging interventions. When Lisa tells me about her neck lift, lower and upper eyelift surgeries, and ongoing Botox shots, hers is a story of reconnecting her interior self to her physical appearance. Lisa's description of her appearance, post-intervention, centers on the return of her authentic self, one that is familiar to herself and to others:

> Now I think that's more me. It's more the me I want to be. . . . I was in New York with a couple of college friends this week and they said, "You look more the way you looked in college and the way you looked in your twenties, you look more the way we remember you." . . . You know, there's something about—if you look at yourself and you don't like what you see, it's like you have to take this little leap all the time, like, "It doesn't matter, it doesn't matter." And so I don't have to take that leap in the same way now when I look at my face.

Anne, who is a retired social worker and currently an artist, experiences her post-surgery face in a similar way. Anne is sixty-five and she has had two facelifts. Anne's facelifts have brought the return of her old face, the face she has "known and loved" for many years, the face that more authentically reflects the "compassionate, fun-loving, intelligent woman" she feels she is. Anne prefers the term "supportive aging" surgery to "anti-aging" surgery. She is grateful for the opportunity for cosmetic intervention because it allows women to "support the nice things about ourselves for as long as we can" and because "it makes us . . . feel more comfortable within ourselves." Anne explains her reasons for having her facelifts as follows:

> I've always liked my looks. I've always been proud of myself in that way. I think that as I grew older, and I began to see the changes in my body, I wanted to continue to like the way that I looked, as I always had. I decided that I wanted to have some cosmetic surgery so that I would still feel my old attractive self.

And how she feels afterwards:

> I've had two facelifts. I had one when I was fifty-six and one when I was sixty-four. And the first one was more major and I was delighted with it. And I felt the face that I had known and loved came back. I felt very *young* and I felt very *attractive* and I felt very *happy*. I mean, I have a smiley, sort of compassionate, fun-loving, intelligent woman in there. And I feel that, you know, it's coming through more, or something like that, I suppose. . . . I guess I feel like I'm just sort of continuing to support the face I always knew. It's like, "Yes, I remember!" My sister said to me—when I had it done, she said, "Oh!" She cried, actually, and she said, "Oh, this is how I remember you."

Anne's interpretation of her facelifts as "supportive" aging is shared among many of the women I spoke to. Caroline carefully distinguishes what she calls "corrective," or "restorative" surgery from "enhancing" surgery—she points to breast implants as a prime example of the latter. Cosmetic anti-aging intervention is about correcting (or undoing) age-driven signs on the face and body and reverting to the face you've always known. It is not about creating a new and different face or body from the one you were born with. Barbara, who is a retired program director for a mental health facility and currently a part-time childcare provider, also shares this perspective. Barbara is fifty-nine years old. She has had an eyelift and a facelift and is planning to have a second facelift, and possibility a neck lift, around the time of her upcoming sixtieth birthday.

Barbara's past (and probable future) surgeries are not a matter of "Gee, I hate my nose," or "I want to be beautiful," even though, as she puts it, "I've always hated my nose" and "I've never gotten anywhere with my looks." Instead she simply wants to get rid of "something that came on with age," something that she calls her "jowls," "puffy eyes," and "sags." She explains her facelift experience as follows:

> I just don't like jowls. I mean, it's very simple. It's not that I want to be beautiful. I would think it would be real sick if somebody hated the way they looked, and hated themselves and was going to look entirely different. Because I did not look like a different person *at all*. I looked like a person that didn't have the puffy eyes, and didn't have as many sags. *That's it*. So it's not going to change you, it's not going to make you beautiful.

Through having cosmetic anti-aging interventions, these women seek to reconstruct their faces to resemble the faces they remember. They hope to resurrect, and even to preserve, their pre-age-marked faces. From Anne's perspective, her two facelifts have literally protected her from having to witness age-driven changes in her face:

> My face just continued to be the same. I think it comes from liking my face from the beginning so that I never really faced my face in a negative way and *then* felt bad about it and *then* felt good about it. It's just like, I didn't wait that long [before having the facelifts] for that to happen to me. Maybe I was protecting myself from that, from experiencing my face where I didn't like it.

"A NEW START."—WENDY

Most women spoke about their cosmetic procedures as a means to reclaim and preserve their former, authentic selves. However, several women equated their cosmetic procedures with a desire to discard, and free themselves from, certain aspects of their past lived experiences. For these women, cosmetic intervention serves as a method of disposal but also a first step towards constructing a new exterior appearance—an appearance that corresponds with the new selves they have become. Wendy believes that her experiences of stress and crying caused by her unhappy marriage and the death of her mother created the marks of aging on her face. She describes to me how two rounds of upper and lower eyelift surgeries and ongoing Botox shots erased the marks of aging on her face and created a new look to match her new and happier self:

> I know that I used to wear my sunglasses a lot to hide my eyes. I no longer look in the mirror and see—this is deep—I don't see my mother's eyes, which I used to see. I didn't have a good relationship with my mother. I see a me, *me*. And I see me as a younger woman. I look at myself now in the mirror and I see, I can go back to my twenties. Now I really feel like I look like [I did] *then*. And that could be compounded by the fact that I'm remarried in a very youthful relationship and [I] have a new start. So maybe that's why I go back to my twenties. But I do feel I look young, that I see that youthfulness, that awakening, you know, so to speak. Now [that] I have the eyes awakened, the whole self has.

Wendy experiences her surgeries as constructing a new appearance that more accurately reflects her new self. Even further, she perceives the surgeries themselves as helping to "awaken" that new self. And yet, Wendy also treats her new awakened self as a youthful self, a former self still untouched by the pain of a difficult marriage and her mother's death. Her new, post-surgery look means "I look like then," and "I see me as a younger woman." In this way, Wendy, similar to many women in this chapter, experiences her post-surgery face as a return to familiar ground, to a face she remembers. She says:

> I'm back before age twenty-seven, before age twenty-five, before I got married. The first five years of my twenties, when things were good—those are the times that I remember most feeling like I looked terrific and felt terrific. Back again! I'm very lucky.

For Wendy, the surgical experience appears to represent both a resurrection of a past, younger, happier version of herself not yet tainted by painful life experiences, and the birth of a new version of herself that has successfully survived and moved beyond these difficult periods. As she puts it:

Before [the surgeries] I just had this pulled-down, heavier look that made me look sad and tired. Now I feel like I look fresh and ready and, you know, just pulled together. It's terrific. You know, I wanted to care for myself and take care of myself and that's very positive going forward.

Like Wendy, Melissa also frames her surgery as a return to a previous, and familiar, self on the one hand—"I wanted to look like me again"— and a symbolic embrace of a new self, and a fresh start, on the other. Melissa is fifty-three years old and currently unemployed. She has had one facelift and plans to have a second facelift in the near future. She explains her reasons for getting her first facelift as follows:

It's not an issue of my nose being too big or whatever, but I wanted to look like me, what I thought I should look like, not what I actually looked like. . . . I was looking older than I felt, and that was freaking me out. . . . I wanted to look like me again. Before [my facelift] I didn't think I looked like me anymore.

But, Melissa's decision to get a facelift was also about reflecting her newly sober self, creating a fresh look that she felt represented and rewarded the new and improved self she had become. In this respect, Melissa interprets her surgery as a kind of investment, or even a vote of confidence, in her new and improved self. And this investment, as she puts it, "helped me amazingly:"

I had my first facelift when I was thirty-nine—which is sort of young, but I felt very jowly. And it made a big difference in my appearance. And I thought about it for a long time and at the time I spent a lot of money, like half my salary, on it. And I financed it over three years. And it was a big decision. But, you know, part of the thing with me, when I was a teenager . . . well, I had a drug problem for a long time. And it's amazing in how many ways that facelift actually helped me. Investing in myself. And, you know, when I actually had the facelift, I said, "Well, I'm not going to go through all this aggravation and spend all this money and then look droopy-faced because I'm walking around like all high on something." So it helped me amazingly.

Choosing Intervention

Over and over again, women shared with me their stories of cosmetic anti-aging invention as a means to reconnect physical exteriors to interior selves. Whether that concept of the self is fixed and unchanging over time, or newly achieved, they equate their cosmetic procedures with the motivation and desired goal to acquire a physical appearance that more accurately reflects who they feel they are. My interviewees' narratives are also filled with talk about the decision-making process itself: many were eager to explain to me how they ultimately made the decision to go ahead and have the cosmetic procedures done. These decision-making accounts are immersed in a language of the self that is fluid and positively evolving over time. Age-driven changes on the exterior of the face and body are viewed negatively. And yet, ironically, most women attribute their decisions to have cosmetic anti-aging procedures to a new and improved self that comes with age.

"WHAT I LOOKED LIKE MATTERED TO ME."—LISA

Lisa and Anne explained to me that, as they have gotten older, they have come to know themselves better, and to more easily acknowledge what is important to them. For Lisa, this means being able to admit that her looks really matter to her. While on some level Lisa wishes that she didn't care about her appearance, with age she has been able to accept that she does care. As she puts it:

> I think what's interesting is, what I looked like *mattered* to me. You know, maybe at some level, I think it shouldn't. But I learned that it *did*. It *shouldn't matter* what we look like. You know, [life] isn't just about vanity . . . It *shouldn't matter at all*. What matters is your mind and your soul and how you feel and think and not [your] physical attributes. . . . So, [a] part of it was acknowledging that it was *okay*, that it was *okay* for me to say, "No, I do care and it does make a difference to me and I can, and *why not* let myself do this [have the surgeries]?"

Anne, like Lisa, attributes her decision to have cosmetic anti-aging surgery to an improved capacity for honesty and self-awareness that comes with age. Age has enabled her to be "really real" with her feelings and to admit that how she looks is important to her. But Anne also credits growing older with her increasingly realistic view of the world. She explains that the wisdom she has gained with age has enabled her to accept the fact that looks do indeed matter, not only to her, but to society as well. She expresses sadness and disappointment with this realization on the one hand. On the other, growing older has helped her to see herself, and reality, more clearly:

> It's just amazing in this country what outside appearance—how it effects people's reactions and thoughts and beliefs. It's very, very interesting. It's too bad. It's very superficial. And, you know, there's that part of me that felt that I was succumbing to that and that politically I shouldn't [have the facelifts]. But, I think that as you get older, and you aren't as idealistic, you're more really *real* with your feelings and admit that actually you really *don't* like it [looking old] and that you would like to look like you used to and feel the same way about your appearance. If you admit it, you know, if you're really honest, more people would *do it* [have cosmetic anti-aging intervention] than say, "Well, I'm not going to buy into that no matter how I feel," or not know how they feel, or deny how they feel.

Anne continues to struggle as she attempts to make sense of her decision to have her surgeries, acknowledging that in some ways it was about giving in to superficial, dominant cultural values like looks, and youth, and beauty. However, she also believes that those women who choose not to have cosmetic anti-aging interventions, and who continue to fight the culture, may simply not be in touch with how they feel, or be denying how they truly feel. And for Anne, the prospect of cosmetic intervention is easier than fighting the culture—after all, the culture is a part of her and giving in to it means not "trying to pretend that I'm somebody else":

> Obviously, I think there's beauty in thirty, in forty, in fifty, in all ages, there *really* is. I don't know—you know, if I think that, then why did I have a facelift? Because I was beautiful, too, at that age, in where I was. But I think that my past and my upbringing and my culture is also a part of me

and that had a big effect on me. And I didn't want to fight it. It was like, "Okay, if I would *feel better* by giving in to it, then I'm going to." Instead of trying to pretend that I'm somebody else.

"I CAN TOTALLY *JUSTIFY* DOING THIS."—AMY

I heard a lot from the women I spoke to about how age enables them to be more honest, aware, realistic, and accepting of what is important to themselves, and to society—namely, that "looks matter" on both counts. Many also spoke to me about how, with age, they have more time to focus on themselves and feel more "comfortable" and more able to "justify" putting themselves first. They have earned the right to treat, reward, and pamper themselves, after years of hard work and putting the demands and needs of others before their own. Choosing cosmetic anti-aging intervention means making time for the self and prioritizing your own wants and desires over those of others. Amy is a retired business-woman and currently a stay-at-home mom who is forty-eight years old. She has had a tummy tuck and is considering having an eyelift in the near future. Amy's articulation of her surgical decision-making process epitomizes the "putting myself first" perspective:

> I got laid off from my job about three and half years ago. I'd worked for decades, which was a wonderful thing, and I was getting severance for two years because I'd been there for so long. And I thought, you know what, I can *totally justify* doing this [having cosmetic anti-aging interven-tion]. And [the tummy tuck] was like six or seven thousand dollars. And I just thought, "I'm doing this." And my husband didn't love the idea that I was going to be put under and thinks any elective surgery is a bad thing. But I said to him, "You know what? I *really want this.*"

Similarly, Lisa, who is also recently retired, attributes her decision to have her neck- and eye-lift surgeries to being able to focus on herself after many years of mothering and working at a demanding job:

> During those years when I was being a mother, I was working full time at a very intense job . . . I didn't focus on myself. There's something about focusing on myself, [and] being *comfortable* with focusing on myself.

Barbara also frames her decision to have cosmetic intervention as a kind of earned right, or self-reward. She does not explicitly associate this right with having paid her dues over time, so to speak, or with becoming a certain age. Yet, it is her self-growth and evolution over her lifespan, including the successful achievement of her sobriety, which warrants the celebration of a facelift. Barbara includes her facelift in a "whole list" of other things she went about "fixing" after she got sober, including her teeth, her house, and her car:

> I got sober and I just did everything. Everything that perturbed me, I fixed. I just wanted everything to be right. There was a whole list. Everything had changed and I just wanted to change for the positive everything that I could. Everything. I threw myself a fiftieth birthday party. And then . . . I started thinking about my face. And I hated my jowls. So I went in to a place [to have a lower facelift].

"I'M MORE MY OWN PERSON."—LISA

My interview subjects' self-reward explanations for their surgical and technological decisions—I'm finally doing something "just for me"—are often coupled with stories of increased independence, self-esteem, and self-confidence over time. Associations between this increased independence and age are both explicit and implicit. Yet, whether or not age is mentioned directly, many, like Barbara, frame their decision to have and use cosmetic anti-aging surgeries and technologies as a narrative of progress and as evidence of a new, improved, and more empowered self. Lisa explicitly attributes her decision to have her neck- and eye-lift surgeries and ongoing Botox shots to increased independence with age:

> I'm more independent. I'm more *comfortable* with being more independent. I'm less dependent on what other people think and I think that's an aging thing. I think that comes with age. . . . I'm more my own person. It's more about what *I* want and not about what everybody else wants.

For Amy, the decision to have a tummy tuck is about asserting herself and standing up for what she wants, even in the face of opposition from others. While she does not mention age directly, standing up to her husband is something she may not have had the confidence to do in the past:

He says, "You're beautiful the way you are." And I say, "You know what? I mean, I love you, but I'm not doing it for you, I'm doing it for *me*." So I don't know if I'll get my eyes done at some point, but, if I do, he's just going to have to accept that it's what *I want*. [Because] he'll say to me, "You don't need to do anything. You look *beautiful*." But it's not about you, *it's about me*.

Like Lisa and Amy, Wendy also attributes her decision to have her eyelift surgeries to her increased capacity for self-confidence, independence, and assertiveness over time. Her first husband did not approve and would not allow her to have cosmetic surgery. When she remarried, though, her new husband was very supportive of her decision. He also paid for the procedures. However, even if Wendy had remained single, she believes she would have found a way to have the surgeries—precisely because she equates them with being able to assert herself and "be myself again":

In my first marriage I would have had [the surgeries] and not told my husband. First of all he wouldn't have provided the money. And then, if he knew I had the money, he would have made it difficult for me to spend the money. Very controlling. No, it would not have happened. Truthfully, it might not have happened in the marriage but it would have happened if I were out there alone. Because once I got out, and was on my own, I was able to be myself again. And, I think I would have begged, robbed, and stolen to have it done down the line.

Taking Action: Health, Fitness, and Self-Care

The decision to have cosmetic intervention, according to the women I spoke to who chose to have it, reflects a new and improved person who has become increasingly wise, confident, and able to assert her individual needs and wants over time. This is also a person who understands the importance of taking individual responsibility and practical action to fight the signs of aging on her face and body. Women who have cosmetic anti-aging procedures "feel good" about themselves and they "take good care" of themselves. Self and body collapse into one as women point to their cosmetic interventions as evidence of the fact that they are not "letting themselves go," and as they equate their cosmetic procedures with improved mental health and physical fitness.

"WE'RE OPEN TO DOING SOMETHING."—CLAIRE

When women spoke to me about their cosmetic anti-aging procedures, and their plans to have more of these procedures in the future, I frequently heard about how their embrace of these procedures reflects a "can-do" spirit and attitude. A woman who chooses to have cosmetic anti-aging procedures is a "doer." She is someone who takes personal responsibility and practical action—she does not sit passively back and let herself look older and older. Claire places herself, and her friends, in this positive camp of doers: "My friends are people who say they're going to definitely *do something*. Within my circle . . . we're open to doing something." Having cosmetic anti-aging intervention also proves that you are open-minded and up for trying new things. Women can attribute their decision to have cosmetic intervention to a kind of positive evolution of the self that comes with age. Becoming more emboldened with age is another one of these positive age-based evolutions of the self—a topic that emerged in many discussions with interviewees. And, having cosmetic anti-aging procedures showcases this new, age-induced capacity for risk-taking. As Lisa explains:

> I think [having cosmetic anti-aging intervention] is just about being a little bit older and saying, "Hey . . . come on, take a risk." You know, you only live once, and if a little goes wrong, it won't be such a bad thing.

Christina is a former businesswoman and currently a stay-at-home mom who is fifty-one years old. Christina has ongoing Botox shots and indicates that she will likely have more cosmetic anti-aging procedures in the future. Christina decided to try Botox because, upon turning fifty, she was up for "some fun" and saw it as a "personal experiment." Indeed, some women feel proud of the fact that they have the courage and guts to go under the knife. For example, Debra, who is fifty-six, a musician, and has had two eyelifts and laser resurfacing and is "likely" to have more procedures in the future, describes her decision to have her surgeries as a "brave" one, whereas her sister would "never" have cosmetic intervention because she's "a baby about pain."

"I TRY TO TAKE CARE OF MYSELF."—WENDY

The collection of positive attributes and characteristics reflected in a woman's decision to have cosmetic anti-aging intervention continued to expand as I listened to women share their stories. Several women told me that their decision to have cosmetic anti-aging procedures reflected their high self-esteem. Wendy decided to have her eyelift surgeries at a time in her life when she was feeling "really good" about herself. As Amy puts it: "I think most of the women I know who have gotten plastic surgery feel really good about themselves and I would put myself in that category." I also heard a lot about cosmetic procedures as a form of self-care. Wendy's explanation for her eyelift surgeries—"I wanted to care for myself"—was a common refrain. Indeed, most women placed their cosmetic anti-aging procedures within a larger framework of "healthful" bodily practices. Cosmetic interventions were on the list of disciplined body activities—like eating well and working out—that informed a woman's health and fitness regime.

Caroline draws a parallel between the exercise routine she follows to keep her body in shape and the cosmetic technologies (Botox and collagen shots) she uses to reign in and control the signs of aging on her face. She uses exercise to tweak her body and cosmetic technologies to tweak her face: "[With my body] I can sort of tweak things, but your face you really can't tweak unless you're going to use artificial means." Like Caroline, Melissa couches her talk about her cosmetic anti-aging procedures, and her plans to have more procedures in the future, in a language of exercise and fitness. In fact, Melissa explained to me the importance of "taking care of myself"—that is, keeping her body fit and healthy through responsible diet choices and exercise—to ensure its readiness for surgical intervention. As she puts it:

> You've got to give [the plastic surgeon] something to work with. Some things he can help you with and some things he can't. But you can't, like, completely and totally let yourself go and expect a miracle to happen overnight. So that's another reason I do the other stuff. I eat right. I exercise. I do try to take care of myself. So it just sort of fits in with that somehow.

Similarly to Melissa and Caroline, Debra places her cosmetic anti-aging interventions within a narrative of health and self-care. Before having her procedures, Debra explains to me, "I did a lot of damage to my skin." And now, post-cosmetic intervention, she says: "I think [my skin] does look healthy. It's about not looking worn out or worn down."

Doing Femininity

My interview subjects' talk of their cosmetic anti-aging interventions is laden with our cultural preoccupation with youth-health-fitness in this country; their talk is also imbued with a fierce American belief in individualism, pragmatism, and personal responsibility *as the means to achieve it*. Yet, when women couch their cosmetic anti-aging interventions in the language of disciplined and healthful body practices and self-care—evident in Melissa's words, "I eat right, I exercise, I do try to take care of myself"—the implication is, of course, not just physical health, but physical appearance, as well. Health and beauty collapse into one when Debra describes her post-intervention skin as "looking healthy," and her prime motivation for having cosmetic anti-aging intervention as being "about not looking worn out or worn down." In short, for the women in this chapter, to be healthy—to take good care of yourself—means *caring about your physical appearance*.

Many of the women I interviewed suggested that to care for the self, as a woman, is to care about what you look like. This interchangeability of "caring for myself" and "caring about what I look like" clearly points to a conflation between the self, or self-value, and what we might call the markers of traditional heterosexual femininity, including physical attractiveness and sexual desirability. The meaning of the phrase "letting yourself go," and my interview subjects' frequent use of it, also points to a deeply intertwined relationship between the self and physical appearance for women. For the women with whom I spoke, having cosmetic anti-aging intervention means refusing to "let yourself go" and proves your willingness to do the required work to maintain your appearance. Debra's motivation for having cosmetic anti-aging intervention is typical ("I care what I look like") and her description of how she felt before her eyelift surgeries and laser resurfacing ("I didn't like who I was") and how she feels afterwards ("I'm in much better shape now") reflects the tight association between physical appearance and self-value experienced by many.

But Debra's account of her cosmetic anti-aging interventions—like those of most of my interview subjects—also betrays a keen awareness of the equation between a woman's physical appearance, her social value, and her *responsibility* to conform to what is socially and culturally expected of her as a woman. When Debra says that "it's hard to be a fifty-six-year-old woman," she speaks not only from an individual perspective, but also with the knowledge that her "weathered," "sun-damaged" skin falls short of the cultural expectation of youth-beauty for women: "It's hard to be a fifty-six-year-old woman. I did a lot of damage to my skin. My skin survived a real lot. It affects your image." When Anne, Caroline, and Janet say "looks matter," the looks they refer to are those of youthful beauty, and it is women in particular upon whose worth—both social and individual—that looks depend. Claire sums up a woman's responsibility to maintain an attractive (youthful) appearance—and makes clear that she views this as a responsibility to herself, her husband, and society at large—when she says: "I just care. I care. I care for myself. I care for my husband. I care for the way I am going to be viewed in the world."

For my interview subjects, maintaining an appearance of youth-beauty means making the right "choice" to conform to what is socially and culturally expected of you as a woman. As Claire puts it: "Letting yourself go" is a "choice you make and I don't understand that choice. I don't get why a woman would want to walk around in sweatpants with gray hair and no makeup." In this way, cosmetic anti-aging intervention is not only about the literal achievement of a more youthful—and therefore more "physically attractive" and "sexually desirable"—appearance but equally about *choosing to do the required work* to maintain that youthful appearance. Cosmetic anti-aging surgeries and technologies enable the successful *doing of femininity* at an older age.[9] In and through their cosmetic anti-aging interventions, my interview subjects adhere to what Sandra Bartky calls the "disciplinary practices that produce a body which in gesture and appearance is recognizably feminine."[10] Barkty distills these disciplinary practices to three aims: producing a body of a certain appearance; acting out a particular set of bodily gestures, postures, and movements; and displaying the body as an ornamented surface. Whether my interview subjects aspire—via their cosmetic anti-aging interventions—to look good in photographs and in clothes, or to attract admiring glances and attention from others, whether they aim to project a perky and energetic personality, or to apply eye makeup to newly remade eyelids and lipstick to newly plumped lips, each of these aspirations reflect a commitment to "doing femininity," and the desire to embody the image and characteristics of a "feminine" woman.

Pictures, Parties, and Clothes

Achieving a body that is "recognizably feminine" can be a lot of work and typically requires time, pain, and money. Exercising and dieting, applying hair and skin products and makeup, shaving and waxing, buying clothes and accessories, deciding on what to wear—these are but a few examples of the multi-faceted work that millions of American women perform in order to take on "a certain kind of appearance in the world."[11] Women of all ages engage in these kinds of "disciplinary practices." Yet, as women get older, more time, pain, and money is required to produce a "feminine" appearance.

My interview subjects' privileging of how their bodies look—and their fierce commitment to conform to the feminine aesthetic of youth-beauty—is perhaps most overt in their willingness to endure not only the physical risks, bodily discomfort, and pain that can result during and after surgical and non-surgical anti-aging interventions, but also to accept and tolerate longer-term, potentially ongoing, physical effects like sensitivity and numbness. For example, Lisa tells me that her neck, while it does not feel as uncomfortable as it did immediately after surgery, is still sensitive and numb months later:

> I mean, it's still numb up around here [*pointing to her neck*] and sensitive. But not like it was. This was *very sensitive* [*pointing to her neck, again*]. I didn't want anyone *touching* my neck for a while.

Anne continues to experience numbness and tightness in her face nearly a year after her second facelift surgery. Anne explains to me that she is actually glad that she is still experiencing these effects—her first facelift lasted "almost ten years" and she is hoping that she won't even have to think about a third facelift until she's seventy-five—because the tighter her face feels the longer her facelift will last. She says:

I'm still feeling numb on the top of head. That lasts along time. It's all coming back here, and it's very sensitive there [*pointing to different parts of her face*] but I can still feel the tightness. And, from what I understand, you really *want* to because if they don't pull it tight enough, it doesn't last very long.

Through their respective interventions, Lisa and Anne prioritize how their bodies look over how their bodies feel as they endure physical discomfort, sensitivity, and a loss in physical sensation even months after surgery.

For some women, in fact, it is actually seeing two-dimensional images of themselves, or anticipating being seen and photographed at events, that marks a turning point and pivots them towards cosmetic anti-aging intervention. Lisa is one of them. It was only after seeing photos of herself that Lisa was forced to confront the reality that something was "really wrong" with how she looked. Before seeing the photos, Lisa was not even that worried about her neck, nor aware of "how bad it was." As she puts it:

Looking in the mirror I wouldn't necessarily *see the difference* but I started seeing photographs. My sister in law is quite a photographer and she's *always* taking portraits of people. . . . She's snap, snap, snap, snap, snap [*miming someone taking a photo*] and I would get to *look* at these pictures over the last couple of years and I would just be *appalled, appalled* at what I would see. It was like I didn't know that I had this neck that went like this [*gesturing from her chin to her chest*]. A friend of mine calls it the "hangman's dilemma" neck. Like, when you have a chin that kind of goes from your chin to your chest.

For Wendy, it was her upcoming wedding and, specifically, the anticipated pictures of herself at her wedding, that prompted her to "just go for it" and have two rounds of eyelift surgery and several rounds of Botox shots. She explains her thought process like this:

I'm not going to have wedding pictures that *look like that*. I don't want to look like *that* in the wedding pictures. So that was why it was critical for me to just go for it.

Similarly, Claire's decision to begin her first round of Botox shots, and her subsequent decisions to continue with them, was inspired by key family events and by the prospect of being seen and photographed at these events:

> The first decision [to get Botox] was event-driven. My daughter's bat mitzvah. And I think the second one was my next daughter's bat mitzvah or something like that. And then my [step]daughter's wedding . . . "I'll look better in pictures," or whatever.

It was Amy's desire "to feel better about my body in clothes" that motivated her to have a tummy tuck. Amy says:

> I wanted to feel better about my body in clothes . . . and a bathing suit. I mean, you know, not that anybody likes themselves particularly in a bathing suit, but I was *very pleased* with the results. I mean, I just felt like a million bucks. . . . And people are saying to you, "Oh, you look great," and you can wear clothes that you've never worn before, and so that's all, you know, that's all great. I mean, to be able to go into a store and for me to be able to put on size twelve pants—and they looked good! And they were loose! [Before surgery] I never wanted anything that was form-fitting. So going clothes shopping just became *fun*. It was *great*.

Amy's focus on how her body looks in clothes echoes Claire's concern with how her body will be perceived and "seen" by others at important family events. Wendy and Lisa are preoccupied with how their bodies will appear in two-dimensional images. Each of these women's accounts call attention to our increasingly visual culture in the United States today *and* to the particular importance and value of visual, two-dimensional body display for women. As literary critic and cosmetic surgery scholar Virginia Blum summarizes, "the displayed body, the body-in-the-world, the two-dimensional . . . body is what counts."[12]

Younger, Perkier, Sexier

Cosmetic anti-aging interventions enable my interview subjects to "do" heterosexual femininity through achieving a more youthful (physically attractive) appearance and displaying that youthful appearance in the world—at parties, in pictures, and in clothes. Cosmetic anti-aging procedures make possible the participation in ritual practices of femininity, like wearing makeup, and embodying the role of a feminine sex object whose appearance garners attention, admiration, and even sexual desire, from others. Janet's complaint that her "droopy" eyelids made it "impossible" to "get eye shadow on" was one I heard often. Eyelift surgery—as Janet and others happily informed me—makes it possible to successfully apply and wear eye makeup again. Lisa reports, with enthusiasm, the positive attention she receives for her new, more "physically attractive," post-neck lift, post-Botox, appearance, particularly from men:

> You want to look good. You want to look physically attractive, sexually attractive. And I actually thought it was so interesting that I waited until fifty-eight to get fixed in my neck. Because, you know, if I hadn't been married . . . I bet I would have done it sooner. If I was "in the market," and if I'd had the money, I wouldn't have allowed myself to look like this from a physical *attraction* perspective. . . . And I absolutely have proof from the reactions I'm getting from all the men around me that it's true.

Nearly every woman I spoke to equated looking younger with looking more physically attractive and with receiving more attention from others. Janet, for example, tells me that "I really didn't like how I looked," before her eyelift surgery. After her eyelift surgery, by contrast, Janet enjoys the positive attention she receives from others:

> Most of the time, [people] always say, "Oh, you're so young looking!" or something like that. When I show my senior subway pass, or when I have to say my age, they just say, "You look very young," or something like that. But I think, I mean, not that it's *so* important, but I know I don't exactly look sixty-eight.

Anne tells me that before she had her facelifts, unless she was able to start a conversation with someone "who wasn't ageist," and unless that person realized, "as we started to talk," that she had interesting things to say, she simply felt ignored and dismissed by many: "I don't feel as dismissed as I used to feel . . . I used to feel dismissed."

Doing heterosexual femininity means achieving a youthful aesthetic, and displaying that youthful aesthetic to the world. In my interview subjects' complaints about how their wrinkles and sags made them look "worn down," and "worn out," and "tired," lies the implicit assumption that the marks of time and lived experience on their faces and bodies will be met with negative consequences and responses from others. But the disciplinary practices of femininity, as Sandra Bartky reminds us, are not limited to body decoration and display—doing femininity also demands the enactment of particular bodily gestures, postures, and movements. Several women speak about their interventions in light of producing a youthful, perky appearance *and* projecting a youthful, perky personality. When my interview subjects tell me about gaining a brighter and perkier "me" through their cosmetic anti-aging interventions, the implication is the re-embodiment of the look *and* persona of a young, feminine, and sexually desirable woman. Claire's Botox shots, and her probable cosmetic anti-aging surgeries in the future, are inspired by her desire to remain fresh and perky:

> I think I like the expression that I've heard, when I know people that have [had cosmetic anti-aging procedures], and the comment they've got back is, "Oh, you look really well rested. You don't look so tired." I guess that's what I'm looking to get out of it. A little perkier, a little brighter, a little less dragging. . . . My goal would be to do something like my mom [who had a facelift] did, to not deny my age, but to be a perkier version, you know, to lift myself up, for me.

Like Claire, Janet does not want to look weary and worn. Janet tells me that, before her eyelift surgery, she didn't feel like going out and about in the world because she looked "tired," because her eyes looked "terrible" and "droopy," because she couldn't "get the eye shadow on," and because she "just didn't look right." As she elaborates:

> I kept looking at myself when I put my makeup on, and when I went to work, and I said, "These eyes look just *terrible* and *droopy* and I look tired." And I said, "*What is this?*" I really didn't like how I looked.

Before her eyelift surgery, Janet tells me, "I didn't like myself too much." In fact, Janet turns to me, the interviewer, with a question that implies insider and woman-to-woman knowledge—"You know what I mean?"—on the matter of not liking yourself, as a woman, if you look droopy, and not looking "right," as a woman, if you look old:

> I just felt I looked tired and I didn't like myself too much. . . . Then I noticed, "I can't get the eye shadow on." You know, "This doesn't look right. I don't like that *look*." It makes me look *droopy*, kind of tired-looking in a way. You know what I mean?

Post-Intervention Identity Struggles and Contradictions

Women seek out cosmetic anti-aging surgeries and technologies for many reasons: to improve the fit between how they feel on the inside and how they look on the outside; to return to a previous and more familiar-looking face, to create a new face to match the new selves they have become; to fight back against perceived negative age-based characteristics (looking old means looking tired and droopy); to lessen age-based invisibility; to reclaim a more youthful, and therefore, more physically attractive, feminine, persona and look. For every woman, the process of making the decision to have the cosmetic anti-aging intervention(s) is transformative. And yet, while cosmetic anti-aging procedures solve a woman's age-related identity struggles in some respects, new identity struggles and questions can also surface, post-intervention. How different, how much younger, does a woman want to look post-procedure(s)? How does she adjust to her new look? How does she want others to respond to her changed appearance? And how does she respond to the reactions of others?

"I PAY A PRICE FOR IT NOT LOOKING EXACTLY LIKE ME."—CLAIRE

I heard a lot of stories about surgeons and dermatologists suggesting additional procedures and interventions beyond what a woman originally had in mind. For example, a surgeon might point to an "imperfection" or a "problem" about a woman's appearance that she herself was not particularly focused on, worried about, or bothered by. A typical response on the part of my interview subjects—recounted to me often—was one of concession to some but not *all* of the doctors' recommendations. My interview subjects described standing up to the surgeon or dermatologist to insist that not *every* wrinkle and blemish be erased: "I wanted to still look like me," and "I didn't want to look too perfect," were commonly shared sentiments. Despite their resistance to doctors' suggestions, however, some women expressed discomfort with their post-intervention look. For example, Claire has conflicted feelings about the authenticity of her appearance, and about the noticeable changes in her face, post-Botox shots:

> It lifted so much here [*pointing to her forehead*] that it changed . . . just from the Botox, changed my appearance. . . . I think from those little needles and having such a *different* look, like people *noticed*. So I'm always mixed about it. It definitely *brightens* me up, but I feel like I pay a price for it not looking exactly like me.

Claire acknowledges that she got a lot out of her Botox shots, including positive reinforcement from others, "otherwise I wouldn't have done it." Looking different—younger, brighter, less wrinkled—reaps rewards. However, Claire explains, "I actually wish I got less out of it [than] I did," given that one of the prices she paid for looking so different was harassment from her children: "My kids called me a witch." Debra also expresses ambivalence about how different she looks after her eyelift surgeries. On the one hand, she is happy that she looks "younger," "less tired," and more "refreshed." On the other, she feels that the surgeries changed the shape of her eyes too much:

> My eyes were almond shaped. [The surgeries] made my eyes round. I don't like that it did that. I wanted my eyes to stay *my eyes*, just take the fat off the lids. I miss my old eyes, the shape of my old eyes. I feel like I wished I hadn't done it sometimes. I didn't know that my eyes wouldn't be the same shape. But I don't know if it would have stopped me. I'm a little angry . . . that my eyes changed shape . . . they look smaller. I don't know how noticeable it is to other people. But they're not quite my eyes anymore.

Anxiety and frustration about looking "too different" post-procedure doesn't necessarily stop women from considering having more cosmetic anti-aging intervention down the line, but it certainly complicates their feelings about it. Claire is convinced that she'll be "signing right up for a facelift," and is hopeful that new techniques will produce more subtle results. However, she also worries about being sucked into a "different version of me":

> I'll be signing right up for a facelift. I mean that's sort of always been the thing with me. When the time comes and I am really miserable I will do something. I think that I will. However, being that I'm getting closer to that age, I am looking around, and I'm not liking what I'm seeing very much. I'm very hopeful for new technology, but I don't want to be sucked into, you know, a different version of me. As much as I always said I'd be signing up, I don't know in the end if I really will. You will never hear me say, "Oh, it's just great, all those lines," and . . . you know, "I'm going to let my hair go gray and aging is a beautiful thing." For me it doesn't feel that way. Yet, I don't want to create a new face either.

Caroline describes feeling unsettled by how different her mother's eyes look post-eyelift surgery. She expresses nostalgia about her mother's previous eyes and feels that her mother "was prettier" before surgery:

> My mother did her eyes when she was fifty-two. And I think she was prettier before she had them done. [It] might have been the kind of job she had, I don't know. 'Cause I think they took too much. And it still looks great, but I realized . . . she was more hooded than me. Her eyes are more deep set. And now [post-surgery] I think actually they're a little smaller.

Caroline says she will probably have surgery herself in the future. But she also worries about losing the distinctive shape of her eyes:

> I don't think you have too many tries at it. I think you can do work like, once or twice, on your eyes and that's it. I would be really careful. 'Cause I think sometimes you could take somebody who's fifty and she's prettier before work, and that to me is probably the most important thing. It sounds so vain [but] I'd rather be prettier and probably look fifty than give up the prettiness for the five years. I don't want to change too much.

You've got to really get in the right hands, I think. It's got to be as natural as possible and as close to you as possible.

"DON'T YOU NOTICE *ANYTHING?*"—LISA

The conflicted feelings among many women about how different they want to look pre- to post-procedure bleed into how they hope to be perceived by others. How do they want others to react to their post-surgery look? And how do they respond to those reactions? Lisa is enjoying the attention she's receiving post-neck lift surgery and Botox shots. At a recent retirement party, several people came up to her and said things like, "You look so good," and "Retirement really agrees with you." And, at another recent party: "I was the biggest ego maniac by the end of that party because of the number of people that came streaming up to me saying, 'You look fabulous.'" But Lisa also feels somewhat uncomfortable about accepting compliments while knowing that her new look is the result of technological and surgical intervention:

> So people *think* that it's largely related to my not working anymore but I *know*. Of course, I feel a little *guilty* like, "Should I tell them?" I mean, I'm cheating! I've cheated! It's not me!

And yet, when people comment on her neck lift surgery directly, Lisa does not enjoy that either: "Actually, what a number of people have said to me is, they asked me the name of my doctor, 'Who did you?'" Lisa prefers people not noticing her changed look at all to direct questions about who her surgeon was. As she explains: "I think that it's really good [when people don't notice]. I don't *want* people to sort of say, 'Ew, look. She's had plastic surgery.'"

Lisa's struggle with how she wants people to respond to her new look continues, however. On the one hand, she thinks it's good when people don't notice because it means it looks "natural." On the other, she articulates feeling annoyed, surprised, and even disappointed when people don't seem to notice her new post-surgery look:

> I'm *surprised* sometimes. At first I was surprised when, you know, a couple people that I knew quite well with my going, "*Don't you notice*

anything? I just went through this hell and you don't notice anything?" I've literally had to stand there and say, "Come on, *don't you notice anything?*" I was sort of annoyed . . . but then I realized, "No, this is good. This is good."

In a similar vein, Wendy articulates her pleasure about how "natural" her face looks post-lower and upper eyelift surgery and Botox shots. And yet, she also feels upset when people don't comment on, or seem to notice, her post-interventions look. She attributes this failure on their part to low self-esteem or jealousy:

I found that the people who couldn't bring themselves to say, "You look great," were people who have some kind of sadness within themselves and some kind of personal stuff that blocked them from viewing someone else as looking good. Because, you know, those people who are confident with who they are, comfortable with the way they look, were the people who were the most comfortable with it. My husband's mother was raving, every time I saw her. She's a great lady, very confident, you know, tells it as it is. My sister-in-law [was] a little more reticent. You know, maybe she's not in as financially comfortable a position as I am. My husband paid for it, so maybe there were some issues around that.

Wendy prefers people to notice her post-surgery look, but not to comment directly on the fact that she has had surgery. As she puts it:

No one has said to me, precisely, "I'm going to call [the plastic surgeon]. Based on what *you* had done, I'm *calling*." No one has said that. It's always, "You look great," you know, [or] "What are you doing differently?" Or sometimes they say, "You're how old?" You know, I get that.

On the other hand, Wendy continues to wonder aloud and worry about why people *don't* inquire about her surgery, and who her surgeon was, directly:

No. People don't ask me [about her surgery or her surgeon]. Is that good or bad?

"BUT YOU'RE NOT SUPPOSED TO TALK ABOUT IT?"—CLAIRE
Choosing to share, or not to share, the fact that you have had cosmetic anti-aging intervention, gauging the reactions of others, and determining how you are going to respond to those reactions—these are some of the complex and challenging questions my interview subjects face about their own self-perceptions and the perceptions of others. Wendy remains pretty quiet about her surgery although she doesn't actively deny it either. Her position reflects who she is—a "fairly private person." She does believe that it will soon be easier for women to share their surgical stories, however, as social and cultural acceptance for cosmetic intervention grows.

> I don't go around advertising that I've had this done. . . . I tend to be more of a private person. If it's someone that I know and I think they may have heard, that's fine. I don't have a problem with that. But I don't go around saying, "Oh, I can't talk to you now because I just had my eyes done today." So, you know, if it gets out, it gets out, I don't care. I'm not hiding it. I have a friend who was hiding it. She didn't want people to know. I don't feel that way. And I think as the years go on, society's view of it is such that there is more acceptance, and people are less inclined to be critical, and more, "Hmm, maybe I'll do that!"

By contrast, Claire feels very strongly about the importance of being open about it. In Claire's view, her decision to use cosmetic anti-aging technologies and her probable surgery in the future reflects who she truly is, someone who is an open person and who cares about maintaining, and taking care of, her physical appearance. She struggles with trying to understand women who want to keep it private. If you are changing your appearance, according to Claire, it's silly to expect that people won't notice, or comment on, the changes:

> Just by nature I'm a very open person. So I'll be the first one to say, "I'm going in today to have . . ." You know, I'm not going to be hiding [it]. I don't really get that whole thing, to be honest. It's hard for me to get my head around that. Because if I'm going to do it, I'm going to do it because I care about how I look and how I'm perceived. And to pretend . . . it's like, really like, such weirdness around the whole thing.

Claire offers a story about a friend who takes an opposite approach to her own. For Claire, the decision to have cosmetic anti-aging procedures reflects the fact that you care about how you look and you want to look better. Why wouldn't you, then, want people to comment on your new and improved appearance? Her friend's story points to the ongoing contradictions and complexities that surface as cosmetic interventions interact with identity:

> So this one woman who I've known for years had a breast augmentation. I mean, she literally had no breasts whatsoever. She looked like a man. I could completely understand why she wanted to be, like, a D-cup. And she had the surgery, and I heard through the grapevine, and no one's supposed to know. . . . So, meanwhile, I see her after her surgery . . . she looks incredible. And I wanted to say something to her, but I knew better. So I called one of her good friends and asked [if I could] say to Sarah, "You look awesome, congratulations!" [And] she said, "Absolutely, positively not. She doesn't want to talk about it." I've never said a word to her. And that, I think, is fairly typical around plastic surgery. I don't get the whole thing. You're doing something that's for yourself, and somewhat for your view of how you fit into society, but it's clearly something that's physical and out there. It's not some psychological thing you did in your own head. You're showing it to people. But you're not supposed to talk about it? I don't get the code of ethics around the whole thing. . . . Like, who the fuck are you kidding? I don't get it. I just don't. One day Sarah didn't have boobs and one day she had boobs. It's like, "Okay, I'll pretend I don't see them."

"I DON'T THINK YOU'LL BE HAPPY WITH ANYTHING." —WENDY

Many of the women with whom I spoke—both explicitly and implicitly—compare themselves favorably to women who choose not to have cosmetic anti-aging interventions. Recall that for Lisa and Anne, surgery is about the practical realization that "looks matter" in society and the personal admission that how they look matters to them as individuals: if more women were "honest" with themselves and more "in touch" with their feelings, more women would be having cosmetic anti-aging interventions. For Claire and others, having cosmetic anti-aging interventions means "caring" about their looks and being willing to work hard at maintaining an attractive (youthful) appearance; women who choose not to go the surgical route are critiqued for "letting themselves go" and refusing to conform to a youthful feminine aesthetic. From my interview subjects' perspectives, aging naturally reflects a lack of self-awareness, an impractical ignorance of societal demands, and a failure of responsible and disciplined maintenance of an attractive appearance.

In addition to favorably comparing themselves to women who do not partake in cosmetic interventions, however, my interview subjects frequently draw distinctions between themselves and women who get particular cosmetic procedures that they consider too extreme, too superficial, or too dangerous.[13] Amy identifies breast augmentation as an example of elective plastic surgery that is "over the top in our society today." Several women describe breast implants as "ridiculous." Claire and Caroline express concern at a woman's (unwise) decision to put a foreign "substance," or "object," like silicone-filled implants, into her body. Many critique women who look fake and overdone as the result of too many cosmetic anti-aging procedures—these women are living examples of what not to do and what not to look like. Wendy takes pains to separate herself from the woman she saw at the supermarket who had way too much work done and looked like a "disaster," from the "facelifts on people that look ridiculous," and from those women who just keep trying and trying to get their faces perfect and end up "screwing it up."

As women "who feel really good" about themselves, who are "content" with who they are but just "want to look a little better," my interview subjects distinguish themselves from cosmetic surgery patients who have "poor self-esteem" and expect surgery to be their "cure-all." Wendy recalls an encounter she had with a woman in her surgeon's waiting room as an example of one of these "problem" patients, and as evidence of her difference from them:

> When I had my eyes done, I was very happy . . . 'cause, you know, you have to remember, *a lot* was taken off. So it was like, "Wow!" So, I went back in for my follow-up . . . [and] there was a woman in the office . . . sitting there waiting with me. . . . It was her follow-up visit. She'd had [her eyes] done the same day, I think, that I did. She was *unhappy*. She said to me, "I don't like the way it looks," and "He should have done this and he should

have done that." And I was sitting there thinking, 'I don't think you'll be happy with anything.' And then I was thinking, 'He shouldn't have operated on you because you seem like you're not a happy woman.' And if I were a doctor, I'd say, "You should go to some therapy first and then come back to me." But she was just unsatisfied. And I think she expected to wake up and she wouldn't be looking at *herself* in the mirror, you know? And she woke up and looked at herself in the mirror [and] it was like, "I'm still here? . . . He didn't *change* me just the way I wanted him to."

Wendy distances herself from the woman in the waiting room who had unrealistic expectations of her surgery—the woman who was upset because she wasn't changed enough afterwards. But one of the reasons Wendy herself cites for being so "happy" after own surgery is the significant change in her eyes: "You have to remember *a lot* was taken off. So it was like, 'Wow!'" Claire and Caroline express discomfort and even some distain at the prospect of having foreign materials inserted into their breasts; yet they continue to have Botox and collagen injected into their faces. Nearly all critique and distinguish themselves from women who overuse cosmetic anti-aging surgeries and technologies, who look fake, overdone, and pulled too tight. And yet, each of these women, if they have not had more than one surgical or technological procedure already, express, with conviction, the likelihood of having more procedures in the future.[14]

My interview subjects want to look younger *and* to look like themselves, to be without signs of aging on their faces and bodies but not look *fake*. Striking this balance grows trickier, however, as the natural aging process continues and as the list of procedures grows inevitably longer. As Wendy tells me: "In five to ten years, if I need a facelift, I'm going for the facelift. Absolutely . . . Yes . . . there is no question I would do it." Like Wendy, who "will do something when the time comes," Caroline hypothesizes that she'll probably have an eyelift, if not a facelift, in the not-so-distant future. She wants to continue to "shave off a few years," and to look "five to seven years younger" than she is. Claire's Botox use goes on, indefinitely. Amy is considering an eyelift, Barbara another facelift. Indeed, as the years pass, and the interventions pile up, it is hard not to wonder whether distinguishing oneself from those "ridiculous" and "fake-looking" women will become harder to do.

***

Taken together, the women's stories in this chapter illuminate some of the complex ways that aging, and cosmetic anti-aging intervention, inform and shape the relationship between identity and appearance. On the one hand, witnessing age-driven changes in appearance can be unsettling and alienating, and cosmetic anti-aging intervention can bring back a more youthful—and, therefore, more familiar—identity and look. On the other hand, many women felt dissatisfied, and hence, somewhat alienated and disconnected, from their post-intervention faces and bodies because they looked *too* different and unfamiliar. As cosmetic surgery scholars Debra Gimlin and Rebecca Wepsic Ancheta point out, a woman can experience her post-intervention appearance as an "inauthentic representation of the self," and, in this way, cosmetic intervention can create "new masks."[15]

When the women in this chapter have and use cosmetic anti-aging interventions to (re)connect to their bodies, they privilege the importance of the exterior of the body—how the body looks—as an instrumental source of their identity. Ironically, however, this appearance-centered means of connecting to the body can engender what can be read as a dismissive attitude towards the body in other respects. In and through their interventions, the women in this chapter make their bodies "both more and less important."[16] A youthful-looking face and body that draws approving and admiring glances and comments from others, and that looks good in photographs and in clothes, can come at the expense of—albeit to varying degrees and durations—bodily discomfort. Lisa and Anne are pleased with their post-surgery looks, but they also endure numbness and sensitivity that makes them averse to physical touch on their neck and face. Amy cannot contain her excitement about how good her post-intervention body looks in clothes—but what of her scarred stomach, un-clothed? Is she less able to feel the caressing hand of her husband on her abdomen because of the scars?

I got a sobering glimpse of what a woman's stomach looks like after a tummy tuck when I attended a plastic surgery information session. The (male) surgeon showed his (all female) audience a slide of a woman's stomach covered in long, red, raised scars. "See," he said, "The stomach is almost entirely flat, which makes it look great in clothes. And looking great in clothes and a bathing suit matters a lot more to women than how they look without clothes—am I right?" The women in the audience nodded, appreciatively, in response. Breast lifts were next on the menu. The surgeon reminded his audience that breast lift surgery can cause "numbness and reduced physical sensation" and "can reduce the capacity to breastfeed by up to fifty percent." First, he showed us a slide of the woman's naked and scarred post-surgery breasts. Then he showed us the same breasts, clothed, and said: "But they look great under clothes, don't they?"

It was some years ago now—well before today's era of iPhones, iPads, and selfies—when Susan Sontag wrote: "We learn to see ourselves photographically: to regard oneself as attractive is, precisely, to judge that one would look good in a photograph."[17] And yet, Sontag's words couldn't express more precisely what inspired many of the women in this chapter to go ahead and have cosmetic anti-aging interventions. "Without the camera, there could be no cosmetic surgery," is how Virginia Blum puts it.[18] Wanting to achieve a particular appearance in clothes, or being upset by how your pre-intervention body looks in clothes and in photos, or being excited by how your body *will* look in clothes and photos *after* your interventions—these are prime motivations for many women in this chapter. I worry that all of this focus on how the body looks can become a distraction from the fleshy, material body itself.

Still, by and large, the women in this chapter teach us that to embrace intervention—and to achieve a more youthful-looking appearance as a result—is to embody and express identity traits that are valued in contemporary American society, like high self-esteem, independence, rationality and practicality, pro-activity, and emotional and physical health. Indeed, these women present their cosmetic anti-aging interventions as narratives of self-improvement. Self-improvement is a popular and well-respected American pursuit and, as such, the cosmetically altered body is increasingly "coded as signifying a healthy inner self."[19] Post-intervention faces and bodies reflect more authentic, more genuine selves, new and better selves—a self who takes action, a realist self, a courageous self, a more confident self, and so on.

Contradictorily, while the women in this chapter seek cosmetic anti-aging intervention to achieve a more youthful appearance, they often positively attribute their interventions to the wisdom, practicality, and assertiveness they have gained with age. Their interventions enable them to more closely conform to the youth-beauty aesthetic of traditional, heterosexual femininity. Yet, many speak about their interventions in light of having more time and energy to focus on themselves—and being more comfortable doing so—now that they are older, care less about what others think, and are less consumed by the demands of caring for others. Ironically, by more successfully conforming to the youth-beauty imperative of normative heterosexual femininity, these women find it easier to express themselves, and to be seen and heard, as empowered individuals with unique voices.

When it comes to the question of identity, however, the women in this chapter teach us that it is the appearance of the body that matters most. They explicitly speak about their cosmetic anti-aging interventions in terms of not letting themselves go, and they equate caring for themselves with caring about what they look like. In this way, they leave us no choice but to acknowledge the reality that a woman's sense of self—how she feels about herself—continues to depend a great deal upon whether or not she achieves a youthful appearance.

2

"I Am What I Am!"

The Freedom of Growing Older "Naturally"

For many of us living in American culture today, age-driven changes in physical appearance can provoke feelings of alienation, frustration, and loss. For women—whose individual and socio-cultural identity and value still intertwines, to a greater extent than men's, with the perceived success or failure to achieve an appearance of youth and beauty—these feelings can be particularly acute. Women in the previous chapter revealed that age-driven changes in appearance, which are often experienced as unsettling disruptions and challenges to self *and* social identity, can inspire the decision to have and use cosmetic anti-aging surgeries and technologies. Nearly all of the women in this book experience some uncomfortable feelings of identity de-stabilization—or what Susan Sontag calls "a special pain and confusion"—in response to age-driven changes in appearance.[1] But not every woman has cosmetic anti-aging procedures. The women in this chapter choose to opt out of cosmetic anti-aging intervention, and to embrace what they call a "natural" approach to aging, instead.[2]

The self-described "naturally" aging women in this chapter share stories about learning to accept and, in some cases, even appreciate, the age-driven changes in their faces and bodies. That is not to say that they don't experience feelings of loss, anxiety, and frustration as they confront their changing faces and bodies, and in response to a growing invisibility and lessening of sexual desirability in the eyes of others, with age. But they turn to different strategies to manage these feelings, and to survive these age-based realities. Women's decision to have cosmetic anti-aging procedures can be understood as motivated by the desire to maintain a youthful aesthetic, and the value it represents. By contrast, the naturally aging women in this chapter work hard to broaden and diversify their understandings of physical attractiveness and beauty, both inside and outside of the realm of physical appearance. Age-induced non-conformity to biological and social constructions of heterosexual femininity, like reproductive viability and youth-centered physical attractiveness and desirability, can engender new freedoms. For the women in this chapter, growing older opens up new and exciting possibilities for self-expression outside of the traditional feminine roles and expectations of sex object, nurturer, and reproducer.

"The Demanding Arts of Acceptance, Adjustment, and Appreciation"

The women in this chapter—like the women in the previous chapter and multitudes of women growing older in the United States today—encounter varying degrees of shock and surprise, and alienation and betrayal, when confronted with age-driven changes in their physical appearance.[3] Nina, who is fifty-seven years old and a psychotherapist, captures these feelings well when she says, "You think, '*Who* is that person? What happened to my hair? What happened to my skin?'" Nina is living in what feminist age studies scholar Kathleen Woodward calls the "mirror stage" of old age.[4] When older individuals look in the mirror, see themselves in photographs, or catch a glimpse of themselves in a shop window, they can experience feelings of alienation from the image that is projected back at them. Nancy, a clinical social worker who is fifty-nine years old, tells me more about what it's like to live in this "mirror stage":

> There's a long period of your life, from about your teenage years, late teens, 'til you're maybe forty, forty-five, when you sort of *know yourself* when you look in a mirror. And then there's this thing that starts happening, and all of a sudden you don't look like you as much as you used to. And there's this *shock* when that starts to happen. And every once in a while you see yourself and go, "Whoa!" . . . in pictures or one thing or another. And you catch yourself in a mirror and go, "I don't *know* that person anymore."

Like Nina, Nancy, and most of the self-described "naturally aging" women in this chapter, Sonya, who is an artist and fifty-six years old, experiences uncomfortable feelings of betrayal by, and distance from, her aging body. For Sonya, the most painful encounters with her aging body are marked by a gap between how her body *looks* and how she *feels*:

> Sometimes there's just this sort of jarring reality . . . I mean, sometimes I'm walking down the street and I'm feeling really good. You know, I'm having a good hair day and I like what I'm wearing. The sun is shining. I'm looking forward to things. And I arrive at my destination, and I'll happen to see my reflection, and there'll sometimes be this very harsh reminder of reality.

Sonya's uncomfortable encounters with age-driven changes in her appearance do not, however, translate into a decision to have and use cosmetic anti-aging procedures. For Sonya, and the "naturally" aging women in this chapter, the mask of aging—or the gap between "look-age" and "feel-age"—is less thick and static, and more variable and transparent, than it is for women who choose intervention. Instead of experiencing age-driven changes in appearance as an overwhelming and irreconcilable disruption to their sense of self, the women in this chapter approach these changes as part of an identity that is "inevitably layered" and evolving over time.[5] Nina is working on "trying to like" her aging face, and to see her wrinkles as a "good reminder that you are mortal and that life is precious rather than there's something wrong with you." Nancy engages in an ongoing process of "readjustment," and "getting reacquainted," with her changing face as she confronts it in the mirror: "It's like a *constant readjustment*, I think, after maybe forty, or forty-five, where you're constantly sort of getting reacquainted with the looks of this person." Sonya, on the other hand, is preoccupied with the age-driven changes in her appearance on some days, but succeeds in being free from worry on other days: "Sometimes it really strikes me. Sometimes I don't think about it at all."

Nina, Nancy, and Sonya, like each of the women in this chapter, cultivate and practice in different ways what feminist age studies and disabilities scholar Susan Wendell calls the "demanding arts of acceptance, adjustment, and appreciation" as a means to navigate the age-driven changes in their faces and bodies, and as an alternative to cosmetic anti-aging intervention.[6] Instead of fighting age-driven changes in appearance with technology, the women in this chapter seek to integrate these changes into their understandings of who they are, to respect and learn from these changes, and to take them seriously as both new—yet authentic—aspects of a complex and transforming self.

"Not Bad for a Seventy-Two-Year-Old"

Resisting the impulse to compare yourself to how you looked when you were younger, and trying to compare yourself to others your own age, instead, is one strategy women use to feel better about looking older. Margaret, a retired nurse and currently a part-time hospital administrator, age seventy-two, admits that while she doesn't enjoy seeing photographs of herself at her current age, being around others her own age helps her feel better about how she looks:

> When I look at pictures of myself, I really don't like to look at them. But, on the other hand, my husband and I went to our fiftieth high school reunion and I looked at the other people my age, and I thought, "Hmm, you don't look that bad, you look pretty good." I think I'm as attractive now among seventy-two-year-olds as I was among eighteen-year-olds. If you stacked me up against all the other seventy-two-year-olds in the world, I would look okay.

Nancy finds it challenging to "live in this culture" and feel okay about how she looks at fifty-nine years old. Yet, she reminds herself that "there is a kind of beauty that exists at every age," and she tries to apply this reminder to herself as a strategy to feel better about how she looks:

> I don't think you can live in this culture and not be aware of some of the standards that are thrown in your face all the time. But I think there is a kind of beauty that exists at every age. I'm having a hard time looking in the mirror and figuring out that I can be attractive at fifty-nine, instead of comparing myself to when I was thirty, or twenty, or whatever. Just to look at myself as a fifty-nine-year-old and say, "Well, you know, as a fifty-nine-year-old, I'm attractive!" It's like when I look at *others* I can say, "Well, now, as a fifty-nine-year-old, or as a seventy-eight-year-old, this is

an attractive person." But you're looking at them as having the character-istics of a person that age. And that's *different* from comparing yourself to what you looked like at forty or thirty-five.

Nancy finds it easier to see beauty in other people who are at older ages than seeing this same beauty in herself. In her evaluation of others—including some of her own clients who talk to her about their unhappiness with looking older—she can subscribe to a broader under-standing of physical attractiveness that incorporates wrinkles and that isn't just about external appearance. When it comes to herself, however, she gets caught up in the younger self-comparison. Still, Nancy hopes to learn how to draw from different and more age-appropriate criteria of attractiveness that will make it "easier" for her to accept her fifty-nine-year-old appearance:

> I think about my clients who would come in and complain to me about how unattractive they are at a certain age because they have all these wrinkles or one thing or another. And, see, I never knew them when they were another age. And, I think for their age, they are very attrac-tive. They have a beauty that isn't only about their external appearance. It's about their whole selves. So, I wish I could share that with them. But, it's hard for me to share it with myself sometimes. Because, you know, you've always known what you looked like when you were younger. So, I mean, I never thought of myself as beautiful when I was younger, but I thought I was attractive enough. But if I compare myself constantly with my younger self, then I would always come up short. And, I guess, I'm thinking that if you could *just learn* to compare yourself to what it is that you expect from that age, then it would be easier to be accepting.

Like Nancy, Ellen, a sixty-one-year-old businesswoman, struggles with looking older at times. Yet Ellen takes comfort in the fact that just because she hates the way her face looks one morning doesn't mean that she will hate it the next: "With my face, when I look in the mirror, I'm *surprised*. You know, sometimes it looks good and sometimes it doesn't. Sometimes it looks like I think it will, and sometimes it doesn't." In fact, Ellen tells me that she has become more comfortable and accepting of her appearance over time. In contrast to when she was younger and often insecure about her appearance and preoccupied with trying to "improve" it, today she actually likes her looks more than she used to:

> I'm more comfortable as I get older. It's almost like, finally I am what I am and that's all that I am. You know, I'm *okay* with it. The other thing that I've known about myself as I've been in my twenties going all the way up, is that sometimes I *love* the way I look and sometimes I *don't* like the way I look. And more and more, I *like* the way I look. And I know that if I don't like the way I look, that probably next week I will again. And it doesn't last very long. I used to, you know, when I was younger, "Oh I hate the way I look," you know, "If I change my hair. . . ." But now it's just passing, it's just the way I'm feeling, or the way the mirror looks right now, but it's okay, it'll pass.

"I'm Better Looking as an Older Person"

As she's grown older, Ellen has become less critical of her body. Yet, while Ellen has become more comfortable with her appearance over time, some women feel that they are better looking, and more physically attractive now, at an older age, than they were when they were younger. Lucy, who is a recently retired shop owner and sixty-two years old, is one of them:

> You know, it's funny. I think my coloring is much better now that I've gone gray, than it ever was with my hair dark. This sounds vain, but I've gotten more compliments as an older person than I ever did as a younger person. I think I'm better looking as an older person than I was [as a] young person.

Similarly, Joan, an artist who is seventy-six, sees herself as more physically beautiful now, and receives more compliments for being a beautiful woman, than she did when she was younger:

> When I see earlier photographs of myself, it's a totally uninteresting face. I mean, people would say I was pretty when I was in high school and junior college, but when I look at those pictures, it's like, "*Really? Pretty?*

That's not somebody I consider pretty." But now people say, "Oh, you're so beautiful, Joan," and they would not have said that years ago.

Joan's understanding of herself as more attractive now, at an older age, and the compliments she continues to receive from others for her beauty, has become a source of confidence and support for her as she navigates growing older. She draws upon her beauty for self-assurance in social situations and to bring her comfort when she feels down about growing older:

> This is a real confession. . . . When I'm tired, or pushed too far, or when I go into a room of people at a party, or whatever, I say to myself, if I'm not quite sure, I say to myself, and I can say it over and over again, "Joan, you're a beautiful woman." And that's like a little prop I have inside of me . . . and so I say that a lot to myself, "Joan, you're a beautiful woman." And so it eases the pain of seeing myself getting older. . . . It's just a little something that reassures me sometimes if I need it.

Redefining Beauty

Joan and Lucy's experiences of increased beauty with age—feeling more physically beautiful themselves and receiving positive social feedback for their beauty from others—is not one that is widely shared among the women I spoke to who are aging naturally. However, expanding the beauty canon to include the faces and bodies of older women is *integral* to the natural aging approach. When Nancy says, "There is a kind of beauty that exists at every age," and Ellen tells me, "More and more, I *like* the way I look," they are resisting and pushing back against what Margaret Cruikshank calls the "almost inescapable" judgment that older women's bodies are unattractive.[7] Many of the women in this chapter succeed in finding beauty in age-related physical characteristics, like white hair and wrinkles. But they also find beauty in the increased capacity of the aging body to communicate the complexity of lived experience, and inner character, over time. And, sometimes, they find that, with age, a person's inner beauty supersedes the relevance of the body altogether: beauty isn't only about "external appearance, it's about whole selves," to steal Nancy's language.

"Getting Used to the Changes"

Nina attempts to train herself away from her initial impulse to read her gray hair and wrinkles as unattractive. Instead, she is trying to like them, and to reframe them as a reminder of the preciousness of life:

> You look in the mirror and say, "Ah, look at that! You shouldn't have that. Who is that? You didn't used to have those. You shouldn't have those." But, I think that's a normal thing, getting used to the changes, particularly in your face that you see all the time in the mirror. Or, you comb your hair and you think it feels different and it looks different and you have to keep coming to grips with who you are now, or what the changes are. But I think it's a good reminder that you are mortal and that life is precious rather than there's something wrong with you.

For Nina, the work of "getting used to the changes" is a continuous, demanding, and "normal" part of aging:

> Mostly I don't like it. But I'm trying to like it. I'm trying to like it. I'm pretty good now with the wrinkles on the side here, but when I look at the wrinkles in my forehead it tells me that I'm taking something too *seriously* and I don't like that. . . . And, you know, you get these little bumps and discolorations and it's mostly just something to get used to. I'm trying to just appreciate them. That's what I'm working on. I'm working on it. I'm working on just accepting it for what it is.

We have learned already from Ellen that she is more accepting of her body's shape now than she was when she was younger. Ellen's body is heavier, and has changed shape, with age. Yet, unlike Nina who is "working" to accept the age-driven changes in her appearance, Ellen is happy and comfortable with her older body and judges it less harshly:

> When I was younger, I wasn't as accepting of however my body was. I wanted to improve it and *work* on it. And *now*, I want to be *healthy* so I want to be in good shape, but my body's shape has changed and I think that is [the way it's] *supposed to be*. And when I was young, if my body's

shape had changed I thought I should *do something* about that and get that back in shape. And now this *is [its] shape.*

Ellen is not alone in her new appreciation for the body she used to criticize and feel self-conscious about she was younger. Helen, a homemaker, age fifty-nine, says: "I'm in love with my body now." Helen has moved from beating her body up and hating her "chubby" thighs, to loving and appreciating them:

> I now call my thighs my aunties. They've been so kind to me over the years . . . and, you know, I have mistreated these legs. I have called them names and been unkind to them and they hold me up and I don't have hip problems and I don't have knee problems. And I'm like, "You know what, aunties, where do you want to go today? Let's do something fun!"

Diane, a therapist, age fifty-seven, tells me that she can, on occasion, appreciate the heavier and more rounded body she has acquired with age.[8] She recounts the following example:

> A couple months ago, I was at my yoga class, and one of the reasons I like it is because the woman does a ten-minute blurb—she was reading some Rumi poem—and it was something about my flesh being my temple and all of a sudden I thought, "Oh my God, you know, I can actually hold that idea. I can, like, get in the bathtub and look at all my fat places and say, 'Oh, look at all this nice skin,' instead of being horribly grossed out. You know, when I'm in the right mode, I can actually say, 'Oh, it's so soft, it's so lovely, it's so wonderful.'" I mean that's *definitely* a function of middle age, to think that fleshiness is anything other than grotesque!

In addition to being able to experience her age-acquired fleshiness as attractive to herself, Diane is pleased that men her own age find her fleshier body "attractive," as well. With age, according to Diane, sensuality and physical attractiveness, both in her own eyes and in the eyes of others, are less dependent upon being thin:

> I was just in the Virgin Islands with ten of my friends, and we're all about the same age, and I know I'm attractive to the men in that group and that's

kind of *nice*. But it's just that, with age, I know that sexuality and sensuality aren't by any means exclusively attached to how thin you are. . . . To be able to feel like a sensual person is quite sufficient, so you don't have to worry about exactly how many pounds you weigh.

"A Softness I Love"

The women in this chapter eagerly and enthusiastically share stories and memories about the beautiful older women in their lives. Nina recounts a vivid, physical memory of her great-grandmother from when she was a young girl:

> I had a great-grandmother [who] I thought was beautiful and she had very white skin and very clear wrinkles and very white hair and no eyelashes and no eyebrows. . . . I loved to comb her hair. It was very long and she wore this little bun and I got to braid it.

Alison, a homemaker, age fifty-five, remembers her grandmother's "beautiful silver-white hair and blue eyes" and exclaims: "She was just a beautiful older woman, old lady!" Ellen recalls her mother's "softest, most wonderful skin," and describes the pleasure she derives from observing a ninety-year-old woman who lives in her apartment building:

> Well, there's a woman in my apartment building, she's probably ninety, and I just love to stare at her. She's just *beautiful*. It's just a softness and a sweetness and a naturalness, that's what *it is*. It isn't tight, it isn't makeup, and it's just a softness I love.

Sarah, a writer, age fifty-five, explains how she finds beauty in the colorful outfits and elegance of an older woman who walks through her neighborhood:

> There's a woman who lives somewhere in the neighborhood . . . and she wears her hair back in a chignon of some kind, and she's always got these amazing clothes on. And she's one of the most beautiful characters, I see her moving along, and I'm delighted to see her. I get so much pleasure out of seeing her walk. She wears beautiful, bright, wild kind of clothes.

"A Very Special Beauty"

Women who opt out of cosmetic intervention articulate an appreciation of physical beauty in their own aging faces and bodies, and in their memories and interactions with older women around them. But their experiences of older beauty are not limited to the physical realm. As they distinguish old beauty from young beauty, more complex understandings of beauty, and the interaction between physical appearance and lived experience, emerge. Several women explain that young beauty is easier to notice, and to achieve, than old beauty. For this reason, Ellen finds the beauty in older women more impressive than in young women. As she puts it:

> I think that an older woman is *so much* more attractive. A beautiful older woman is so much more wonderful than a young woman, 'cause I kind of think, like, anybody can do the young stuff, you know.

Elizabeth, a painter who is sixty-one, highlights a similar distinction between young and old beauty. Elizabeth sees new and different aspects in old beauty when compared to young beauty. Young beauty is more immediately linked to physical characteristics. Older beauty, on the other hand, becomes more about the relationship between physical characteristics and the expression of inner character. Even further, because that inner character has developed and grown more complex over time, the face—as a medium for communication of that character—becomes more arresting. Elizabeth explains:

> Young beauty is almost always beautiful no matter what. The thing about beauty is that the quality of a person is so much more defining of what beautiful is as time goes on. . . . I think that the character of how someone has lived a life, and is living a life, becomes very evident in their physical being. Because we really are what we eat, what we do. We do become what our practices are. And it becomes more and more clear, as time goes on. There's something very beautiful, a very special beauty, when one has really lived a long life. Sometimes I think that a person of that [age] is so much *more beautiful* . . . . I have a friend who was extraordinarily beautiful as a young woman. But she's so much more beautiful now. Because

so much of her character, and her integrity, and all those things, come through.

Sarah can appreciate the young beauty she sees in the teenage girls that her sons bring by the house these days. And yet, like Elizabeth, she also finds their young, "unformed" beauty less intriguing than old beauty in some respects. Sarah finds herself being more interested in looking at, and seeking out, beauty in people her own age and older:

> Both of my boys are getting interested in girls. And they'll bring girls home, who are these *little*, you know, just these *little, adorable, unformed beings*. . . . I look at their beauty, which is this *very virginal* kind of beauty, and I love to see it because it's very pretty. But I don't want it. I don't want it for myself. It's for my kids, it's for them to discover themselves in their lives. . . . It doesn't look as beautiful to me, as it does to my kids. . . . And I sort of want to look at other images to find my place of what really is appealing, or interesting, to me. It's not that they're not interesting, but it isn't something I want to *dwell on*.

Rebecca, a flute-maker, age fifty-eight, likens young beauty to the easily evident and luscious beauty of her grandson, and old beauty to snapdragons as they dry out and their shapes become less straight and pure, more complex and unusual:

> It might not be the same kind of beauty. Obviously, it's not like looking at my three-year-old grandson, who's just like this gorgeous little critter. You know, like these snapdragons are drying out, but the shapes and the way they're transforming is still beautiful. And they're not, like, standing up straight and perfect.

Catherine, a retired career counselor, age sixty-one, finds that with age, she increasingly sees beauty as a combination of physical and spiritual beauty. Like the women described above, Catherine finds the physical characteristics of an older face more intriguing in some respects, and more reflective of the complexity of lived experience, than younger faces: "I think often I find that the face of people as they get older becomes more interesting. It has a different aspect to it, rather than just the smooth beauty of the face." Catherine tells me that she is "awed" by the faces and bodies of some of her elderly friends. Of her friend, who is ninety-five, whom she visits often, she says:

> All of a sudden, you see her skeletal form, where actually you see the bone of her forehead, and it's kind of odd, but it's kind of mesmerizing. . . . I'm fascinated by what's happened to her body.

And yet, Catherine is also "awed" by the declining relevance of the physical body altogether, and by the increasing significance of a person's character and spirit, with age: "But it's her *spirit* that fills that little room," she says of her ninety-five-year-old friend. Catherine elaborates further on what she calls the "real potential for beauty" in the aging process:

> I definitely feel that I'm just awed sometimes by some of these elderly people. I mean, really, the definition of beauty shifts, and it shifts increasingly to the beauty of the spirit. The way I see it is that, as the body begins to shift, and eventually is going to fall away, that's where the real potential for beauty comes. As the spirit deepens and ages, that's where, if that is happening in the life of the person, that is what really comes through. All the wrinkling and the aging is within the context of that deepening of the spirit.

"I Like What I Radiate"

Catherine, like most women I spoke to who refuse cosmetic anti-aging intervention, is shifting and expanding her interpretation of beauty with age—she moves beyond strict definitions of physical beauty (as equated with youth) and re-conceptualizes beauty to include non-physical aspects, like the spirit, as well. This does not preclude the fact that Catherine, like most of her "naturally aging" counterparts, continues to value how she looks and to take care of her physical appearance. Most women I spoke to who are saying "no" to cosmetic anti-aging intervention express a keen interest in the clothes they wear and enjoy dressing up. Many wear jewelry, some wear makeup regularly, and several color their hair. Some talk about how much they enjoy traveling to countries outside of the United States where older women are considered attractive, and where, as an older woman, they have received appreciative looks on the street and a greater degree of attentiveness from men in general than they do in the United States. France, in particular, is singled out by several women as a country wherein beauty does not have to be exclusively limited to youth. In France, Sarah explains, women are looked at no matter what their age:

> One of things I love to do is—I love to go to France. And I know I'll love going there when I'm eighty because men will look at me. You're not anonymous at any age [there], people *look*. And women look at you as well. People whistle at you at whatever age you are. They make eye contact and they check you out! But in a lot of cultures, people don't look. I mean, here [in the United States]—we don't look at each other. And I can't understand that. It's horrible!

Alison makes similar observations about French culture and laments that the United States is not more like France in this respect. She appreciates the fact that French women of older ages continue to be admired and considered attractive without having to look young, and without having to have cosmetic anti-aging interventions. She recounts a party she went to in France where there were many middle-aged and older women present, all of whom looked "beautiful" and were wearing "great colors." And yet, as Alison puts it, "I didn't see one facelift!"

Indeed, most women often make note of the fact that, with age, they receive fewer looks from men and are considered less physically attractive than younger women. As Eva, a psychologist, age fifty-one, puts it:

> One thing I do notice is, it seems like places like the gym, or even walking down the street, that men in their twenties and thirties, they don't look anymore. I mean, you sort of felt like, like when I was younger, that you're sort of being checked out. . . . But, men in their twenties and thirties are not checking me out. You realize that, you know, I'm their mother's age, and so if they're smiling, it's probably because maybe I reminded them of their mother, not because they thought I was cute!

Catherine looks at photographs of herself when she was younger with some nostalgia. She admits that part of that nostalgia stems from feelings of vanity—she used to like how she looked in photographs but current photographs of herself are harder for her to enjoy. Catherine associates the less friendly camera lens with the less attentive gaze of others. Just as she likes herself less in photographs, she experiences fewer looks from others:

> When I look at early photographs of myself . . . photographs when I was like, in my twenties and saw long, black hair, I thought, *Oh, yeah*, okay. When I look at photographs of myself now, that's not the way I feel. I look at myself and I say, "Oh, I wish you had taken that from a little farther away," or "I wish I'd had a chance to *raise my chin* when you took that photograph." . . . So, I'd be a *liar* if I didn't say I have that kind of vanity. Because you definitely notice those things, like what happens. So, *very definitely* I have noticed that you lose—well, the kind of thing also that you experience is, I remember a time where I'd walk down the street and I could get a *look*. Well, you get to a certain age . . . and, *goodbye to all that.*

Catherine gets fewer looks on the street, and is less enthusiastic about the way she looks in photographs. She struggles with the age-driven changes in her face like the "flutta butta" under her chin, and the "wrinkles around my eyes." But Catherine doesn't feel that all of her beauty and attractiveness, both to herself and to others, is lost as a result of growing older. She continues to enjoy getting dressed up for parties and going out, wearing a nice outfit, earrings, and a little blush and mascara. In addition, she takes comfort in the fact that her personality and her energy—in short, her spirit—continue to emanate through her face and to engage others and attract people to her. As she explains:

> It's interesting, I still do feel—I still have the experience in a group or with certain men, of the attraction to my energy, to my own spirit. Which is a lovely thing, and that is when I think, "Okay, bow your head." You know, God willing, that will never get up and walk away.

Catherine's successful strategy of redefining her attractiveness, both to herself and to others, by drawing from a combination of physical and non-physical aspects, is shared and practiced by many women who subscribe to the natural aging approach. Helen finds it reassuring, for instance, that her smiley personality will always call people to her, regardless of her age:

> I actually really do like the way I present myself . . . there's something in me that invites another human being to smile back at me, even if I haven't smiled at them. I don't know what that is, I don't know where it came from. But that feeds my soul. So I can't imagine that would ever go away, unless I went into a deep, deep depression of some sort. And I don't want to go there and don't intend to go there, so. . . . I like what I radiate, I guess.

"I *Had* My Day"

The women in this chapter fight back against the universal tendency to read older faces and bodies as unattractive. They develop new, more inclusive, and age-friendly beauty criteria and apply these criteria to themselves and to others. Still, age-based invisibility continues to be a frequent, and painful, experience for many of them. Stories proliferate about being ignored, or being paid very little attention to, by virtue of being an older woman who is considered less physically attractive and sexually desirable in the eyes of others.

Catherine echoes the sentiments of many when she describes her own encounters with invisibility as a "primary," and "painful," part of the aging process. By attributing what she calls the "shift" in her "perceived attractiveness" to nature and biology, however, Catherine assuages some of the hurt that comes with age-induced invisibility. In the following account, Catherine describes her experiences of invisibility as "probably pretty biological," and as she attributes this invisibility, particularly in the eyes of men, to being "noticeably no longer childbearing age":

> I think probably the most *primary* way in which I've experienced [aging] is the *shift*. I think, and I've talked with other friends too, that shift of when you're younger as a woman, the perceived attractiveness in terms of viability. That definitely is a shift, there's no question about that. The way I think about it is—and, of course, this is pure rationale because there isn't a damn thing you can do about it unless you do want to go out and change your face—but, way I look at it, it's probably pretty biological. If

you look at all the animal kingdom, as a friend of mine said, "Men can't help it, their job is to spread their sperm." Women are really *noticeably no longer* childbearing age. It isn't that they *want children*, it's that I think it really *works on* men and so, in *that sense*, you aren't, you're not front and center viable. And that's the kind of thing that I think is really the shift that is *hard* for all of us as women to make. It's hard, when we get to be our age, to really recognize, you know, to *allow* that to happen.

Adopting an explanation like nature and biology helps to de-personalize age-induced invisibility. Yet, painful feelings persist. As Catherine says: "You know, that's *not easy*, because that's an idea, it's not a feeling. If you're feeling that way it's very painful." Even if you accept that invisibility is inevitable, it is still disappointing that a woman's physical attractiveness—her visibility in others' eyes—is so caught up in having a youthful appearance. Catherine puts it like this: "Part of it, too, is really the bowing of the head. And humor, just to say, 'Well, wouldn't it be nice? Wouldn't that be nice? Isn't it too bad that that's what it hangs on?'"

Catherine's strategy of treating invisibility as inevitable—while not without its limitations—is a commonly shared practice. Alison also draws from a life-cycle narrative to help her understand and accept the fact that heads turn to look at her less often than they used to when she enters a room. Alison remembers a time when heads did turn to look at her. She had the very same experience that young women are having now. Alison sees her evolution from younger to older woman as a kind of universal experience—the young women now will too grow older—and she takes comfort in the universality of it. As she puts it:

I have to be perfectly honest. When I was, you know, twenty-five years old I *had* my day. You know, I looked pretty good and I thought I looked pretty good. And I loved to get dressed or go out . . . I enjoyed it! And that's, but that's *past*.

Like Alison, Sarah applies a life-cycle perspective, and uses a language of inevitability, as she gives advice to a friend who is struggling with looking older than her daughter. Everybody has a turn at youthful beauty and once your turn is up, Sarah tells her friend, it's time to let someone else take theirs:

It's their turn. You know, and that's actually something I said to a woman who was really having an issue about looking so much older than her daughter. I said, "Well, you know, it's her turn, it's not your turn, you've had your turn, so move on, you know, get into your own things, you're not competing with your daughter to be that."

Indeed, understanding that young beauty is something "we all get for a little while," may help women move beyond it *and* continue to take pleasure in it. As Elizabeth explains:

I mean there is something, there always will be something intoxicating about someone very, very young. It's like a baby, this young skin and those beautiful clear eyes, and these beautiful forms, you just love to look at . . . I mean that's what we all get for a little while. And then it moves along and we're getting new things. And it's a mistake to think that's the prize, I think, for me.

Nature, biology, and life cycle explanations are tools that help women accept and understand the diminishing attention they receive from others solely on the basis of how they look. But, as is also evident in the language quoted above, not all experiences and feelings are limited to loss. Women encounter gains as they leave youthful beauty behind, as well. Sarah and Elizabeth talk about getting into "your own things," or "getting into new things." It's a mistake, Elizabeth feels, to see young beauty as "the prize." In some ways, Sarah is glad to have moved beyond the stage of youthful beauty (as represented by the teenage girls her sons are spending time with) and feels more comfortable where she is now:

I look at these girls, and I think, "You know, I was one of those once." And they're kind of ditsy, you know, they're kind of all over the map, and they are finding their way, and they're just forming themselves as people. And I often think, "I'm *so glad* I'm not there anymore." You know, I had my turn. I did this. But I don't envy them.

"Living from the Inside Out"

Elizabeth and Sarah don't want youthful beauty back. To leave youthful beauty behind is to experience new freedoms: freedom from worrying about how you look, freedom from worrying about attracting the male gaze, freedom from the discomfort of being the target of the male gaze, freedom from the physical and emotional demands of mothering young children. In each of these ways, the women in this chapter embrace aging as a welcome and exciting opportunity for self-discovery outside of the traditional feminine mandates of sexual desirability and reproduction. Nancy calls this new phase of age-produced freedom "living from the inside out." As she explains:

> You know, I think living a beautiful life is . . . living it from the inside out. . . . I think the only time I ever am aware of my body from the *outside in* is when I'm looking at a picture, or looking in the mirror, or getting dressed in the morning, or getting in bed with my husband. And those are the times when, I mean, you know, they're certainly part of my everyday life, but they're just not places where I dwell on. I'm too busy living from the inside out. You know, too busy interacting with the world and life to be conscious of how I look to others, or to myself in the mirror, or whatever.

Helen echoes Nancy's sentiments: "I'm not as consumed by my appearance now. . . . My identity is definitely less wrapped up in it." For Sarah, being less preoccupied with how she looks, and less anxious about whether she looks "hot enough" to attract male interest and attention, is a clear advantage to aging:

> I'm *a lot less vain*. You know, I think I used to worry about, you know, was my mascara all right, you know, or did I look ok? I mean, I certainly remember the anxieties of the dating scene. Just that *terrible* time you go through of, you know, "Are you beautiful enough? Will this guy love me? Do I look hot enough?" I'm *so happy* to be out of that life. I'm just so happy that it's gone.

"I'm Perfectly Free"

Diane continues to take care of her appearance and to "look as pretty" as she can. But, like Sarah and others, she is enjoying the freedom of being let "off the hook"—the freedom from worrying about sexually attracting others—that age grants her. As she explains:

> I've gained ten pounds in the last year, so I have put on this middle age thing. You know, people put weight on around here, and I've done that. But, I don't mind as much as I did. I think some of that is that I'm over the hill sexually, you know, that sense of, I mean one can say, "No you're not," but, you know, there's this part of me that's sort of like "Well, I'm off the hook." I was never beautiful, but now I don't have to worry about it anymore. Who cares? You know, it's like, "Oh good," now I'm not in the marketplace anymore in terms of men looking at me or women looking at me. I can't say that I feel that every moment but, you know, sometimes I do. I really do genuinely feel like it really doesn't matter how I look when apparently it mattered before. . . . But, it doesn't matter very much. And that doesn't mean I don't like to buy nice clothes and look as pretty as I can and stuff. But it's, you know, there's a lot of freedom that comes with, and who knows what, what the age is. But, I mean at fifty I still felt like in my forties, so maybe it is fifty-five that I began to think, "Oh well, I'm perfectly free." And it is freeing to be older. Actually, that's a really big feeling, that's a really important feeling. It's very, *very nice*. It's sort of like, it's not that I'm asexual, and sexuality is still important, and it's still present, but one's attractiveness isn't as important.

When she was younger, Elizabeth experienced feelings of inadequacy and self-consciousness that hinged on her physical appearance and on the evaluations of others:

> I had this sense of inadequacy that I just had from the time I can remember. I felt inhibited in my body. I didn't feel free to move around freely. I felt that I was being measured constantly by this label of beauty, which was very *disturbing*, because it's so ephemeral, and it's so nebulous, you don't really know what it *means*. And so you're sort of always a little

anxious about how you're comporting yourself, or how you're presenting yourself, or whatever.

Now, at an older age, Elizabeth feels freer from her own worries about her physical appearance *and* from the judgments of others:

> It's a very liberating thing for me. I don't have a lot of the inhibitions and focuses on the exterior that I used to have. And I have a lot of freedom that I didn't have. So even though it's a little disturbing sometimes to look in the mirror, and to feel things like stomach muscles going, and stuff like that, it's really *nice*.

With age, women step outside the sexually objectifying gaze of others. They are also freed from the anxiety of attracting it. New space opens up for previously hidden aspects of themselves to emerge, and for new aspects of themselves to develop. Alison tells me that she enjoyed being checked out by others when she was younger. But she doesn't want that being-looked-at-identity—what feminist film critic Laura Mulvey calls "to-be-looked-at-ness"—back.[9] Like many of the women in this chapter, Alison is increasingly interested in "what a person is like on the inside," and finds herself more focused on "inner personal qualities over external appearance as a measure of human worth," as she grows older.[10] Alison wants people to get to know the real "me," or, as she puts it, "who I am, my insides":

> I walked into a room, and I knew people were checking me out. I knew that and it was *great*. And I'm not going to have that back. . . . And who wants it? I mean find out about *me*, who *I am*, my *insides*.

For Rebecca, not being evaluated as a sexual object, and not being worried about being picked up, has allowed her to be less self-scrutinizing and more relaxed about her appearance:

> I figure, you know, I'm fifty-eight, and people aren't looking at me like they did when I was twenty, obviously. And I find that really comfortable. I always felt, "Somebody's looking at me and I should look good." And now I feel like, "Oh, you know what, no one's really going to look if I've

got this little piece of hair falling down." And they're not really looking at me that much anymore, which is nice. So it's a relief. It's a relief and I figure, "So my pants aren't quite hemmed right," or, "I've got some bleach stains on these pants which I'm going to wear to work." So I don't really care.

Feeling less "self-conscious" about her appearance has enabled Rebecca to come out of her shell and to enjoy interacting with others more than she used to: "I'm not so self-conscious about my looks anymore, which is really good. It makes me more open, I think, to people in general. I have a better time with people." Because she doesn't have to worry about how she looks as much, and because she doesn't have to worry about someone's motives—in other words, whether or not someone is talking to her with the intent to "pick her up," or "hit on her"—Rebecca feels more free to engage in conversations:

> I'm not as self-conscious about it [her appearance] as I used to be. Which makes me really happy, 'cause I think I was overly self-conscious about it. And it works out much better, because I find that people respond more happily and I do too. We do with each other, in general, 'cause I'm not so self-conscious about that. And I don't have to worry about, if somebody wanted to pick me up or. . . . It's just, you know, "Hi, how are you?" and have a conversation.

"I Enjoy the Invisibility of My Age"

Rebecca and Elizabeth were never entirely comfortable with the attention they received for their looks when they were younger. It made them uneasy and self-conscious, and it was difficult for them to find themselves, to know themselves, amongst the desiring and objectifying gazes directed at them by others. Alison felt more comfortable, and actually enjoyed, receiving attention for how she looked when she was younger. But whether she felt unease or enjoyment (or both) under the male gaze, each woman experiences her (age-driven) release from the male gaze not only as a loss, but also as a gain, of self. With the lifting of the male gaze, it is now possible for people to see, in Alison's words, "who I really am, my insides."

As Rebecca steps outside of the role of sexual object, and out from under the desiring and evaluative male gaze, she discovers new space for authentic self-expression and genuine interaction with others. Rebecca acknowledges that she is grateful to be pleasant enough looking that people don't turn away from her. Ironically, however, it is the freedom from the physical appearance of her youth, and from the sex-object identity that accompanied it (an identity that felt ill-fitting, artificial and externally imposed), that enables Rebecca to see herself more clearly and others to more clearly see her. As she tells it:

I'm much more comfortable with it [her appearance] now. Not that I didn't enjoy being pretty. Maybe I didn't enjoy being pretty, come to think of it. Maybe it's easier now that I'm more comfortable with it. And people still seem to like me, which is nice. And they don't turn away cause I'm ugly or something like that. Not that they would. But nobody looks aside when I walk down the street. They say, "Hello," and they talk to me, and so I guess I feel comfortable with my looks as far as that goes. And then, on the other hand, I don't feel the pressure of being really pretty, like, when I was in my twenties, where it really made me self-conscious. I don't have to deal with that anymore. So I'm much more comfortable, I think, with my looks now. They've kind of come down to a medium area. People still smile and find me friendly. Somehow they don't turn away. They like me. People seem to like me. I don't know why this surprises me, but clerks in the stores and people just going by when I'm working in the garden always stop to talk. And I don't feel it's because they want to hit on me anymore. It's just nicer. It's really nicer for me.

Like Rebecca, Diane finds that the erosion of her sexual desirability in the eyes of others, and the decreasing primacy of her sex-object identity, enables her to participate in the world in new ways. For Diane, being freed from the evaluation and gaze of others empowers her to enjoy the art of observation herself:

I actually *enjoy* the invisibility of my age. . . . I have this mental image of sitting at a café someplace, in some foreign country or something, just sitting there and watching everything that is going on, and having tremendous pleasure at watching everything, because I'm invisible. So there's a great kind of comfort in that. . . . But, anyway, I kind of enjoy the invisibility. . . . I'm fifty-five, it's like if you're over the hill, that can be *good* rather than *bad*. It's sort of like you're *totally free*, it's like, you know, who the heck cares what you look like . . . you're just free to observe and be part of it in whatever way you want. The exterior stuff just doesn't get in the way, either in terms of people's perception of you, or your perception of yourself.

"My Body, It's Mine Now"

Aging can offer a welcome departure from the acute self-consciousness and worry about physical appearance and sexual desirability many endured as younger women. As the anxiety and pressure to attract and hold the admiring gaze of others lessens, new space opens up for self-exploration and self-expression. On the other hand, growing older, and embodying a post-menopausal body, can also provide an exciting opportunity for women to connect to their bodies in new ways. When the focus on sexual desirability, reproduction, and nurturing children lessens, women's bodies become more their own to do what they want with. Rebecca puts it like this:

> As I get older . . . I'm not going to be childbearing anymore, so I figure, my body, it's *mine now*. I don't have to be responsible for another being inside there and nurturing it. I can drink all the tea, and some alcohol, if I want to, cause I'm not nursing. . . . My body's not a temple for another human being at this point. That's a big responsibility gone.

Rebecca, like many of the women I spoke to, feels less constrained by her body after menopause. Rebecca enjoys a new sense of freedom, autonomy, and control in her relationship to her body. She doesn't have to worry about when she's going to get her period, or about spending money on menstrual products, and she can wear whatever she wants. She says:

> I don't spend any money on all those products. And I was never regular, so I was like, Is it going to happen today? And then I'd have PMS for a

week. . . . But *out the door with that one!* Now I can wear white underwear and it always stays white.

"This Is Your Time"

"Menopause definitely changes one's focus," Elizabeth tells me. Nina agrees. She uses libratory language to speak about her life in her post-menopausal body. Since going through menopause, Nina's physical and emotional energy is less wholly consumed by the nurturance of her children. Menopause is a time to shed the primacy of her role as mother, and to channel her newly released energy into self-nurturance and self-development. As she explains:

> It's not that you stop being a mother totally, but that part of your life where your main identity and focus—I mean even though I was working and all this other stuff—is about nurturing your *children.* That it can be about nurturing the *world* or the things that you value. . . . It's more a time for your self and your self in a larger sense. You know, whether it's community or spirituality. . . . With the idea of menses stopping, and not ovulating, and not thinking that you're kind of there for nurturing in a physical way, the job you have is to figure out your importance in a bigger way. And that it's important to let go of your children in some sense too, that you're not responsible in the same way. And you can celebrate *their* going off and being their own selves in a full way, and making their own decisions, and appreciating that but not feeling that responsibility. And then you have all this energy for *whatever else.* And the idea that you're not *losing,* even physical, like *blood,* every month, it's within your own self. So it's kind of a reminder that you can nurture yourself, and that this is your time to do whatever feels really important, and really right.

Nina distinguishes herself from her own mother, who, according to Nina, was somewhat lost, and unable to find meaning and value in life, once her phase of active reproduction and hand's on childrearing ended:

> I think my mother never realized that there was something beyond, she just kind of felt empty, I think, and didn't figure out what the next phase

was about for her. But for me this phase is very exciting. It's not all just looking back, or looking to your kids . . . it's good.

In addition to her regular job as a psychotherapist, Nina has become involved in working on political, environmental, and social justice issues in her community. This involvement has been "helpful," and given her a new "sense of purpose." Nina also recently expanded her home to incorporate a new room for her weaving—an action that she describes as "making space for what I love and what I want to do":

> So now I'm going to have a space for weaving that's really *perfect* and right. And, it's a kind of a symbol, making space for what I love and what I want to do. For my own creativity, so that's good. And that feels like a good part of *aging*, really.

Nancy echoes Nina's sentiments. Like Nina, she celebrates having more time and energy for herself, now that she is older. Not having children in the home means that she has more time to devote to herself and to doing things that she enjoys. She doesn't have to worry about getting the kids ready for school, for instance, so she can have more leisurely mornings. Age and seniority have also empowered Nancy to push back the start to her workday (she recently decided not to schedule any clients "before nine o'clock"). She says:

> In recent years [I have the] *freedom* to not have as many demands on my time. And my energy. I have more time. For instance, like I do the yoga in the mornings, and I can *do that*, because I don't have to rush to work. . . . And that just feels so *luxurious* after raising a child, a couple of children, actually, my stepson and my daughter. And, you know, just to have that time is nice. So that's one of the things about aging that's helpful.

* * *

To age naturally is to challenge what Cynthia Rich calls "society's revulsion of aging flesh."[11] The women in this chapter subscribe to a "new and more democratic aesthetics of the body," as they incorporate age-coded markers, like heavier bodies, gray hair, and wrinkles, into their conceptualizations of beauty. At the same time, however, to release beauty from "the narrow limits within which it is now confined," means finding beauty in non-physical attributes, like personality, character, and spirit.[12] To respect the aging face and body means appreciating how it reflects and communicates the unique and evolving lived experiences and emotions of an individual over time. To respect the aging face and body also means accepting that aging is an inevitable process beyond individual control.

These are some of the ways that the naturally aging women in this chapter embody what Susan Wendell calls "the demanding arts of adjustment, acceptance, and appreciation."[13] Yet, their practice of these demanding arts—particularly that of appreciation—extends well beyond the matter of an aging appearance. They also welcome the opportunity to develop new identities, and new sources of agency and empowerment, outside of physical appearance altogether. When their sexual desirability in the eyes of others abates, and the evaluative male gaze erodes and softens, some women feel more comfortable freely expressing themselves as individuals. To hear Rebecca and Elizabeth talk about this age-produced identity shift from self-conscious object to acting subject demands that we confront the ongoing sexual objectification of young women, and the reality that it continues to overwhelmingly be men who act and look upon them: "Men act and women appear. Men look at women. Women watch themselves being looked at."[14] For Diane, invisibility brings freedom. No longer a target of the male gaze, she newly inhabits the role of observer. Freed from being looked at, she looks back.[15]

To grow older naturally can bring a welcome, and liberating, shift away from the woman-as-sexual-object identity, and the companion anxieties about physical attractiveness and sexual desirability in the eyes of others. Aging also frees women from the mandate of reproduction, which, together with a youthful appearance and sexual desirability, remain required criteria to achieve hetero-normative femininity. For the women in this chapter, to move beyond menstruation, and the biological and socio-cultural realities and expectations that accompany it, is to reclaim the body for the self. And, now that pregnancy, childbirth, and intensive mothering are behind them, they can begin to prioritize their own needs and wants more fully—in short, to more fully care for themselves.

3

"Age Changes You, but Not Like Surgery"

Refusing Cosmetic Intervention

Thus far in this book, women have shared their pro-intervention approaches to aging. We have also heard from women who are growing older without intervention. But on what specific grounds does a woman decide against having cosmetic anti-aging procedures? This question warrants more attention. As the next chapter reveals, critical perspectives on cosmetic anti-aging intervention are hard to find in a media and popular culture that celebrates youthfulness, and in a society wherein we are saturated with medical advertising for cosmetic anti-aging procedures. Indeed, it is this overwhelming pro-intervention message that makes hearing from the women in this chapter about why, exactly, they refuse intervention all the more urgent.

"A Lot of Money for Nonsense"

Teresa, who is sixty-two and a yoga instructor, tells me that aging is about "making the shift" from eliciting attention and admiration for external beauty to "letting the beauty come from within, the energy come from within." Whether this identity shift from "outside-in," to "inside-out," as Nancy puts it, is easy and welcome, or frustrating and difficult, most of the women I interviewed who refuse intervention subscribe to an age-based perspective that, at least to some extent, "rejects surface readings of the body and appreciates the inner being."[1] Cosmetic anti-aging intervention reintroduces the importance of physical appearance just at a time when, to repeat Helen's words, "my identity is less wrapped up in it." Spending money, time, and energy on "improving" your exterior doesn't make a whole lot of sense—and can even seem vain and superficial—especially if your own focus has shifted to the value of alternative attributes.

Some women told me that they would rather spend their money in other ways; others simply don't have the money to spend in the first place. And several question the ethics of spending money on cosmetic anti-aging procedures instead of directing that money towards humanitarian and social justice causes. Sonya, the fifty-six-year-old artist introduced in chapter 2. talks about how the combination of the cost of cosmetic intervention, and her lack of preoccupation with her physical appearance, means that it is "one of the farthest things" from her mind:

> Well, first of all . . . there's the economic issue. Maybe you don't even think about plastic surgery unless you're in a certain income bracket. . . . I mean, it's probably one of the farthest things from my mind. In terms of improving myself, my own appearance is probably the farthest thing from my mind.

Lucy, the sixty-two-year-old shop owner introduced in chapter 2, explains that if she had more money, she'd rather spend it on "going out to dinner every week" than on getting Botox. Lucy also critiques Botox from a practical perspective: it's "a lot of money for nonsense," she says. Eileen, a higher education advisor, age fifty-three, thinks of cosmetic procedures as "this huge, expensive deal." She feels alienated from the cost of cosmetic intervention, but also from the prospect of placing so much emphasis on physical appearance. She seeks to surround herself instead with people who, like herself, "don't care about appearances":

> I'm beginning to find people who are like-minded to me, who don't care about appearances, who look deeper, who I share some real interests with.

Eileen is also frustrated that people spend their money on cosmetic procedures instead of directing their money towards helping others:

> I guess it just makes me angry or frustrated when I hear people who have the money to do this, or that, or the other thing, and it's not really necessary. That gets me frustrated. I think, "Well, why don't they spend money on other things?" I think it costs a lot of money to change yourself, and

if you don't need to do it for medical reasons, the money is better spent elsewhere. There are plenty of children who need surgery for medical reasons, for example.

Like Eileen, Teresa worries that women who have cosmetic anti-aging procedures are too self-focused. They are "more concerned with themselves" than with others, she says.

Diane, the fifty-seven-year-old therapist who has come to appreciate her more rounded body with age, objects to cosmetic anti-aging intervention on moral and ideological grounds. She explains that she herself could never have cosmetic surgery because she just doesn't "think it's right," and because it "separates the rich from the poor":

> I might want to do it because other people were doing it and I thought it would make me look better. But when I ultimately had to make the decision, I wouldn't do it because I don't like it. I just don't think it's *right*. So it really would be *ideological*. I just wouldn't do it. I just don't like it. I think it *stinks*. It's just so *scary* to me. . . . I think it's *immoral*. But then I ask myself: "Well, if you think it's immoral, why do you think it's immoral?" And I can say, "Well, it separates the rich from the poor so that makes it immoral."

"A Wolf in Lamb's Clothing"

Many of the self-described natural agers I spoke to equate cosmetic anti-aging intervention with a kind of deception, fakery, and a lack of authenticity. For these women, such interventions mean pretending to be something that you are not—deceiving those around you into thinking you're younger than you really are. Further, some are uncomfortable with the literal prospect of changing their faces and bodies through the use of cosmetic surgeries and technologies. They worry about not looking like themselves—not recognizing themselves—after such procedures. Elizabeth is the sixty-one-year-old artist introduced in chapter 2. She explains:

> Changing my face would be so disorienting. I couldn't imagine if I looked in the mirror and didn't recognize who I was. It would be horrible.

Elizabeth continues, equating her rejection of cosmetic anti-aging procedures with her fear of fraudulence:

> I think there is a kind of terror, a real *terror of fraudulence* to me. There is some kind of thing I personally have which is mixed up with that . . . the truth business. I don't know what it is, but it is some very deep-lying fear of fraudulence, of something misrepresenting what it is.

For Elizabeth, the prospect for identity transformation via cosmetic anti-aging intervention is not an appealing one. Elizabeth tells me that our society is moving in a "strange direction," as she likens a woman who has had cosmetic anti-intervention to a wolf in lamb's clothing:

> You think you're dealing with one thing, and in fact you're dealing with something entirely different . . . sort of like a wolf in lamb's clothing. And I think that this whole thing about changing your identity is *very* tied up in that. . . . Our society is certainly moving in a strange direction. I mean, like, you know, these reality shows, where people are getting these makeovers.

Sonya shares Elizabeth's discomfort at the prospect of changing her face, and hence her identity, through cosmetic surgeries and technologies. She states:

> Besides the fact that I have wrinkles and some little funny things that appear on my skin, you know, I feel that's me. I think it would be the weirdest thing to look in the mirror after having looked at one's self for fifty-seven years, and suddenly be a different person.

"This Is *Me*"

On the one hand, women's rejection of cosmetic anti-aging intervention reflects their distancing from their bodily exteriors—and from physical appearance—with age. On the other hand, many women—like Elizabeth and Sonya—convey deep and visceral feelings of *connection* to their bodies as they articulate their anti-intervention position. They use phrases like "this is me," and "this is who I am," in reference to their un-cosmetically-altered faces and bodies (gray hair, wrinkles, sags, and all). They negatively equate cosmetic procedures with "changing your identity," and becoming "a different person," to explain their lack of interest in having cosmetic anti-aging procedures. Margaret, the seventy-two-year-old retired nurse and part-time hospital administrator, who, as discussed in chapter 2, feels pretty good about how she looks when she compares herself to others her own age, puts it this way:

> This is who I am. You know when I was twenty-five, I looked twenty-five. When I was twenty, I looked fifteen. I looked very young until I hit twenty-five. But all through life, I think—although some people say that's not true—I've pretty much looked very close to my age and that's *okay* . . . If I had anything done now, at this age, I would feel totally phony. Although I really don't like these [*pointing to the wrinkles around her eyes*], this is *me*, this is who I am. I can't imagine looking fifty. Even though I feel fifty, I can't imagine looking that way. I'd probably embarrass my kids.

Margaret's description of her seventy-two-year-old face—"this is who I am"—communicates a deeply integrated relationship between self and body. Like Elizabeth and Sonya, Margaret worries that getting rid of her wrinkles via cosmetic intervention risks erasing or misrepresenting who she is. Would she "recognize" herself? Would others recognize this "different person"?

Margaret and others who reject cosmetic anti-aging procedures call attention to the continued relevance of the exterior of a woman's body in old age. A woman's older face and body offer a powerful canvas for self-expression and lived experience, and reflect the unique evolution of the self over time. Joan, the seventy-six-year-old artist introduced in chapter 2, enjoys witnessing the layers of lived experience that emanate through the faces of older women around her. According to Joan, cosmetic anti-aging intervention inhibits this facial potentiality for rich and complex self-expression:

> I think the older women that I know who are natural, to me, are the most beautiful. I love seeing the character that's still there, and that's really

erased with cosmetic surgery, totally erased. At least [that's the case] with my friend and with a few other people I know who've had facelifts.

By contrast, Joan tells me about a friend of hers who is in her nineties and who has not had any cosmetic anti-aging procedures. Joan finds inspiration and takes pleasure in her friend's aging face and body and in the many different life phases and experiences that are communicated through them:

> She's in her early nineties and I think she is *so* beautiful, so incredibly beautiful. I *love* to see her, just love to look at her. And she's just a prime example that I can think of, of an absolutely beautiful woman. I mean, the way she moves, her body, that big tall angular, almost awkward body of hers. She's just a great, great beauty to me. And I can sometimes look at her and I can see what she looked like when she was young. You can just get this sort of flash of, 'Oh my God, she was so beautiful.' You can't beat it. No amount of cosmetic surgery can accomplish that, at all . . . She didn't erase it. She didn't erase it with any kind of cosmetic surgery. And you can see those levels and it's so rich. It's so enriching.

Joan's description of her friend who is in her nineties and aging without intervention articulates a changeable, yet familiar, face, one wherein new and old selves and experiences emerge and recede and emerge again. When Joan talks about being around friends and acquaintances who have had cosmetic anti-aging procedures, however, she stresses her feelings of disorientation and loss in response to a new and entirely different face—a face that is more fixed and opaque and less open and porous. According to Joan, cosmetic anti-aging intervention more definitively changes a person's appearance than aging itself. And, this definitive change to the surface of the body makes it less able to communicate the unique history, biography, and lived experiences of the individual who inhabits it:

> It's so erased. And so you have to get used to what they look like now. But you long to get back to that person that you knew. I mean, age changes you, but not like surgery. It's so definitive, surgery.

"It's the Coward's Way Out"

Women's refusal of cosmetic anti-aging intervention is imbued with a language of the self. This language of the self reveals a deep connection to the aging exterior of the body. At the same time, much of this talk about the self centers on honesty, morality, integrity, and inner character. For instance, Elizabeth's equation between cosmetic anti-aging intervention and "fraudulence" communicates an integrated self-body relationship *and* a moral aversion to false self-representation. And, when Diane and others reject cosmetic intervention on the grounds of its superficiality and expense, they express what they understand to be a fundamental aspect of their character. Margaret clearly experiences her aging physical appearance as a formative aspect of who she is. Yet, when she uses the word "genuine" to describe herself and the kind of person she aspires to be, she refers not only to her naturally aging exterior, but to her inner character, too. Margaret tells me that her decision not to have cosmetic anti-aging intervention is about her commitment to being genuine both in terms of how she looks and in terms of how she behaves. She says:

> I try to be as genuine as I can be. We all have to be a little phony sometimes, in some situations, but basically I try to be as genuine I can be. And this is who I am and if I had surgery I wouldn't recognize myself and no one would recognize me and I wouldn't even know how to behave. Because basically I'm a combination of everything that has happened to me and part of it is how people have reacted to what I look like.

Like Margaret, Joan draws from the concept of an authentic inner self as she articulates her critique of cosmetic anti-aging procedures. Joan tells me that she will not have cosmetic anti-aging intervention because doing so would require her to be dishonest with herself, and with others, about who she really is. Joan doesn't think of herself as someone who would submit to cultural pressures to have a "patch-up" in her words. Why should she feel shame about looking old? It is her age, and her life experiences that inform it, that make her who she is. As she puts it:

> It's a betrayal of something very deep in one's self, to go that route. It's almost the coward's way out. It's almost too easy to just give into it and

have a patch-up. Yeah, for me, that would be a betrayal, even though I might toy with the idea. But it would just be a betrayal of who I really am, who I think I am, and that person I think I am would not do that, would never in a million years do that. Even though it sometimes tempts me. It's just a betrayal.

Just as Margaret uses the word "genuine" to describe who she aspires to be and to explain her lack of interest in cosmetic anti-aging intervention, Joan calls the prospect of intervention a "betrayal." When Joan says, "I can't be dishonest with myself," and "I can't fool myself," she expresses a strong commitment to an inner honest self *and* to her aging body whose surface authentically communicates and expresses that self. She elaborates:

As you grow up and have all these life experiences, I think you build up a belief in yourself, who you are. I mean, you get tested so in life, always tested, and a lot of times you fail and make a mess of things and so forth. But . . . it's part of that picture, [that] belief in yourself. I can't be dishonest with myself. I can't fool myself. I have to hold on to where I am, what I've gone through, and where I feel I am with myself in the world and in my body.

Joan associates cosmetic anti-aging intervention with superficiality. She thinks of herself as someone who is deeper and more real than someone who spends a lot of money on making her appearance look younger: "I mean it's almost like I couldn't live with myself if I gave into this contemporary world of commercialism and so forth." Joan also experiences her aging appearance as a fundamental part of who she is and this makes the prospect of changing it unappealing: "I've held onto it for so long that even during these years when you age and you could change things . . . that would be so dishonest." When Joan tells me that her rejection of cosmetic intervention is rooted in a "sense of integrity," her use of the word "integrity" has a double meaning. On the one hand, she offers a moral and ethical perspective: she doesn't want to deceive herself and others into thinking she is younger than she is, and therefore, someone she is not. On the other hand, Joan equates integrity with an organic structure of the self, unchanging and continuous over time: "your core," and what is "quintessential in the person." According to Joan, to have cosmetic anti-aging intervention is to fundamentally change "who you are":

> I guess it's a kind of sense of integrity that I feel I want to hold onto. You might feel the same inside, but people perceive you as changing, as being different. At least the ones I've seen with plastic surgery. I don't know, I think it probably changes your personality to have it. Because you've lost your core. You've lost what was originally holding you together when you were young. You lose that by [having] somebody else [tamper] with the vision of you and who you are.

Joan asserts that changing the exterior of your body through cosmetic anti-aging intervention also means fundamentally changing yourself. And, like many of my interview subjects who refuse intervention, Joan frames this change not as self-improvement, but, instead, as a troubling loss:

> Once you go through that, you've really lost part of your soul probably. It almost seems like you've lost something quintessential in the person. Maybe they feel like they've evolved into a much better version, but I don't see it that way.

"Somebody Else's Idea of Beautiful"

My interview subjects who reject cosmetic anti-aging intervention talk a lot about the importance of having autonomy over their own bodies. To refuse intervention means that you are not comfortable with giving your body over to be remade in somebody else's (the surgeon or dermatologist, for example) image. Refusing intervention also means appreciating your own body's unique and distinctive characteristics and not conforming to the contemporary mainstream ideals of youth and beauty. Alison, the fifty-five-year-old homemaker introduced in chapter 2, wonders what, if anything, will be left of a woman's face that makes it unique after she has had cosmetic anti-aging procedures:

> My aunt says, who's a *lovely* lady and takes good care of herself, and has beautiful gray hair, "You know, what's going to happen to all these people?

They're going to be like cookies in a microwave, they're going to revert back to their original state, like glumpy dough." I mean, if you keep doing it, how much can you do it? And once you start, I don't think you can stop!

Elizabeth is also disturbed by the prospect of conforming to the mainstream norms of youth and beauty that cosmetic anti-aging intervention offers, and by the potential loss of an individual woman's unique appearance as a result. She states:

> But I just can't, it's our uniqueness that is such a thing to celebrate. And that is the destructive aspect of society that makes one think that everybody's got to look like, whatever it is now, the current, whoever it is, 'sex and the single girl,' you know.

I heard a lot of critique and concern from my interview subjects who refuse intervention about the prospect of putting your body into someone else's hands and allowing someone else to determine how you are going to look. Joan puts it this way:

> It's another person imposing your face on you. Their idea of your face. And that would disturb me. . . . It's a second person who's deciding how you would look better. You certainly have no control over that. I mean they can make mistakes. It's somebody else's imposition of your face over the one that's really you. I think it's a scary, scary thing—plastic surgery.

Alison, like Joan, is deeply troubled by what she understands as the giving up of control over your body that cosmetic intervention requires. She says:

> First of all, I wouldn't trust anyone. If I could do it myself, maybe. I'm such a control freak and I'm very good with my hands. I probably would be a very good surgeon! The thought of trusting someone, thinking, "Okay, they know just how much to tighten up." If I told them I want a natural look, and I come out and my lips are around my ears—I mean, "No thanks!" *Who knows* what you're gonna get and *that's it!* I'm gonna trust someone that thinks they know what's gonna look good on me? No, I'd rather have my sagging jowls!

Like many of the natural agers introduced in chapter 2, Nina, who is a psychotherapist, and fifty-seven, doesn't want to risk being turned into someone else's vision of what is beautiful. And, when Nina says, "It would be turning me into something that I'm *not*," the deep connection many of my naturally aging interview subjects feel to their bodies reemerges, even as they struggle, at times, to accept the age-driven changes on their bodily exteriors. She elaborates:

> I don't think I would ever have plastic surgery for cosmetic reasons. It sort of goes against my sense of what's right and it would be giving in to somebody else's idea of beautiful and that that could change, you know? It's not about *me*. It would be turning me into something that I'm *not* and so I don't really want to do that.

"Putting Yourself in Danger"

Intentionally cutting the face and the body, causing bleeding and bruising, and injecting synthetic and chemical substances into the skin to look younger is a concept that is difficult to grasp for the women I spoke to who reject intervention. Most identify the prospective physical pain, violence, and health risks that accompany cosmetic anti-aging procedures as fundamental to the formulation of their anti-intervention perspective. Alison tells me: "Yuck, the bruising and the pain too, that's scary. Why would I want to do that to myself? Never." Joan shares an episode in which a friend experienced troubling side effects after having collagen and steroids injected into her hands to make them look younger:

> My friend had steroids put into her hands, and she has great trouble with them because they swell up. That was a disaster. It [the collagen] started moving around . . . I visited her once out in Aspen and she couldn't lift anything because it had all become infected and it was just such a mess and I thought, "Oh Susan, Susan, what you're going to go through."

Catherine—the retired career counselor, age sixty-one, introduced in chapter 2—is disturbed by the idea of "cutting your skin." The objections Catherine raises to having "somebody cut my face and be black and blue" echo some of the anti-intervention perspectives articulated by women earlier in this chapter. When Catherine calls cosmetic anti-aging intervention "self-abusive" she communicates a deeply integrated self-body relationship. When she equates intervention with "a kind of hubris," the earlier associations between those who have cosmetic anti-aging procedures and "self-centeredness" and "superficiality" reemerges as a theme. Finally, Catherine's description of cosmetic anti-aging intervention as a "mask" evokes a deep connection to the aging exterior of the body and contributes to the often-expressed critique of intervention as a kind of deception and dishonesty. Here is how Catherine puts it:

> There's something, I have to say, about cutting your skin, and reconfiguring your face . . . for me, it would be disturbing. I wouldn't do that to myself. It feels like, to disfigure myself in order to look differently is, like, you know what it is? It is like a kind of hubris I guess. I don't know, I just wouldn't do that—you know, have somebody cut my face and be black and blue and whatever else you have to do. It feels a little self-abusive in order to get something that is basically—it's really a *mask*.

For Nina, like Catherine, Alison, and others, to have cosmetic anti-aging intervention is to be "hurting" your body in some way. And when someone hurts their body, they are hurting themselves. Nina says:

> I think it's hurting their body in some form. Whether it's Botox, which is a toxin, whether it's cutting—you wouldn't want to, you know, self-mutilate—and yet it is kind of self-mutilating. It is kind of like self-mutilating in a way. You might be going under anesthesia, and that's dangerous, and at what point do you *stop*?

Nina elaborates on what she means by cosmetic intervention as "self-mutilating" through sharing her experience of caring for a woman who suffered a botched facelift:

> I had a very sad experience when I was working in the psychiatric emergency room, and this woman had had a facelift. And it was pulling apart, you know she had had it done very dramatically, *a lot* of it, and she was beside herself. She was extremely depressed and just about psychotic and

she looked like a horror movie to me. It had been about two weeks, and it was pulling apart, and it was *horrible*. And that actually had *quite* an impact on me—that she had *chosen* to have this thing, that she wanted to be more *beautiful*, and she didn't want to have any wrinkles, and *look what she got*.

Nina presents the facelift-gone-wrong story as a cautionary tale: if you seek to look younger and therefore "more beautiful" through cosmetic intervention, be warned that you may mutilate your body beyond recognition. And, if you have cosmetic intervention to improve your self-esteem and to achieve greater self-fulfillment and happiness, you may be disappointed. It is misguided, in Nina's view, to believe that you are going to improve your interior self by changing the surface of your body to make it look younger:

> It just made such an impression and made me realize . . . that probably she had felt she needed to have this surgery because she felt so bad about herself. And it wasn't going to fix it, and not only was it not going to fix it inside, but this was turning out to even be *worse*.

Nina tells me that this woman would have been better off seeking psychotherapy—not cosmetic surgery—to help her feel better about herself:

> I felt *so bad*, if only she could have done psychotherapy instead of a face-lift. She went to the wrong specialist, I think!

According to Nina, choosing the cosmetic anti-aging intervention route instead of choosing another option, like therapy, means losing out on the potential for truly meaningful, deeper, and more lasting self-help and self-improvement. Not only can cosmetic anti-aging intervention risk physical harm, but it is also only a temporary solution to feeling better about yourself. Nina elaborates on this point by drawing from her story one final time:

> It was very sad. I don't know what happened to her. I'm sure she had a lot of deep sadness and regret. But she was literally—she had created this self-mutilating thing in my mind, and I'm sure, yes, she felt like a victim,

but she had chosen this. And even if it hadn't been that dramatic, the message was loud and clear to me that this is mutilating, this is hurting you, this is putting yourself in danger. And no matter how much you do, it's never going to be enough. It's never going to be enough.

"Change Is a Good Thing"

The prospect of changing one's face or body through cosmetic anti-aging intervention is viscerally disturbing to many who subscribe to a natural aging approach. They view cosmetic anti-aging procedures as deceptive and dishonest acts, and worry about not recognizing them-selves, and losing a core part of themselves, to such procedures. On the other hand, these women are not strangers to change. They attribute the changes in their bodily exteriors to cumulative life experiences and they appreciate these changes—like wrinkles, sags, and bags—as expressions of individual character. Further, many also understand these changes as *natural*, as inevitable, and as a phenomenon that is *supposed to happen* with age. Change is about an evolving self with unique life experiences, but it is also a natural process. To age naturally, as Ellen puts it, is about "trusting the process."

"*I Feel Pretty* Normal"

For Ellen, a sixty-one-year-old businesswoman who shared her embrace of natural aging in chapter 2, understanding the age-driven changes in her face and body as natural, as what is "supposed to happen," helps her to accept them. She reads these changes both as signs of lived experience *and* the course of nature:

> I love *scars*. I think they tell a *whole story*. Well, so do the lines in your face. I just think that if you weren't *supposed* to have those lines and wrin-kles, you *wouldn't*. But there must be a *purpose* for them, you know? This just happens, and it *should happen* if it *happens*. So, *why take that away?*

While these age-driven changes startle and unsettle Ellen at times, see-ing the changes happening in women around her, especially in her older sister, helps her prepare for them:

My sister is six years older than I am and so she experiences it first and then I get to watch it and every time something happens, like a change in the body, or a change in anything, I say, "That's her, that's not going to happen to me!" And six years later, I'm there, and I think, "I can't believe *this really happened* to me!"

Ellen says that she continues to find the age-driven changes in her face and body "surprising" and "strange." But knowing that they happen "to everybody" reminds her that she is "pretty normal":

Sometimes I look in the mirror when I'm undressed and I think, "Oh my God," you know, "I don't ever want to have to share this look with anyone." But I think, you know, "*It's okay*." But it's kind of *shocking* to *see it*. And once again I've seen my sister's body, and then I see mine, and *there it is*, you know, it's like, "Wow, that'll happen to me too." It's so surprising. It's just very strange. But it is *interesting*. I mean, I think it's interesting because it happens to everybody. You know, that's just the thing. 'Cause I feel pretty *normal*.

Ellen also expresses a curiosity and respect for the natural mystery of the aging process: "I wonder, what's going to happen next?" She tells me that she wants to bear witness to what is happening to her body over time, and to see what it looks like "at the end." As she puts it:

I find it fascinating. I think it's a privilege every year I get to experience something new. . . . I find it *so interesting* just to see what's *happening* to me. I think life is such a mystery, and I think that there is a master plan, and I don't want to mess up that master plan. I want to see what's in store for me at the end. And I want to see what I look like. I *don't want to change that*. I want to see what I look like at the end. And I want my *kids* to see what I look like at the end.

"Almost Like Adolescence Again"

In chapter 2, Nina told us about her ongoing struggles to adjust to the age-driven changes in her appearance. One change that she is particularly preoccupied with right now is her hair:

At the moment, I'm having trouble with accepting my *hair* or figuring out how to deal with it. It's different. It's more *wild*, and it's more wiry, as the grayer hair comes in. And I'm not a fusser-with-my-hair-person, but it's *annoying* to me.

Still, Nina works to accept, and even to appreciate, her changing hair:

I'm trying to appreciate it. I think on the whole I'm feeling less defensive and more comfortable with it. I think I'm still okay, and beautiful at times, and just okay at other times. But every now and then, something is harder for me. Like right now, it's my hair. Like, how do you deal with this different texture? My first reaction is it's less pretty, or less beautiful, but I think it's just a matter of figuring out how to adjust to it. It's definitely a challenge. So, I think I'm feeling fine about it. It's just that it keeps tricking me.

When Nina says that "it's just a matter of figuring out how to adjust to it," she clearly conveys her understanding of the age-driven changes in her face and body as an inevitable process, beyond her control. Nina compares these age-driven changes to the physical and biological changes that happen during adolescence. Nina tells me that just as her appearance was fairly constant "between about thirty and fifty," so too was her childhood body, pre-puberty. And, just as her bodily changes began to happen quickly around the age of fifty, so too did her body begin changing "all of sudden" when adolescence began. As she puts it:

It really does feel almost like adolescence again in a way, that you're trying to get used to these changes, because you're fairly stable physically for such a chunk of time, and then there are all these changes to incorporate.

Nina hopes that the age-driven changes in her appearance will become easier to accommodate over time. Right now her feelings are comparable to being in the middle of adolescence, when the body is changing—or "molting," as she puts it—practically on a daily basis. She hopes, just as with adolescence, that she will reach the other side, a period where the changes have leveled off somewhat, a period of greater stability where major changes "have happened" already. A time when, for example, her hair has become entirely, instead of partially, gray. As she explains:

> I wonder if it's *easier* when you're used to being older. You know, it seemed to be the same for that chunk of time, it was just who I was, and now, there are just more changes, and *more changes* . . . . Maybe at some point, I imagine when I'm like, I don't know, seventy or something, *most* of the changes will have *happened*? It'll just be *all changed*. So then it may be easier to feel like it's the way it is: it's whatever, it's beautiful, or it's attractive, or it's okay. And now it's still molting or something.

"Eventually the Sucker Is Going to Fall"

Coping with age-driven changes in appearance can be challenging, even for the women who opt out of having cosmetic anti-aging intervention. And yet, to minimize these changes through intervention is not an appealing or viable option. Because they experience the changes in their exteriors as growing evidence of a lived life *and* as part of the natural life cycle, cosmetic anti-aging intervention risks an erasure of life experiences and the false promise of disrupting nature's path. Cosmetic anti-aging intervention means looking backwards and not forwards; living in the past and not in the present; and denying the future. Cosmetic anti-aging procedures can make you look younger, but they don't actually turn back the clock.

In Elizabeth's view, women who have cosmetic anti-aging procedures are fooling themselves. She asserts that cosmetic anti-aging surgeries and technologies create merely the "illusion" of starting over:

> I don't have any envy at all about having facelifts, or Botox treatments, or any of those things. I don't understand how somebody can think that doing something like that is going to really make any difference, or really make you a twenty-year-old again. I think that is why people want to take away all their wrinkles and their sags and their this's and that's. I think that the illusion is that, maybe you'll be twenty-five again and you'll have all that appeal to the opposite sex or to society. You'll be able to start fresh. To me, it just seems like such a weird way to look for it. It's just like, *hello!* I can't *understand* it.

Elizabeth feels sad for women who have cosmetic anti-aging procedures because they can't enjoy the current phase that they are in—instead, they are constantly looking back and wanting to be younger:

> I feel kind of sad that they are focusing on that and they can't be enjoying where they are. It feels like a *loss* for them. And it certainly is sad for children and grandchildren—imagine all the people around somebody. I don't know, it's just sad to be looking to these very superficial ways to find happiness.

As Elizabeth mentioned in chapter 2, she is actually enjoying being less concerned about her appearance than she used to be. For Elizabeth, to be focused on physical appearance at her age, and to have cosmetic anti-aging procedures, would be a "crazy way to live." She elaborates:

> I guess it does make me feel, "Oh, that's where they are." I mean, it's a little arrogant of me, but it's a little bit, "Well, *that's* where their focus is," you know. And I'm thinking of one person in particular—it's a strange thing to me that she continues to have this kind of *focus*. Whereas, I mean, I wouldn't give anything to be focused on my body right now. I would not be a happy camper.

Catherine certainly understands the temptation of having cosmetic anti-aging procedures:

> I *completely understand*. It would really be nice to remove this area under my eye. Or sometimes I think, "Oh, wouldn't it be nice to pull this back up?" Certainly every woman I've talked to my age, we *laugh*, we've *laughed* about it. "Boy, wouldn't it be nice? Wouldn't it be nice to take that little flutter butter away?," or, you know, "take a nip or a tuck here." I can absolutely understand somebody doing that.

And yet, she continues to move forward, and to leave behind the preoccupation with physical appearance and youthful beauty that cosmetic anti-aging procedures require:

> My energies are going farther and farther away from that. I'm not *going in that direction*. I'm not even sure what I would be fixing *myself up for*.

Now it might be completely different, I might feel completely different, if my *driving need* was to marry again. But I'm not obsessed with that focus. So, I don't know quite why I would do it. To look at myself in the mirror? Because, I think even if I got a facelift, I still wouldn't get the looks on the street.

In the last chapter, comments from Catherine showed how she uses a nature and biology framework to help her to understand and accept her lessening of sexual desirability in the eyes of others, particularly men, with age. But Catherine also talks about menopause, specifically, as a natural, biological, and inevitable process that brings the quieting of her own sexual urges and desires. And this too makes her disappearing sexual desirability in the eyes of others easier to accept:

> I think, at least for me, it is coming to a recognition that you *can't* hold on to it. It isn't that you wouldn't want to—I mean, if I could I would. But, I think energies shift as you get older. You know, once you're past menopause, your libido doesn't have that kind of intensity. It's not that it *isn't there*. It's *very much* there, but it *does shift*. I mean it shifts in the sense that it doesn't have the *urgency* that the libido of a woman who is of childbearing age has, and it's a lucky thing.

For Catherine, the shift in libido initiated by menopause signals a new and different life phase and knowing that it is part of the natural and biological "design" of things brings her comfort:

> It *quiets* a little bit, that's the way I experience it. Because otherwise you'd be driven *mad*. Imagine having all that libido and you're in a sixty-year-old body. So *that's*, I think, very much part of the *design*. It makes all the *sense in the world*.

Like Catherine, Elizabeth speaks about aging, and menopause specifically, as a shift away not only from the reality and expectation of her own sexual desirability in the eyes of others, but from her own body's sexual feelings and desires, as well. Elizabeth doesn't couch this change in a language of loss. Instead, she frames it positively as an opportunity to focus more time and energy on interior self-development. As she puts it:

Once one goes into menopause, at least for me, it sort of relieves you from the sexual fixations of one's body, or the leadings in that direction. You feel as though that's not laid to rest at all *totally*, but it's just on the back burner. And it's an interesting thing, because I think it's time as we grow towards the end of life, there are these opportunities to really focus on the *interior* work, which I think is really what we're all about. So, if the libido isn't beating at the door, it's an opportunity to really focus on that.

Just at a time when Catherine is working to develop and value aspects of who she is outside of what she calls the "external," cosmetic anti-aging intervention threatens to reel her back in. Catherine struggles more than Elizabeth does with the age-driven changes in her appearance, and with her growing invisibility in the eyes of others. "Just because it makes sense doesn't make it easy," Catherine tells me. From Catherine's perspective, however, to be distracted by the surgical or technological pull brings "trouble." Ultimately, aging is a natural, biological, and "inevitable process," and the prospect of cosmetic anti-aging intervention interferes with a woman's ability to confront this reality. Catherine puts it this way:

It makes me feel sad in a way. Because it just seems misdirected. I think what happens is—it's like anything that moves you farther away from your spirit. I think when you have that kind of focus on the external, which we all do—God knows I do, I mean, I'm not outside of that *at all*—but I just *know*, from my own experience, it's most apt to get me in trouble. So, to go in and do all this work on your face, I guess it just seems like a kind of misdirected energy in a way. I just think it takes you out into a place where you're putting your hopes on something that *basically* is like staving off an *inevitable process*. Because one way or another you've got to bow your head. You can have your face lifted, but eventually the sucker is going to fall.

Nina continues to work on accepting, or "growing through," the age-driven changes in her face and body. Nina often feels like she's trying to "catch up" with herself—yet, for her, there is no alternative but to "keep trying" to get used the changes. She says:

Sometimes there are phases that I grow through where I think it doesn't feel like me, or I'm becoming something that I wasn't, and then I'm trying to catch up with myself all the time. And certain things seem to happen all of a *sudden*. You know, you just go along and all of a sudden, whether it's my hair, or certain wrinkles, or it's like a bump or something that never used to be there. You know, you think, "Oh, that feels funny," or "Oh, it didn't used to be like that!" And it's sort of feeling like it shouldn't be there, or it isn't me. But it *is me*. And so you have to keep trying to get used to that.

For Nina, understanding these changes as part of the natural order of things—recall her earlier description of these changes as a reminder that we are "mortal," and that "life is precious"—is important and makes accepting them easier. Just as she compares these changes to the physical and biological process of adolescence, she also compares them to the physical and biological changes that occurred during her pregnancies. Sometimes Nina felt alienated from her changing appearance in adolescence and in pregnancy; sometimes she feels her aging appearance "isn't me." But, as Nina points out, "it *is* me." She elaborates:

Being pregnant, there were so many changes so *fast* that I keep going to back to [feeling like], "Well, maybe it's kind of like that, you're just getting to know what it's like to be *different*," but you're still you, and you're still the same.

On the other hand, however, Nina interprets these changes as evidence of positive self-evolution—these changes in her appearance reflect not only a natural, biological process but also her own unique experiences and development over time:

So I'm trying to see it all as a gift and as a way to see yourself evolving and changing. And change is a good thing. It's a development. I'm trying to see it as wisdom, of all different kinds.

"Change is a good thing," says Nina. In fact, part of what worries her about women who have cosmetic anti-aging intervention is their *inability* to embrace change:

Plastic surgery says the *opposite*. That to be yourself, to be you, you can stay at *this point*, but then you're not really preparing yourself very well for the next stages. If you try to *stop that process*, you're really trying to stay at a certain level that probably isn't realistic. I think it holds you up spiritually. My general take is that if you have plastic surgery, you're hurting yourself in some way and you're trying to stay in the same place, rather than move to the next place.

***

To understand aging as a natural process—as what's "supposed to happen" in Ellen's words—proves a useful framework for accepting and adjusting to aging faces and bodies. In addition to assuaging some of the emotional hurt and pain that comes with eroding sexual desirability in others' eyes, this natural-process narrative comes to signify the opportunity to develop new parts of the self *outside* of the confines of the body as sexual object and reproductive vessel. Self-proclaimed natural agers treat the age-driven changes in their faces and bodies as prompts for self-growth and self-development. These changes are signals to push themselves in new directions, and to evolve in new ways.

At the same time, however, many who subscribe to a natural aging approach articulate an increasingly reflexive and integrated relationship between their bodies, and their own unique biographies, with age. Bodily changes prompt self-development, but they also reflect and express the lived experiences of the self. The body transforms from a more fixed and opaque exterior in youth to a more open and porous surface with age. Older faces and bodies can become more powerful mediums for self-expression, and for the communication of lived experiences— reflective of individual women's evolution and development over time— than younger ones. For these self-proclaimed natural agers, the degree to which their bodies "reflect who I am" increases with age.[2]

It is this understanding of the self and the body as inextricably linked that lies at the heart of women's rejection of cosmetic anti-aging intervention. For the women who opt out of cosmetic anti-aging procedures, the body and the self are continuously "formed and reformed in a dialectical relationship."[3] To have an integrated understanding of the body and the self—the body "reminds me my life experiences," "tells me what I've gone through," and "where I feel I am with myself in the world"—is to find cosmetic intervention unappealing. Cosmetic anti-aging intervention, from Joan's perspective, produces a wider gap between the body and the self than aging itself. And, because the aging body and the self are interwoven, the pain and violence of intervention is not only about what is being done to the body, but also about what is *being done to the self*—not just abuse of the body, but "self-abuse," as Catherine puts it.

4

"Can We Just Stop the Clock Here?"

Promise and Peril in the Anti-Aging Explosion

Women in the United States today cannot go online, watch TV, or visit their doctors' offices without being bombarded with images and information about age-related "symptoms"—aesthetic and otherwise—and the products and procedures required to "fix" them. Every woman I interviewed—regardless of whether she embraces or refuses intervention—is keenly aware of our youth-centric culture *and* the increasing prevalence of cosmetic anti-aging procedures. Nina, who is not interested in having cosmetic anti-aging intervention, still feels an overwhelming pressure to look young: "You feel like you're fighting it all the time. You're supposed to look younger. You're not supposed to look your age." And, when I asked Caroline, who is a Botox user, how she first became familiar with Botox, she replied: "Oh, I don't even know. I heard other women were doing it. I really don't know. It's out there. You see the ads. I saw it maybe on a couple of friends. I don't really know." Caroline's difficulty pinpointing exactly how she learned about options for cosmetic intervention is not surprising. It is as if she learned about Botox through osmosis, through simply living and breathing in the cultural soup of everyday life. The media images of youthful beauty, the middle-aged and older movie stars who look young because they have had cosmetic procedures, the print and television advertising, the brochures in doctors' offices—these are cultural elements most women confront on a regular, if not daily, basis in our country today.

The women I interviewed who choose intervention generally greet the anti-aging explosion with enthusiasm. They welcome the opportunity to embody and project a more youthful image and they express faith and optimism in the power of technology to fight back against the natural aging process. They appreciate the advertising and marketing campaigns as a source of information about new and improved cosmetic

technologies. However, maintaining a youthful appearance can be physically and emotionally exhausting and expensive. The marketing and
availability of new and less invasive procedures can lead women—both
those who have *and* refuse intervention—to feel worse about their aging
faces and bodies, to stigmatize themselves for looking older, and to feel
pressure to "do something" about it. Women's reverence for and investment in youth-sustaining technologies to make them look younger may
also leave them ill-equipped to confront and navigate the realities of
aging that cannot be so easily "fixed" with technology.

"There's a Whole Arsenal Out There!"

Maya, a stay-at-home-mom who is forty-nine, represents the sentiments
of many who embrace intervention when she expresses enthusiasm for
the ever-expanding range of cosmetic anti-aging technologies to choose
from: "I feel like, 'Oh, there's a whole arsenal out there! Great. No problem!'" Knowing that this "arsenal" of cosmetic anti-aging technologies
exists and can be relied upon to fight and minimize age-driven changes
in appearance brings comfort and reassurance to Julia—the forty-seven-
year-old mom first introduced in chapter 1—as well. She explains that
she is grateful that the technologies are available *and* that she can afford
to use them:

> I feel very, very privileged. I mean, we have this amazing life materially.
> And that makes things a lot easier too. I don't know what it's like to be
> aging and not have the money to say, "Okay, remove this, remove that." I
> have the wherewithal to go fix what needs fixing. I feel like it's comforting
> in the back of my mind to know like, "Okay, if I get to the point where I'm
> horrified by something, I can go fix it."

Several women articulate positive perspectives on the explosion of
medical and pharmaceutical advertising that targets older people and
that calls attention to new cosmetic anti-aging technologies and procedures, in particular. Maya shares her feeling that the plethora of medical advertising that centers on older individuals makes her feel better
about her own age-driven physical ailments by normalizing and de-
stigmatizing them. She explains:

I think that so much more advertising is being done, marketed towards, you know, the older, aging population. Which I think is very helpful in terms of being more comfortable—knowing that many more people in this world have, you know, reflux or bladder control or . . . You know, it's so helpful knowing that other people are going through the same thing that we might be going through.

In addition to the comfort of knowing that she is not alone in her experience of age-driven changes in her body, Maya also appreciates that the advertising—and the new products and technologies themselves—offer her a relatively easy and practical means to fight back against these changes. Maya's knowledge of these new drugs and treatments empowers her to take things into her own hands. She says: "Yeah, I think it's great. So you got reflux, so does everybody else. You know, deal with it. Isn't it great, some of these drugs aren't even prescription anymore! You know, it's like, 'Okay, we can take care of this ourselves.'"

If I get to the point where I'm horrified by something I can go fix it, says Julia. *Deal with it*, Maya proclaims. Janet, the sixty-eight-year-old retired airline ticket agent introduced in chapter 1, shares her own real life example of doing just that. Janet was feeling bad about how she looked, and especially about her "droopy" eyes. Then she read an article about a doctor who developed a new eyelift technique. Then she decided to explore what could be done about her condition, called the doctor for an appointment, and, shortly thereafter, had the surgery. She tells the story:

I kept looking at myself when I put my makeup on and when I went to work and said, "These eyes look just *terrible*, and *droopy* and I look tired." I said, "*What is this?*" I really didn't like how I looked. And then it was just in the newspaper that I read about this surgery. I mean you read so much about it. It's everywhere. But I read about this doctor who had actually started this whole laser thing, many years ago already, from Harvard Medical School. . . . And I said, "Well, let me see," and I called him for an appointment.

Janet actually saved the article (it was in her local paper) that influenced her to seek the intervention and showed it to me:

You see, this is what I saw: "Crows Feet, Removing Unwanted Eye Wrinkles." This was the article. This is what got me going. And I read more and more, and I said, "Gee, you know, I want to see what can be done about this."

"Who Knows What They'll Have in Ten Years?"

I listened as women shared with me, over and over again, their pleasure and excitement about ongoing innovation in the cosmetic anti-aging industry. They expressed a heady enthusiasm for the fast pace of technological innovation that is producing new and better procedures, less invasive *and* more effective, than ever before. The user-friendly aspect of these new cosmetic anti-aging technologies also enables women to "test the waters," without having to make the kind of major commitment in time and money—at least not right away—that more invasive procedures, like surgery, require.

Caroline, the forty-seven-year-old radio producer who has ongoing Botox and collagen injections to combat signs of aging, is thrilled with the speed of technological advancement and hopeful that these advancements will mean she can keep "tweaking" without ever having to do "major work." As she puts it:

> I think it's great that there are things out there. . . . I'm trying to play back conversations with friends and we always say, "Yeah, it's great, who knows what they'll have in 10 years?" I think the less invasive, the better. So all these little advances mean that you can keep tweaking, without really having to do major work. You know, why not? "Keep working in your labs," that's all I have to say! "Keep at it!"

Janet is also pleased with the increasing range of options for less invasive procedures. Now that she knows about the mini-facelift (while watching her local evening news, she learned about a doctor who performs the relatively quick and easy procedure at a local hospital) she tells me that she is more likely to go ahead and have the procedure. She explains:

> Let's say in ten years, you know, I'll be seventy-eight. Why not? If things are really falling apart. Really drooping. I mean nothing *big*. I would

never go for a full facelift. But they do now so many things, just a little bit, a mini-lift. There was a whole story on the news one evening—they interviewed the doctor. I was looking at it, you know, I happened to watch the news, and then I said, "This is interesting." Like you go in Friday, and you can go to work on Monday, because they just put, like, two things here and just a little bit of pull to lift this here. I would do that tomorrow if I really wanted it. I am not against anything like that.

Christina, who is a recently retired businesswoman-turned-stay-at-home-mom, age fifty-one, tells me that when her dermatologist suggested she try Botox because "it's not bad, it's fun," she decided to go for it:

I was not invited to a Botox party. It was none of that. Yeah, everybody reads the articles, but there was none of that. It was just my dermatologist saying, "You know, it's not bad. It's fun." So, it's like a couple of pinpricks. They use a needle and they put in four injections. Like, two minutes. If you think of it, just go "Boom, boom, boom, boom." They just clean the surface, do it, done.

Christina is pleased that "instead of having the facelifts you can do these things," and she is hopeful about the continuing evolution of less invasive technologies: "I think the technology's going to change, and I'm so glad about that." Sadie, a stay-at-home mom, age fifty-three, shares Christina's enthusiasm. She describes her first encounter with Botox as a quick and practically painless experience:

I looked in the mirror one morning and thought, "Oh gosh, look at this." So I called [her dermatologist] up. And he said, "Oh well, come on by and we'll see." And I went, bang, and he said, "You know, we can put something in there for you if you like." And I thought, "Will it hurt, will it hurt?" And he said, "Done." I said, "Oh!" It was nothing. It's just amazing.

New and less invasive procedures are less daunting and intimidating—"it wasn't scary," as Christina says about her first Botox treatment—than full-fledged surgery. Still, by using these cutting-edge technologies, women can fancy themselves forward-looking and hip participants in the anti-aging wave. Christina describes her Botox use as a "personal experiment." She says: "I'm always curious. And my doctor is so open that I can just ask, 'Okay, so what is this and what is that?'" Sadie is also "curious" about Botox and other new and less invasive cosmetic anti-aging options:

> I thought, "Well, you know, I'll try it." I was curious. And I've done it. And I've done this bit here and I think to myself, "Well, let's just see how that goes." I just thought I'd try it, you know, and see what it was all about.

Stepping into the world of cosmetic anti-aging intervention via user-friendly technologies like Botox can also make it easier to contemplate having more invasive procedures later on. Christina describes herself as "dabbling." Relatively quick and painless procedures, such as Botox injections, enable a woman to play around the edges of the world of intervention, to dip her toes in here and there, without great risk or commitment. Christina tells me a story about her friend who was unhappy with her aging face. This friend had been considering having a facelift for some time, but was too afraid of surgery to follow through with it. Christina offered this suggestion: "Why don't you try Botox instead?"

"It's Almost Like Magic"

Women celebrate the growing "arsenal" of options for cosmetic anti-aging intervention. They welcome the ease and accessibility of new and less invasive techniques and procedures. They also marvel at the sheer power of technology to literally erase signs of aging from their faces and bodies. Amy, age forty-eight, recently left the business world to become a stay-at-home mom. She exclaims, in a tone of wonder and amazement, how her tummy-tuck surgery made her sagging stomach like new again: "I was *very pleased* with the results. I mean, I just felt like a million bucks. I felt like, 'Oh my God, it's amazing this thing that I never could get rid of is gone!'" Amy describes her surgical experience as "almost like magic." She finds the power of cosmetic intervention to make aging flesh disappear "very enticing." While Amy resisted her surgeon's pressure to have "a lot more done" at the time—including liposuction on her hips, thighs, and vaginal area—she explains that she certainly will take advantage of more cosmetic anti-aging surgeries in the future:

> It's almost like magic and I *totally can see* how women, especially as we age, get seduced into "Oh, let me do a little bit of this," because it is *very enticing*. Going in, my line was: "This is all I'm ever going to do," like I've drawn the line and that was it. [But] afterwards, I kind of sat there and thought, "Oh, you know, I might get an eye job at some point," and "Yeah, I mean, never a full facelift, but I can see, you know, a little bit here and there . . ."

When she was in the recovery room, in fact, Amy experienced some pangs of regret about not having had more surgery done. She muses that maybe if her husband hadn't been opposed to her having surgery in the first place (due to his worries about the potential health and safety risks of surgery), she would have woken up to the pleasure of even more of her age-touched flesh having been miraculously "whisked away":

> But I *do remember* when I was recovering in the recovery room, there was a woman next to me who also had the same doctor operate on her, and she said, "You know what? I did the full thing." She did the thighs, she did the hips and everything. . . . And I don't know how she looked because I was too drugged and I never saw her afterwards. But to a certain extent, if Daniel [Amy's husband] hadn't been so adamant about, "I don't even want you to do it," to a certain extent I could see it. You're under [anesthesia]. It's not that much more in terms of money. I mean the recovery I can't imagine is *that much worse*. So, I don't know. Afterwards I definitely sort of thought, hmm, maybe, I mean, you know, 'cause it is nice to think of this notion that it can just sort of be all *whisked away*.

Like Amy, Janet is ecstatic about the power of cosmetic technology to rid the evidence of aging from her bodily exterior. Janet's eyelift gives Mother Nature a run for her money. As she puts it:

> You don't exactly cheat on Mother Nature, but you kind of, you know, get a handle on this particular aging process by getting rid of all that skin. And I felt like I could go back a few years and look the way I used to look.

"Sixty Is the New Fifty"

When Janet says, "I felt like I could go back a few years and look the way I used to look," she blurs the lines between looking younger and being younger. For Janet, like for many of the woman I spoke to, cosmetic anti-aging intervention is not only about achieving a youthful appearance. It also signifies a youthful attitude and lifestyle and offers the prospect of extending youth and, even, life itself. Amy generally feels that she is "going in a good direction" when it comes to growing older, *except* for what is happening to her body. She tells me how, by having her tummy tuck and likely future cosmetic anti-aging surgeries, she can reverse and change her body's course from a bad direction to a good one:

> All of a sudden something feels drastically *better* . . . . And it's kind of like, "Wow, I can keep going," as opposed to with the aging process you feel like you're going in a good direction from many respects but from your body's respect, it's tough. It's tough. And all of a sudden something's been reversed and it's like, "Wow, I can really go off in this direction!"

The women I spoke to commonly equate their embrace of cosmetic anti-aging procedures with their commitment to living a long and healthy life. I heard a lot from women about how technology and science make longer life possible. Maya puts it like this: "I love the idea that, you know, sixty is the new fifty. I think that's the best attitude going. It's a really great way of thinking. And people do live longer. And, you know, there's so much more you can do." My interview subjects' faith in contemporary technological and scientific advancements—cosmetic and otherwise—is also evident in the way many favorably compare their own generation to that of their parents. Unlike their parents, who were "old before their time," these women strive to look and feel young for as long as possible. Nora, age sixty-two, a restaurant owner who has had eyelift surgery, distinguishes herself from her mother and father when they were her age, and even from when they were younger than she is now. She says: "My mother already started acting old . . . well, actually they both did, like when they were forty."

Lisa, the fifty-eight-year-old retired financial planner who told us about her neck lift and eyelift in chapter 1, draws a stark contrast between her own attitude towards aging and that of her mother's. According to Lisa, her mother, and women of her mother's generation, were more "accepting" of age-driven changes in their faces and bodies, and of aging more generally, than women are today. Lisa tells me that her mother engaged in a notably lower maintenance beauty routine than she does now:

> I mean, she made herself look *attractive*, dressed nicely, and she wouldn't totally let herself go, but my mother never had a manicure, never had a pedicure. I mean she did her nails herself, never had a facial. She cut her own hair.

Lisa's mother didn't "work" on her body the way Lisa does, nor did she feel compelled to fight age-driven changes in her appearance. As Lisa puts it:

> I was looking at some photographs of my mother in her early sixties, and, you know, she had very *white hair* . . . . She never *worked* on her body. And she always looked nice, but she was just more accepting of, "That's *just the way I am.*"

Lisa's mother was less well-off financially than Lisa is today. Lisa's mother wasn't living in our current era wherein beautifying and age-defying products and technologies proliferate and are more aggressively marketed than ever before. Yet, Lisa believes that her mother wouldn't have been interested in things like manicures, pedicures, facials, and hairdressers even if she could have afforded them: "She didn't have as much money as I did, but even if she had *had* more, I don't think she would have spent money that way." Lisa is also convinced that her mother would "*never*" have had any cosmetic anti-aging intervention whatsoever:

> My mother would never—I mean, there wasn't that kind of money in my family, but my mother would *never*, she wouldn't have done that. She would have thought it was *unnecessary*.

Like many of the women I spoke to, Lisa tells me that she had her cosmetic anti-aging interventions to look more like herself again. Implicit in this explanation, however, is the sentiment of not wanting to look *old*. Lisa says: "I talk about it in terms of, 'I didn't like the way I looked.' But the way I looked is a normal aging process for some people." Lisa reiterates that even though she didn't openly talk a lot about it, wanting to look younger was an underlying motivation for her neck- and eye-lift surgeries: "Even though I didn't sit around and say, 'I'm going to do this because I want to look younger,' obviously that was *it*, I mean at some *larger level*." The power of cosmetic anti-aging intervention is limited to the realm of aesthetics. But that doesn't stop Lisa (and Janet and others) from conflating their cosmetic procedures with extended youth. Lisa and her friends "hate" growing older and she wonders aloud whether their cosmetic anti-aging procedures are a "grasp" at staying young:

> I don't know if this is a *grasp* at staying young. I mean, there is something about this, I'm sure that has to do with—you know, you're almost sixty years old. And my mother's generation thought sixty was *old*. And my generation is *primarily* trying to make sixty young. I mean, I don't sit around thinking, "Oh, I want to be twenty-five." But I think that there is no question that my friends will say, "Hey, I'm not old." We *hate* the fact that we are, *hate* it.

Working on the body, fighting age-driven changes in appearance, not wanting to be old, these are feelings and activities that Lisa explicitly identifies as "much more a part of our generation" than her mother's. "It's different now" than it was then:

> I think of my mother talking much more like, "Okay, now we're old." I always got the sense she was *much* more accepting. For years, she would say, "I'm ready to die. I'm ready to go." Whereas everyone I know is like, "Can we just stop the clock here?"

Lisa candidly shares her feelings about not wanting to grow old and not wanting to die:

I really, really don't like thinking about the fact that in twenty years I'll be eighty. I mean, I *really* don't like thinking about that. I *really* don't want to die. I really don't want to get old—I don't want to be feeble. . . . So, when I talk to my friends about it, I think that a lot of us are feeling that way.

And Lisa identifies her neck- and eye-lift surgeries as an expression and reflection of these feelings, as an indication of *refusing* to accept aging and death in contrast to her mother's acceptance of it:

I think that it's about not wanting to become frail, not wanting to die. Not wanting to *leave*. Not wanting to have things end. I don't like things *ending* . . . . What I mind is that it's going to *end*. I'm not accepting of that in a way that I think my mother was.

Claire, the forty-nine-year-old personal trainer who has already told us about her Botox shots and expressed her openness to surgical anti-aging interventions in the future, also expresses a deep aversion to growing older. Like Amy, she bemoans the age-driven changes in her appearance and her body's physical deterioration with age:

The aging process and the physical self, it sucks. There's not one good thing about it. It completely, one-hundred-percent sucks. . . . I mean, *what's* good about everything aging? I mean, what's good about it? I'm not talking mentally and spiritually. I'm talking about physically. I mean, your internal organs are aging. I mean, nothing's going in the positive direction.

Claire also echoes the sentiments of Amy, and many others, when she tells me that there have been a lot of positive aspects to aging for her: "In general it's been positive. . . . It's been *awesome*, especially in the last ten years. . . . I finally have defined my role [and I'm] feeling comfortable with myself." However, now that Claire is content with herself, her life, and where things are at, she doesn't want things to change again: "It took me a long time to get there and now it's going to go away and it's going to change again." The changes Claire anticipates make her apprehensive because she likes her life "just the way it is." She says: "I think it's going to be a little bit of a roller coaster, to be really honest. I don't want my kids to leave my home. I don't. I like my life just the way it is."

Like Lisa, Claire doesn't like "things ending." Like Lisa, Claire connects her dread of aging to her fear of death:

> What I'm not okay with is I have a huge fear of death. And it's something I'm trying to work on. It's like one of my biggest goals right now, doing some work around that. In that regard I can't totally separate aging from the fear of death.

Claire hopes to be able to confront and overcome her fear of death so that she can live more fully in the moment. She puts it like this: "So I'd like to be able to embrace that a little bit more so that I can let that go. And, you know, fully be present in the age that I'm at." Yet, despite Claire's plans to embrace aging and the eventuality of death, she continues with her Botox shots and articulates a desire to have more invasive cosmetic anti-aging procedures in the future. Claire and Lisa's sentiments and actions certainly seem to confirm that—to steal Nina's language—cosmetic anti-aging intervention is about "trying to stay in one place rather than move to the next place." This is a concern that is echoed by social theorists who argue that our contemporary cultural "obsession" to "belie the ultimate limits of the body" leaves us anxious, vulnerable, and ill-prepared to confront the eventuality of death.[1]

"It's the Culture around Us That Makes Us Feel Bad"

Like many who opt out of intervention, however, and who raise critiques and concerns about it, Nina is not immune to feeling bad about herself when she is exposed to relentless youthful images in the media: "I can still be kind of critical of myself after exposure," she tells me. Nina has dramatically cut back on her television viewing as one protectionist strategy. Yet, looking at magazines, or going to the movies can be a "such a *downer.*" She elaborates:

> Well, it really affects me. I'm not immune to it. I've actually chosen, for a lot of reasons, but that's one—I mean we're too busy and we have other things we want to do—but we don't watch much television at all. And I

notice if I'm looking at certain kinds of magazines, like in a waiting room, and looking at *Glamour* or something, you really can feel worse about yourself. Now I'm kind of getting immune to it, but it's such a *downer*. And certainly movies, and things like that, can be really a mixed bag. At this point, I'm not totally immune.

I heard a lot frustration expressed, both from women who are having and refusing intervention, about the dearth of women who are aging naturally—that is, women who actually *look* their age, in contemporary American media, television, and film. Catherine, who is sixty-one and who, as mentioned earlier, refuses cosmetic anti-aging intervention, identifies actress Katharine Hepburn as a role model precisely because she continued to act into her old age without having plastic surgery. In fact, Catherine can't think of *any* contemporary actresses who are following Hepburn's example:

> The actresses I think that are just *fabulous*, are the actresses who really have taken their looks and moved them right into old age. And [the] best ones who've done it are the—I can't think of anybody today—but Katharine Hepburn to me, she is like a classic example. I mean, first of all, she's a wonderful actress, but part of that was, look at that woman's spirit—she was fierce!—and she just went from one role to the next to the next as she *got older.*

Elizabeth, the sixty-one-year-old artist who also refuses intervention, shares her disappointment and dismay in several older actresses, including Susan Sarandon, whom she admires and whom she suspects have had cosmetic anti-aging procedures: "Somebody like Susan Sarandon, who always had a great face—she had those wonderful big-lidded eyes. She looks like everybody else now." Catherine and Elizabeth feel strongly that having more women growing older naturally in the public eye would go a long way towards de-stigmatizing the aesthetic aging process for ordinary, everyday women. Catherine describes Katharine Hepburn as an actress who provided "a service" to all women: "That does *such a service.* It's just good that there are *some women* who really feel comfortable being, *literally*, in their own skin." Catherine and Elizabeth speak for many when they articulate a desperate need for more women to stand up and counter the trend of agelessness in Hollywood. As Catherine puts it: "Because it's a voice to put side by side with that other side, which could be a perfectly legitimate argument: 'This technology is here,' you know, 'I'm going to use it and I'm going to look the best that I can.'" Elizabeth makes this plea for more "powerful women" to "stand up" to the pressure to have cosmetic anti-aging procedures:

> I know there is a tremendous amount of pressure. But I think that if Meryl Streep and some of these people would stand up to the media and just say, "No, I'm not doing it," it just would be a great favor to society. If [only] some of these powerful women, these screen creatures, would stand up!

Julia is the forty-seven-year-old stay-at-home mom who takes a pro-intervention stance to aging. And yet, like many of the women I spoke with who refuse intervention, Julia laments our youth-centered culture as the source of the pressure she feels to have cosmetic procedures. Julia tells me that aging *could* be a "beautiful" process if only the culture didn't make us feel bad about it: "I think that it could be a really beautiful process and I think it's mostly the culture around us that makes us feel bad." Julia would be "happy" to accept her wrinkles and age naturally if everybody else "would let me be okay with it." She elaborates:

> I could look in the mirror and see these wrinkles and think, "Okay, that's what's happening, if everybody else will let me be okay with it." And, if we'll all stop, if we'll all age gracefully and naturally, I'm happy to do it. But, you know, who wants to be the one hag in the room?

Julia uses the phrase "media culture" as she continues to express her frustration with what she experiences as coerced anxiety about her aging appearance: "I think it's mostly from the media culture." Like Nina, Julia feels worse about her aging face and body after exposure to the media images of youthful beauty embodied by young *and* middle-aged and older actresses and reality stars. She is convinced that she would "spend a lot less time worrying," and that we would all be a "little happier with how we look," if we could escape the relentless media "bombardment." As she puts it:

I think that I could spend a lot less time worrying about this if I didn't see the magazine covers that I see. And I think that our culture, well, I don't watch TV, but I certainly know enough about what's going on with these *Desperate Housewives* and *Sex and the City*. These are the icons that are plastered everywhere. I don't look like Angelina Jolie and I can't get away from her picture. And I think that if we were less bombarded, we could all be a little happier with how we look.

Laura, a fifty-one-year-old higher education advisor who is not planning to have any cosmetic anti-aging procedures, agrees. Laura keeps trying to remind herself that the age-driven changes in her face and body are "normal." But the culture we live in doesn't "allow aging" and tells us "aging is not good":

I think things like your face growing lined, and the thickening of the middle if you've had children, and all that stuff is *normal*. And I guess I don't really like people not being able to accept that. So I guess what I think is, the culture is ridiculous, because it doesn't allow aging, or says, "aging is not good." 'Cause it's happening to me, it happens to everybody, and so it's ridiculous when people can't accept that.

"This Is a *Choice* You're Making"

The overwhelming imagery and embodiment of youthful beauty in contemporary media and popular culture can make a woman feel bad about her own aging face and body. Yet, knowing that there is a rapidly expanding pool of new cosmetic anti-aging technologies available to you—being directly marketed to you—can make a woman feel worse. Maya encapsulates the feelings of many when she celebrates what she calls the growing "arsenal" of cosmetic anti-aging treatments and procedures. However, others greet the cosmetic anti-aging explosion with dismay. Aesthetic changes in the face and body, once thought of as simply part of the natural aging process, are now in need of "fixing." More and more options for intervention can mean that women are made to feel personally responsible for—blamed for—looking old. Aging becomes their *fault*. Laura puts it like this: "If you look the way you do, it's because you've made a choice. You have to feel hard on yourself because you have no one but yourself to blame." Feminist and social gerontologist Martha Holstein agrees: "We may be viewed askance—at the simplest level for 'letting ourselves go' when 'control' is putatively within our grasp—and, more problematically, as moral failures for being complicit in our own aging."[2]

When Laura asserts that contemporary American culture "doesn't allow aging," she calls out the ubiquitous images of youthful faces and bodies that surround her, the dizzying number of options for cosmetic anti-aging intervention at her disposal, *and* an ideology and expectation of taking personal responsibility for working on her aging body. Unlike Lisa's mother and women of prior generations, who, according to Lisa, were able to "accept" aging and who would have felt that fighting aging was "unnecessary," Laura feels compelled to take advantage of modern science to maintain a youthful appearance. It's hard to counter the mainstream logic put so succinctly by Catherine: "'This technology is here . . . I'm going to use it and I'm going to look the best that I can.'" Laura alternates between using the phrases "modern times," "modern science," and simply, "the culture," to identify the source of the acute pressure she feels to stay fit, healthy, and young. Laura can't hide from the images of women who are her age and older who are free of flab and wrinkles. And, it's impossible for her to ignore the message that she too can look like that by choosing to work hard on her body, and by saying "yes" to cosmetic anti-aging intervention:

> I think modern times tells us that you don't *have* to look like this. So then you just have to be hard on yourself because I'm *choosing* in some respect to look like this. Because look at Jane Fonda, and look at a myriad of woman my age, who don't have extra flab. So now it feels like a choice. How can you feel comfortable with being twenty pounds more than maybe you would like to be when you have [a] choice?

It's tough, Laura says, to feel "comfortable" with the heavier body she has in middle age—and to accept these bodily changes as a "normal stage of life"—when the culture is telling her that it's "not necessarily so." She puts it like this:

Now modern times have proven that it's possible, instead of just saying this is the normal stage of life and you move through it, and there's the thickening in the middle for women, and your breasts aren't perky anymore, that would be good if you could just say that, but *no*, we have to say this is a *choice* you're making. You *could* look like, think of somebody my age, actresses like Susan Sarandon or Goldie Hawn, Michelle Pfeiffer, all those people. So it's hard to feel good about aging, having your body do what it naturally does around this age, when the culture is telling you that that's not necessarily so.

Laura wishes she lived in a culture that conveyed a natural aging message like "relax, women your age are supposed to look like that," but instead, she is made to feel guilty about looking her age because "it could be otherwise":

> It'd be much easier if I had a culture supporting me, saying, "Relax, women your age are supposed to look like that." But no, modern science tells me, "No, that's not true. It could be otherwise." And there's a sense of guilt, an added source of guilt for women, I think, to say you're just choosing this because "we've proven otherwise."

There must be other cultures out there, Laura imagines, where you can "slow down," and "get old," because that's just "what happens." Here in the United States, however, that's not an option. In our culture, all the choice has become a "burden," that makes aging "our fault":

> The choice in all the matter can be a burden because we constantly feel that when we age or get older-looking, it's partly our fault, and there are things that you can do to undo effects of aging. And so there's just more guilt there. I don't think other cultures have that. You get old, that's what happens. You slow down. But we have this feeling that it's bad to do that.

"Oh My God, Everybody Must Be Doing This!"

Nina feels bad about her aging face and body after exposure to young-looking faces and bodies in the media. The expanding options for intervention, and the growing pressure to take advantage of these options, make Laura feel worse still. Women were eager to share more with me about what it's like to be the direct target of cosmetic anti-aging advertising and marketing campaigns. Several call attention to doctors' offices as a site wherein they are acutely aware of being marketed to. Julia tells me that every time she goes to her gynecologist, or to her dentist, she learns about new options for intervention. In fact, Julia first learned about new laser hair removal and age spot removal technologies at her gynecologist's office, where she continues to have these and other cosmetic anti-aging procedures performed. She explains:

> When I go for my yearly check ups, they now have brochures and fliers in the office. It's "Attention Patients: We Now Are Offering Our Patients These Services." You go to her because she's your doctor, and then you notice, while you're in there for your yeast infection, or your whatever, that "We're now offering blah, blah, blah." I'll stand there, paying the receptionist my co-payment. And I look and I pick up this brochure and I think, "Oh, they do X, Y, and Z." I hadn't really considered doing X, Y, and Z, but if it's convenient and it's right there . . .

We have already heard from Lucy, who is sixty-two and a retired shopkeeper, that she is not interested in having cosmetic anti-aging procedures. Yet, she tells me, it seems like the advertisements for new cosmetic anti-aging technologies are "in your face a lot," pointing out problems "I didn't know I had." Like Julia, Lucy talks about being bombarded with new cosmetic anti-aging procedures at her doctor's office. She understands that doctors make a lot of money off of these procedures and therefore have an incentive to pressure women into having them. Even so, seeing the posters and brochures while on a visit to her primary care doctor makes her feel worse about her own aging body and worry that everybody else is doing it—should she be doing it too? As she puts it:

> You go in and there's this huge sign in the hall about all the cosmetic surgeries they offer now. Yeah, there [are] a lot of people out there and they might as well get you. It's a moneymaker for health organizations. It's a

huge moneymaker, I guess. It makes you stop and think, "Oh my God, everybody must be doing this!"

In contrast to Lucy, who, despite her vulnerability to the marketing of cosmetic anti-aging procedures, remains opposed to having cosmetic anti-aging intervention of any kind, Julia has already had varicose veins and age spots removed via laser, and plans to move on to Botox, collagen, and probably even surgical procedures in the future. Yet, like Lucy, who says that the marketing and advertising points out "problems I didn't know I had," Julia is having a difficult time figuring out whether her motives for having these procedures are her own, or stem from her exposure to the marketing and advertising campaigns. Julia describes this as a "chicken and egg" dilemma: Do her negative feelings about her aging appearance, and her need to "do something" about it, come from within, or would she be perfectly content if these technologies weren't available and relentlessly marketed to her? She elaborates:

> What I resent is that I can't look in the mirror and just be happy. I have to look and think, "Oh, are these too saggy? Do you think I should be doing something down the road? Or, should I fix this?" I had my first varicose veins treatments this year. It's available. It's out there. I can afford it. It's marketed. I can't read [the newspaper] without seeing all these ads: *Before, After.* So I don't know what comes first, the chicken or the egg. Am I dissatisfied with myself and I want to fix it? Or, am I minding my own business, the media is showing me all these ads and I'm thinking, "Oh, maybe I need to do this"?

Mia, a fifty-nine-year-old real estate agent who is committed to aging naturally, criticizes the advertising of cosmetic anti-aging surgeries and technologies as "morally wrong." Such advertising, according to Mia, creates an "artificial demand" among consumers to spend money on procedures and products they don't really need:

> I think it's wrong. And I think the major reason it's being pushed is just to make money for the companies. It's an artificial demand. It's not helping

somebody. So I'm really opposed to direct consumer advertising. I think it's morally wrong.

Mia articulates a nuanced understanding of the moneymaking motives on the part of the companies that create and market cosmetic anti-aging products and procedures to women. She is quick to say that the marketing and advertising "doesn't impact me," and to describe herself as "fairly immune" to it. But Mia also admits that seeing it "all the time" makes her worry that there is something wrong with her for *not* being more concerned with looking younger. As she puts it:

> It doesn't impact me. I'm fairly immune to a lot of advertising. But you see it all the time and it makes you think, "Oh, is that something I should be thinking about?" Or, "am I so out of the mainstream, or I'm so weird, that I don't care about this?"

The more Julia thinks about it, the more she is convinced that the exploding availability of options for cosmetic anti-aging intervention are to blame for her preoccupation with her aging appearance: "Because if the products and services weren't available, I wouldn't be thinking about it." Julia holds the marketing and advertising accountable "for the fact that I spend as much time as I do thinking . . . 'Should I get the veins done?,' or 'should I get another treatment?,' or 'should I get this?'" Mia agrees. She tells me that her exposure to the marketing and advertising for cosmetic anti-aging products and procedures increases her anxiety about her changing appearance with age. Mia also shares her concern that the marketing and advertising sends the "wrong message," by making women feel worse about looking older and by heightening men's expectations about what women *should* look like. As she puts it:

> I think it tries to increase one's anxiety. And I think it's a wrong message that society sends to all parts of the population. Not only the women, who can feel it, but also for the expectations for men. It's really unhealthy.

Like Laura, Mia is now made to feel "apologetic" about growing older because she is unavoidably "aware of what the possibilities are," and because she has to make a "conscious choice not to use them." It's like the

Botox advertisement proclaims: "You can choose to live with wrinkles. Or you can choose to live without them." In Mia's view, the advertising and marketing certainly "does make one feel worse about growing older," and does *not* help "one's self-esteem." She elaborates:

> I think it does make one aware of what the possibilities are. And I think that now one has to make a conscious choice not to use them—whereas before it wouldn't have been on one's radar screen. So I think it does make one feel worse about getting older, because these products are designed to make one look younger. So I think it makes one feel either apologetic or, "Gee, I'm getting older and things are just getting worse." It does not help one's self-esteem.

***

The exploding field of cosmetic anti-aging intervention offers the possibility of fighting aesthetic signs of aging with technology. And this brings many women comfort and cheer. Women who embrace intervention feel better about aging—not because they are coming to terms with the age-driven changes in their faces and bodies and coming to accept aging as a normal and natural process—but because their interventions make them look and feel *younger*. They practice what Martha Holstein calls "age-avoidance" as they "take advantage" of an ever-growing stockpile of new cosmetic anti-aging products and procedures in "pursuit of youthfulness."[3]

On the other hand, however, the fear among women who refuse intervention that the anti-aging craze will "only devalue old age and intensify existing cultural attitudes about aging," also rings true.[4] For women who aspire to grow older without intervention, this rapidly expanding "arsenal" of anti-aging options transforms their naturally aging bodies into "problem bodies" in need of repair.[5] The growing marketing, advertising, and availability of cosmetic anti-aging products and procedures raise questions, not only about the acceptability of older-looking faces and bodies, but also about the mental health of the women who inhabit them. Why look old when you don't have to? "Letting yourself go" is a "choice and I don't understand that choice," Claire proclaims. Or, as Laura puts it, "You have no one but yourself to blame."

"Why Should I Be the Ugly One?"

Social Circles of Intervention

Critical and feminist gerontologists agree that our individual experiences and attitudes about aging are "formed and given meaning in culture."[1] We are "aged by culture," as Margaret Morganroth Gullette succinctly puts it.[2] Over and over again, I listened as women threaded what they call simply "the culture," into their narratives about growing older, and as they pointed to its influence. For the women in this book, "the culture" is code for an *anti-aging* culture. Like so many American women today, they make sense of their aging faces and bodies in a landscape filled with dizzying options for cosmetic anti-aging intervention, media images of youthful beauty, and an obsession with fitness. Whether a woman decides to have, or refuse, intervention, she inevitably confronts the anti-aging explosion.

But the women in this book also depend on their social relationships—the social interactions that enliven their communities and their social worlds—as a source for understanding and evaluating their aging exteriors. Sociologists of the school of symbolic interaction have long argued that the self is "essentially a social structure" that "arises in social experience."[3] According to George Herbert Mead, it is only through interacting with others and adopting the "social attitudes of the given social group or community," that people can develop a strong and secure sense of who they are as individuals.[4] Contemporary critical gerontologists and sociologists of the body draw from this perspective when they argue that individuals create their own "vision of age identity from the expectations of others."[5] Appearance is "socially mediated" and "given meaning through social interaction." Our social interactions, as Rebecca Wepsic Ancheta points out, work like a "human mirror." It is through social interactions that individuals "internalize" and develop a sense of what they "'look' like to others." They transform the "reactions of another" into their own "view of self."[6]

The women in this book interpret the age-driven changes in their faces and bodies—and how to respond to them—through the social worlds they inhabit. This means mirroring the social mores, expectations, attitudes, and behaviors of their social worlds *and* experiencing their own attitudes and behaviors reflected in them. This means coming to see themselves, and their aging faces and bodies, through the "human mirrors" that populate their daily lives—work colleagues, female friends and acquaintances, other moms in the neighborhood, romantic partners, doctors, and children. In this chapter, the women who embrace intervention introduce us to their social environment. They tell us about the social expectations that inform their own pro-intervention stance on aging, and about the social relationships and interactions that directly impact their own decisions to have and use cosmetic anti-aging procedures.

"It's Stupid Not to Do Everything You Can"

I heard a lot from women who embrace intervention about how looks matter—and how looking *young* matters—particularly for women. Women repeatedly expressed this attitude as reflecting an empirical reality, but also a kind of moral duty. To be a woman means to care about how you look, and to maintain as youthful an appearance as possible. To be a woman, therefore, means to have cosmetic anti-aging intervention. In chapter 1, readers were introduced to fifty-nine-year-old Barbara, who has had a facelift and an eyelift already, and who is considering having another facelift and a neck lift in celebration of her upcoming sixtieth birthday. For Barbara, cosmetic anti-aging procedures are a "no-brainer." "Who wouldn't take advantage of surgery?" she asks, incredulous at the thought that any woman would not do just that. Julia will "absolutely avail myself" of cosmetic anti-aging procedures and is astonished that some women seem unbothered by the age-driven changes in their appearance: "It amazes me that these things don't bother them . . . it amazes me when I see women who . . . do nothing." Debra, the fifty-six-year-old musician who told us about her two eyelifts in chapter 1, puts it this way: "If women can afford to do it, *they should do it.*" Mary, a semi-retired commercial realtor, who is seventy-two, agrees: "I mean, why not? You might as well do what you can."

According to Mary, having a facelift was one of the best decisions she's made in her life: "I have no regrets. Absolutely. It's the smartest thing I ever did." This is because, Mary tells me, "needing to look good" (i.e., to look young) is undeniably important for a woman's social acceptance and professional success. As she puts it:

> Looks, let's face it, have a lot to do with it, whether you like it or not. We all talk about how terrible that is, but it's absolutely the reality. . . . Because that is the way we live in this world. And I think it's a bunch of crock when you read all this stuff, "Oh, it doesn't matter and we have to love people for who they are." Sure, I mean, in *theory*. But that is simply not the way human nature works.

Mary describes her work in the commercial real estate and development business as a "man's world" punctuated by very few women, all of whom are young. She is "competing in a professional world" where "it helps to look good." Mary also attributes her facelift to the difficulties of being a single woman in middle age: "I found that being single and being middle-aged is not easy. I was out there as a single woman. And that's a life-changing experience. And I found that looks were very important. For good or ill." After having her facelift, Mary's social life, and her experience of single life, improved. As she puts it:

> I think I had an easier time of it. I think I was more self-confident, because I knew I looked good. And youthful for my age. And age wasn't the factor that it might have been otherwise. I didn't have to think to myself, "My God, I look ancient," at a singles group, or cocktail party, or whatever it happened to be. Or, if I met somebody new, I found that the people I met were pleased that I looked good.

Mary describes herself as an "advocate" for having facelifts. As someone who knows how tough it is to work in a "world of men" and to be a single woman in middle age, and as someone who credits her facelift with helping her to overcome these difficulties, Mary encourages other women to do the same. Even though women "don't want to talk about" the difficulties of looking older, particularly if they are single, it is, as Mary puts it, "a major thing." Mary feels strongly that to "hold your own" out there means having cosmetic anti-aging intervention. "It's stupid not do everything you can," she says, and she is not shy about sharing her feelings with other women her age:

> I'm very glad I did it [had a facelift]. I've talked to a lot of women about it since then and been kind of an advocate for it. . . . I encouraged them if they had any inclination at all, to at least consider doing it. . . . You just have to do what you can with what you have. And I think it's stupid not to do everything you can, particularly if you're single. So that's my speech. And I've given that speech to a lot of women, I might add.

And yet, Mary tells me that having her facelift to look younger "wasn't even a question of remarrying" (though she did happen to meet her second husband post-facelift). Even more than being successful in the singles scene, or in her professional life, for Mary, having her facelift was about something more basic and fundamental. It was about not being an outcast, not being isolated, not being invisible, or, to repeat Anne's language, "not being dismissed." As Mary puts it: "It was just about having friends and, you know, having something to do, socially. Being socially acceptable."

"You're Always Looking at Everybody Else"

When women who embrace intervention share their feelings about their aging appearance, they often talk about their habit of "checking out" the women their age around them. The women you see at work, at your children's schools, in the grocery store, in the neighborhood— they all serve as a kind of barometer for evaluating just how well you are doing in the battle against aging. Maya is the forty-nine-year-old stay-at-home mom introduced in chapter 4 who is open to having cosmetic anti-aging procedures, but isn't sure she will, and hasn't had any yet. In Maya's experience, competitiveness between women based on physical appearance increases with age. As she explains:

> I used to never even think about how I looked a lot, and now I do a little bit more. But it's hard to go out there and not think about it, cause you're

always looking at everybody else. So you think they must be looking at you, too. You know, as catty as it sounds, we're all doing it. . . . So women check each other out all the time.

Like Maya, Claire, who is forty-nine, and Caroline, who is forty-seven, admit to frequently comparing themselves to other women. Perhaps at younger ages their physical competitiveness with other women was based on characteristics like weight, height, or body shape. Now the aesthetic trait of youthfulness has been added to the list and—for Claire and Caroline—other women become a measuring stick for how well they are aging. Claire puts it this way:

> Because I do compare myself. Like, I will—there's no question—walk into one of my kid's schools and go, "Okay, how do I look compared to these other [women]?" For me, that's a natural thing to do. And, feeling that I'm in the better half of that range is like a good thing for me.

Or, as Caroline puts it: "This sounds terrible to say, but I think if you compare yourself, or if you think like what most forty-seven-year-old women look like, I'm very fortunate . . . And as long as I'm not at the bottom of the heap, I'm okay."

Julia, who is forty-seven, also talks about comparing herself to women in her peer group, particularly other mothers at her kids' high school—where a lot of moms are older than she is—and feeling better about how she looks as a result:

> A lot of these women were much older than I was when they had their babies, and this might be their third kid. So these people are like sixty. And they look so frumpy and so old. So I feel really good as a forty-seven-year-old. Do I look really good standing next to a twenty-seven-year-old? No. But in my group, I feel good.

It is not so much her husband, or other men, that Julia wants to look good for at her husband's upcoming office holiday party. Instead, it is the women who will be at the party that have inspired Julia's diet and fitness regimen. Unlike the women at her children's school, these women are not Julia's peers but significantly younger. And she wants these women to think that she looks "pretty good" for her age and after having had three kids. She explains:

> I have my husband's office holiday party. It's next week. He is the boss. So I'm the boss's wife. . . . All the secretaries in their twenties will be there, who look great. And I am extremely conscious that the party's next week, and after being a total pig over Thanksgiving, I am very motivated. And I keep thinking, "Well, Julia, why do you have to look good for the twenty-five-year-old secretaries? Why do you care?" 'Cause in my mind it's not about his other male partners. It's not even so much for Michael [her husband]. It's some competitive thing where I guess I don't want to be embarrassed, or I want them to think, "Oh, she looks pretty good for her age or having had three kids."

"We're in It Together"

Female friendships feature prominently in the narratives of women who look favorably upon cosmetic anti-aging surgeries and technologies. Many identify their female friends as a source of support and camaraderie in light of the age-driven changes in their faces and bodies. They share and commiserate with their friends, and they find comfort in the fact that, like themselves, their friends are confronting changes in their appearance that trouble them. Seeing echoes of their own age-driven changes in the faces and bodies of their friends also brings reassurance. On the other hand, some women are tired of looks being such a common topic of conversation. And others express feeling competitive with friends about who looks best and youngest, and feeling pressure to "keep up" with their friends in the battle against looking old.

Maya tells me how much she appreciates being able to share her frustrations about the age-driven changes in her face and body—aesthetic and otherwise—with close female friends her own age. She and her good friends from college are all are "turning fifty together" and they all know about her tendonitis and her other irritating physical issues and she welcomes hearing about "their stuff" too: "I'm not keeping it a secret. And actually they're all very sympathetic. So then when they need to talk about their stuff, they'll have someone." Trad-

ing stories with her friends about annoying dental work makes it easier
to cope with:

> When your teeth start to go, crowns are something that most people are
> experiencing the need for at this stage of the game. And it's horrible. So
> we all say, "It's horrible. It sucks. It's so much money, oh my God!" But
> as long as you have a camaraderie . . . you have instant sympathy from
> people who are going through it with you. We just laugh and do it. And
> say, "Oh, okay, I'm not the only person in the world who needs to have
> their teeth replaced." And so it makes it a little easier.

Maya also takes solace in the company of friends when it comes to the
"glasses game":

> Oh, and of course, the whole vision thing too. The glasses game. Vi-
> sion, you know, close, far, it's so ridiculous. . . . Everybody's playing the
> glasses game, and the teeth, and so that helps, I think. We just laugh.
> And cry.

Maya is pleased about the growing options available to her for cosmetic anti-aging intervention: "I guess the point is that I feel as if I want
to know about it. So if I wanted to utilize it, you know, maybe I could."
She is glad to know that she can do something about the age-driven
changes in her appearance if she chooses to: "There's more you can do
about it these days." Yet, Maya also measures her own changes in appearance against those she sees in her friends. If she continues to feel that she
and her friends are weathering the aging storm at about the same rate,
she will be less likely to consider having cosmetic anti-aging procedures:

> I guess as long as I'm looking around and I'm seeing what's happening to
> me happen to my contemporaries, then I feel a little more accepting of
> it. . . . A few more wrinkles, those aren't fun to see. . . . So I don't know, as
> long as I look around me, and, you know, I've got my group of friends and
> we're all sort of hanging in there at the same rate, it's bearable.

At the moment, Maya is focused on her neck. And she sees similar age-
driven changes in the neck of a friend who is even younger than she is.

If, however, she starts to feel that she is "way ahead of the curve," she just might sign herself up to have something done:

> The only part of me that I'm thinking about right now is my neck. I'm being very honest. This [*pointing to her neck*] isn't going anywhere. I know. So it's like, "Okay, well, she's got that too. Okay, she's younger than I am. Okay, well, all right." Just let it go, kind of thing. I'm not going to go start cutting. But it's kind of like, "Okay, I could use a little more Retin-A down there." . . . I'm not thinking about it unless I'm looking in the mirror. So I'm not obsessed, but of course it's there. You see the wrinkles, like, "Oh, better change the light bulb, keep the lights dim." But my point is that, as long as I look around and I see something that's happening to me is at a rate that's happening to most people in my age group, then I feel a little better. But if I was way ahead of the curve. . . . I don't know.

Like Maya, Caroline also feels better after seeing age-driven changes in the appearance of her friends that mirror her own. Witnessing changes in her friends' faces and bodies reminds her that everybody ages and this brings her comfort: "I see it on my friends. Maybe it does make me feel a little better, you know, 'cause it isn't just me. It just happens, no matter how much care you take, it's the way it goes."

Caroline tells me that she and her friends "commiserate" about aging and looking older. Lamenting aging together is a "source of comfort." On the other hand, Caroline sometimes wishes it wasn't always on their minds so much and that they could "just talk about something else." Nonetheless, these conversations about appearance always seem to take center stage: "We can't help it. We always seem to lapse into it." Julia spends a lot of time talking about aging and physical appearance with her friends, too. She and her friends support each other's victories over gray hair and weight gain, but they also bond over the various hassles involved in fighting aging all the time. As she describes:

> I do a lot of social things with my women friends and we always say to each other, "Oh, you did your hair, it looks great," or "That color looks so good on you," or "Have you lost weight?" I think we're very supportive and complimentary of each other. By and large, I think people I call my "real friends," we're kind of in it together and we can grouse

about it, or laugh about it, or say, you know, "Oh God, I can't believe my roots are showing again," or "I ate so much over Thanksgiving," or "teeth whitening."

Female friends offer the comfort of shared experience when it comes to aging and age-driven changes in physical appearance. Yet, their faces and bodies also offer a means of comparison and evaluation and can introduce competitive feelings about who looks best. Julia puts it this way:

> I would say though . . . I feel a little bit of competitiveness. Part of my not wanting to be fat, that seems to be more my focus lately, is I don't want to go out to lunch with two of my women friends and be the fat one, or the dumpy one, or not look good.

Caroline tells me that growing up she never had a "hang-up" about having small breasts and that she actually used to like them: "Flat was great." Now, however, "something's shifted." She has started to feel defensive about her natural breast size and like she has to justify it: "Can I help this? I just have, like, no upper body fat and I never did and just won't." Women in Caroline's social circle are getting breast implants: "You start seeing a lot of people getting them. . . . I mean, there were some times I thought about it when I've seen other people get it, and think, 'Oh, it'd be so nice.'" Caroline has decided not get breast implants at the current time. And yet, she would treat herself to bigger breasts if she ever had breast cancer: "If, God forbid, I did have breast cancer . . . I would automatically put them in, no question. And I would go a little bigger!"

Julia sometimes resents all the pressure she feels to have and use cosmetic anti-aging procedures. If only she and her friends could make a pact to age naturally together. But, as she puts it, "Why should *I* be the ugly one?":

> What I really resent is, I feel like if we could all just make a pact, and none of us will do it, then I won't either. But if everybody else is going to get their teeth whitened, and they're going to have plastic surgery, and they're going to do this and they're going to do that, then I'm going to feel like, "Well, why should *I* be the ugly one?"

"They Really *Encouraged* Me to Do It!"

Female friends played a formative role in the decision to have cosmetic anti-aging procedures for many of the women I spoke with. Seeing a friend who looked enviable after having had a procedure, getting a recommendation about a good doctor from a friend, receiving reassurance and encouragement from a friend who had already had the procedure done, getting confirmation from a friend that your dissatisfaction about your appearance was indeed warranted—in each of these ways, women's stories about their embrace of invention illuminates the power and influence of female friends. Unlike Caroline and Julia, who sometimes feel ambivalent about so many of their friends having work done, most women identify the instrumental role female friends play in their path towards intervention as a positive one, and as one reflective of true friendship.

Anne, who is the sixty-five-year-old artist and retired social worker introduced in chapter 1, didn't think she would ever have a second facelift. But, after seeing how good a friend looked after having one, she decided to treat herself to a second as well:

> I didn't think I was ever going to have another one. I thought one is fine. But, things started, as they naturally do—things fall again, and change. . . . And one of my friends had just had it done again. And we were the same age, and she looked so *great*, and I thought, "Oh well, for my sixty-fifth," I thought, "Okay, that's my present to myself. I'm going to have that done once more."

Amy, who is forty-eight, had a similar experience. It was seeing how good her friend looked after tummy-tuck surgery that motivated her to sign up for one herself: "A friend of mine had one . . . she had it done, and she looked *so good*."

Getting a recommendation from a female friend about a particular doctor—either because that friend is in the beauty or skincare business, or knows someone who has used that surgeon or dermatologist, or has used that practitioner herself—can substantially increase a woman's comfort level with having cosmetic anti-aging intervention herself. For example, it was a friend of Amy's who suggested a surgeon for her tummy tuck: "A friend of mine owns a skincare business and I got the name from her. And I knew, you know, that it came highly recommended. And I felt good about the choice because you read these *horrific* horror stories." For Sadie, a retired businesswoman and currently a stay-at-home mom who is fifty-two, it was a combination of seeing that her friend "looked so good" after her Botox shots, and receiving encouragement from this friend and others who had done it and survived, that helped her feel more comfortable with the idea of trying it herself. Exposure to Botox advertisements had already increased her familiarity with it—but actually seeing the results of the injections on her friend, and hearing from her friend that "you should try it, it's really not that bad," made it easier for her to imagine actually doing it herself. As she puts it:

> A friend of mine recently underwent some Botox—she had a line across her forehead—and so she said it was "really good." And I said, "No, I don't know, maybe, but I'm not sure about putting things into my body like that." But she looked so good with it, so I said, "You know, I'll give it a try."

Some women told me about how they actively sought the advice and opinions of female friends about a particular aspect of their aging appearance that was bothering them, and whether or not they should consider cosmetic anti-aging intervention to address it. For instance, Wendy, who, as discussed in chapter 1, has had two eyelifts and continues to have ongoing Botox shots, originally sought out a friend's counsel regarding the lines above her upper lip. Wendy's friend, however, pointed out other problems with her face that required more drastic measures. Wendy hadn't even considered the possibility of having eyelift surgery until having lunch with her friend:

> Well, let's see, I think the reason that I had the surgery was because I was talking to a friend and told her that I thought that I needed something for my upper lip because I was having all of these little fine lines. She's an aesthetician, and she sat there and *she didn't think through her words very carefully*. And she said to me, "Wendy," and she shook her head. She said, "I don't know if I'd be so worried about your upper lip." She said, "If I were you, I would be looking at my under-eyes more than anything." And that

was really earth shattering. It was *shocking* to me that she said it because I *knew* they looked bad, but it pushed me right there. That's all I needed to hear. Because she was *absolutely right*. I mean I was not—because it was an expense, I wasn't thinking about going for the bigger picture. I was thinking about taking care of the smaller problems. But she was right. She's been a friend of mine for twenty-seven years, and she knows where I've come from, and, you know, how I looked, and she wanted to make sure I understood that.

Even though it came as a shock at first, Wendy interprets her friend's suggestion about her eyes as an accurate reality check: her friend was "*absolutely right*." Her friend's suggestion pushed "me right there," or literally, into the surgeon's office. When I asked Wendy to expand on how she felt when her friend made the comment about her eyes, and whether it hurt her feelings, she replied:

No, I wasn't hurt at all. I think I was more *stunned*. I didn't say it to her then, I think I might have said, "Really?" And inside I was thinking, "I can't *believe* she said that." But then, I sort of remember going home that night and looking in the mirror and saying, you know, "God, she's absolutely right, *look at this!*" And I was, you know, I kept thinking about getting married and the pictures and I looked like an old hag! And I said, "She's *right.*" And I think, you know, I immediately consulted with a plastic surgeon and he suggested that "yes," indeed, not only did I have bags under my eyes but that my eye lids were very heavy and had excess skin on them and that those should be done as well. So I agreed and quickly scheduled it! I was getting married in July and I wanted it to be done so that I would have healing time before the wedding.

Wendy's interaction with her friend, and how she responded to it, offers a striking example of the process by which the reactions of another are internalized and transformed into individual self-perception. Wendy's friend acted as a "human mirror": she went home after her friend's assessment, looked in the mirror, and saw herself through her friend's eyes. Despite her initial disbelief at the gall of her friend's suggestion, Wendy is grateful to her friend for forcing her to admit to herself just how bad her eyes looked, and for preventing her from looking like an "old hag" at her upcoming wedding. Indeed, Wendy's friend's critique was not only confirmed, but also expanded on, by her surgeon who identified her "heavy" eyelids in need of repair as well.

Lisa, the fifty-eight-year-old retired financial planner we have gotten to know quite well already in prior chapters, tells me that her female friends played a critical role in her decision to have her neck- and eye-lift surgeries in two key respects. First, because more and more of her friends were having cosmetic anti-aging procedures—a phenomenon that she is quick to point out is reflective of a "larger societal" movement in that direction—it became more conceivable for her to imagine doing it too. As Lisa witnessed her friends around her having cosmetic intervention, and as its general acceptability increased, she began to shed her sixties-era persona and to embrace the prospect for herself:

> I grew up, maybe like a lot of women in their late fifties, in that era when cosmetic surgery was just something that wasn't done. And *then* being a college student in the *sixties*, you know, we didn't wear bras, we didn't wear makeup, and we certainly were not going to dye our hair or have cosmetic surgery. I still don't wear much makeup, but, you know, there was a bit of a stigma around having plastic surgery. It was, you know, *unacceptable*. That came I think both from my upbringing, and from the sixties, a little bit of that generation, yes. I think it took some *time* to really think I would *do this*. But, the fact is, I had more and more friends having plastic surgery. So I had friends through some of my non-profit work where I was kind of seeing this and going, "Wow!" And *then* I had a couple of friends who moved south, to Savannah and Charleston—three as a matter of fact. And every single one of them moved south and then did *something* and said, "Well, Jane, *everyone* down here does."

Second, even though Lisa's interest in intervention was "starting to build," it was her conversations with two of her closest female friends that offered the turning point and provided her with the conviction she needed to move forward with her cosmetic procedures. Her friends validated Lisa's assessment about her neck and encouraged her to have the surgery:

> I really needed to talk through the decision. And so I talked with a couple of good friends, and two in particular I would say who are very, very

good friends. Both said, "You should do this," and they really *encour-aged* me to do it. And I was quite *surprised* when they did that because I thought, "Wow, they, you know, they *notice* it, this *thing* [referring to her neck]." They knew how much it bothered me, but also they kind of gave me *permission*.

Lisa's friends demonstrated true friendship when they sympathized with her unhappy feelings about her neck and supported the surgery as a means to overcome them:

> It was a *relief* in a way, psychologically to say, "Well, if they think this is okay," and they are sort of saying, "Yeah, you should do that," you know, "This is something that we know how much you hate it." And I wore turtlenecks all the time and I never wore necklaces that were around my neck because I didn't think they looked good. I wore turtlenecks and col-lared shirts because of just *hating* the way it was.

Like in Wendy's case, Lisa's friends served as "human mirrors," reflect-ing back to her just how real the problem with her neck really was: "My friend Alice said, 'Yeah, it doesn't look good, you should do it!'"

When Lisa says that her friends gave her "permission" to have the surgery, and talks about feeling "relief" after her friends tell her that it's "okay" to go ahead with it, she also speaks to being able to finally let go of the last vestiges of her sixties-era identity—her worries about superfi-ciality and vanity—and her fears about her mother's disapproval. Earlier Lisa shared feelings about how her mother, who was much more "ac-cepting" of her aging appearance, "would never have done that." By con-firming, "in a nice way," that her neck didn't "look good," Lisa's friends empowered her to move beyond any lingering doubts: "Any kind of little sort of 'Oh Lisa, this is so stupid why are doing this?'—spending eleven thousand dollars for vanity, for what could be interpreted as vanity, that negative thing vanity, and then going back to the sixties and my mother."

Mention of female friends was not uncommon in women's talk about their recoveries from cosmetic anti-aging procedures. Some women told me about how their friends, who had experienced similar procedures themselves, failed to share with them just how painful and traumatic the surgery and recovery process can be. Other women pointed out how helpful their friends were during the recovery process, especially friends who had already had the same procedures. Lisa tells me that if she had known just how painful and uncomfortable the recovery would be, she might have reconsidered her decision to have her neck- and eye-lift surgeries. On the other hand, her decision to go ahead and have the surgeries was one of the "best things" she's ever done for herself. In this way, perhaps by *not* disclosing the extent of the pain of recovery, Lisa's friends were acting in true friendship. All the same, Lisa now warns people. As she puts it:

> I did have friends who had—one friend in particular who had done something very, very similar. And later, after the surgery, I immediately called her and said, "You *lied*"—a lie of omission—"You *never* told me how *painful* this would be!" And she said, "Well, if you told people how painful this would be, they'd never do it!" But I wasn't, and I've talked to other women who said the same thing, I wasn't really expecting as much discomfort as there was. I now actually warn people.

In contrast to Lisa's experience, Wendy's friends were forthcoming with information and assistance throughout her recovery. Wendy's friends offered emotional support and practical advice—often garnered from their own surgical experiences—on such matters as pain management, swelling reduction, and bruise concealment:

> I got phone calls from everyone about how I was doing, and, you know, that night [after the surgery]. I also have a friend who had her eyes done as well, by that same doctor. And she called me up and said, "You need to do this for your eyes," or that, you know, icing, "Don't keep the ice off, keep your head this way, keep your head that way," so everyone was very *supportive*.

"He Didn't Have a Clue"

Mary proclaims that embracing cosmetic anti-aging intervention is about being "socially acceptable." Women "ought to do whatever they can with what they have" and this means having cosmetic anti-aging procedures. This message was reiterated, repeatedly, by many of the pro-intervention women I interviewed. Saying "yes" to cosmetic anti-aging procedures means that you understand that looks matter, and that looking young matters, particularly for women. Mary was one of the few women I spoke to who explicitly talked about men and how they factored in to her decision to have cosmetic anti-aging intervention. She says that, as a woman, "you have to hold your own"—by which she means that you have to look young—when you're working in a predominantly male work environment, and when you're navigating the heterosexual singles scene. When Julia tells me about working on her body in preparation for her husband's office party, men, including her husband, are not first and foremost on her mind. Instead, her motivation for wanting to look good "in tight pants and a tight shirt" comes from the young women she knows will be there. But, in some very real respects, that competitiveness leads right back to men. Julia and the much younger secretaries are vying for her husband's approval and attention. Winning the attention of a man—her husband—symbolizes the ultimate validation of Julia's attractiveness. She says: "Yeah, [it's about] wanting to feel proud. And I want . . . and I want it also to be a reflection on Michael, like they'll think, 'Wow, Michael's wife is . . .'"

Like Mary, Julia brought men into her narrative about her aging appearance several times. She shared examples of women who had been left by their husbands for younger women, or whose husbands had affairs with younger women. These stories unsettle Julia and heighten her insecurity about how she looks. Overall, men are certainly powerfully implicit in nearly every woman's story about her aging appearance. When a woman says that cosmetic anti-aging intervention is the obvious choice to make—a "no-brainer"—this means that she knows that looks, and looking young, matters more for women than for men. Yet, while male surgeons and doctors feature prominently in almost every woman's account of her cosmetic anti-aging interventions, husbands and male partners remain largely peripheral, or absent altogether.

In stark contrast to relationships with female friends—and to the influence of female friendship throughout the process of considering and following through with cosmetic anti-aging interventions—intimate relationships with male partners appear to have little impact on women's decisions to go ahead and have their procedures. Lisa's story of her husband's lack of involvement was typical: "It was more my thing," she says.

Even when it comes to their new and improved post-intervention looks, women do not seem to expect too much from their male partners. Lisa puts it this way: "My husband . . . doesn't exactly stand around saying, 'You look great, you look great,' the way my friends do. But then if I ask him what he thinks, he says, 'Oh yeah, it looks great.' He sort of forgets. I'm not sure now how much he thinks about it." As discussed earlier, Amy's husband didn't want her to have the surgery. About six weeks after her surgery, Amy hosted a surprise party for him and "bought a new outfit for it and everything." It was "nice to hear" her husband say, "Wow, you look *really good*." But, "that's not why I did it," Amy is quick to point out.

Husbands and male partners were generally not in on a woman's process of consideration and decision-making from the beginning. Unlike female friends, intimate male partners often didn't hear anything until a woman had decided to go ahead with the procedure, or, at the very least, start to seriously consider it. Several women didn't tell their husbands at all, even after they had their procedures done. Maybe they were worried about their husbands' disapproval of spending money on something that was "unnecessary" or "frivolous." Or maybe they didn't want to share their "beauty secrets" with male partners. Or maybe they felt that men simply "don't get it," and are not interested in such things.

Sadie's story is a typical among the women who keep their male partners in the dark. Other than her dermatologist and his nurse, one friend, and myself, the interviewer, no one knows about Sadie's Botox shots: "You [meaning me, the interviewer] know now, and my dermatologist and his nurse know. My friend knows, I told her. And I haven't told anybody else. It isn't something I talk about." When I asked Sadie about whether she's thought about sharing it with her children, or with her husband, she replies: "They wouldn't notice . . . and if they asked me, I would be honest. But if they don't ask me, I don't proffer that information. My husband didn't have a clue anyway. He didn't have a clue. He wouldn't. And the kids wouldn't notice."

Most women did open up to their husbands and male partners when they got to the point of seriously considering cosmetic anti-aging intervention. And, in most cases, they found their male partners to be "supportive" of their ultimate decision to move forward with having the procedure(s). In every instance, when my interview subjects described their male partners as "supporting" their decision to have intervention, the intended meaning was not that the men agreed with, and confirmed the need for, intervention, but instead that they supported *their right to make their own decision.*

Men who supported a woman's autonomy, her power to decide for herself whether or not to have cosmetic anti-aging intervention, and who also emphasized that they didn't think she "needed it," were often described as saying "all the right things." Anne recounts how her husband responded to her desire to have a second facelift: "My husband kept saying the right thing: 'I don't think you really need it but if you *want* it, it's up to you.'" Lisa tells me that her husband would never actively encourage or promote her having cosmetic anti-aging procedures. And yet, when she told him that she was considering having neck- and eye-lift surgery, he was "incredibly supportive":

> I would say my *family* never encouraged me, they would never have thought of it. My husband, my kids, would never have *suggested this.* They would never have said anything, never *promoted* it as an idea. But, once I told my husband that I was thinking about it, he was incredibly supportive.

Lisa's husband is "supportive" because he respects her independence and her ability to make her own decisions. He supports her decision to move forward with her surgeries not because her neck bothers him, but because he knows how much it bothers her: "It doesn't bother me but I know how much it bothers you," he told Lisa. Lisa describes both herself, and her husband, as "very independent." Unlike the marriages of some of her friends where a spouse might say, "I *can't* do something," Lisa's husband is "very supportive of things I want to *do* about myself."

Like Lisa, Wendy describes her husband's support of her decision to have eyelift surgery as evidence of his support of her independence—he supports her capacity to choose for herself and make her own decisions. As Wendy puts it: "I asked him how he felt about it, and he's—what's so wonderful about him, is he said, 'How do *you* feel about it? Is it something *you* really want?'" Wendy contrasts the freedom she feels with her current husband, and her ability to be true to herself with him, with how constricted she felt in her first marriage. Her current husband enables her to authentically express that part of herself that cares about how she looks, that part of herself that enjoys wearing makeup and getting her nails done, that part of herself that *wants cosmetic anti-aging intervention*. Her first husband, on the other hand, asked her "not to wear makeup when I went home to visit his family," where "I just stood out like a sore thumb." Wendy's current husband also has the money to support her interest in cosmetic procedures, and is more familiar with the prospect, given that his sister and mother have both had work done.

Out of every woman I spoke to who shared their desire and intention to have cosmetic anti-aging intervention with their male partners, Amy's husband was the only one to raise serious objections. His opposition was not focused on whether or not her wish to do something about her stomach was warranted, but instead arose from his concerns about the risks and potential complications associated with surgery. Unlike the women who celebrated their husbands' support of their independent decision-making power, Amy tells a story of *asserting her independence over and above her husband's wishes*. She makes up her mind to go forward with the surgery with or without her husband's approval: "My husband didn't love the idea that I was going to be put under and thinks any elective surgery is a bad thing. But I said to him, 'You know what? I *really want this*.'"

Amy respectfully listened and took measures to alleviate her husband's concerns. Before she made the final decision, she took him along with her to the consultation with the plastic surgeon. She asked the surgeon all the difficult questions about possible complications and side effects she could think of, in part to reassure her husband about the relative safety of the procedure, and in part to show her husband that she understood the seriousness of what she signing up for:

> I said to my husband, "I don't know that I'm doing this but I'm going to meet with the doctor." . . . He said, "I don't want you to do it." I said, "Look, you can come with me or not come with me but I'm going for the consultation." So we went, and I wasn't *convinced* I was going to do it. And I talked to the doctor, and I walked in and I said, "Look, my husband doesn't want me to do this so I have to ask you every ugly question you ever heard asked." You know, "Has anyone ever died on the table?" because I knew my husband was sitting right there.

At the end of the consultation, Amy decided she wanted to go through with the surgery, regardless of the potential risks and regardless of her husband's concerns: "And so, after the consultation, I was scared out of my mind but I just thought, 'I *really* want to do this, this is *really important* to me.'"

Ultimately, Amy's husband was never completely comfortable with her decision to have the surgery. If she "had to do it all over again," she still doesn't think he would approve, though he didn't prevent her from doing it because "money wasn't an issue" and because "he knew I really wanted it." Amy made the decision to have her tummy-tuck surgery for herself, it was about what she wanted, it was about *her body*: "I said to him, 'It's not your body and you don't have to live in it and it really bugs me.'" In fact, Amy is already considering having more cosmetic surgery in the future, in particular, an eyelift for her fiftieth birthday. She has started to prepare her husband—but, as was the case with her tummy tuck, she's going to do what she wants no matter what he thinks or says:

> I'm standing there saying I never will get a facelift, but I do know you never say never. But I definitely could see—my eyes are looking gross to me—I can start to see signs. And so I said to my husband, "Gee, I think maybe for my fiftieth I'm going to get my eyes done." He said, "Absolutely not!" And I said, "I'm just raising it because I might."

Women's understanding of their decision to have cosmetic anti-aging interventions as "my thing" is clear in their lack of expectation of assistance from their husbands and male partners during the recovery process. Some women were appreciative that their husbands did help out, although they certainly didn't expect them to. Anne's husband took care of her for the first couple of days after her second facelift surgery. Lisa was touched that her husband took a half-day off from work to help take care of her because he "doesn't normally do that." Lisa did not assume her husband was going take care of her, however. She was not offended when he didn't come in with her to the hospital the morning of her surgery. And she jokes about the fact that when her husband came to pick her up afterwards, he didn't escort her out because she looked too terrible and he was embarrassed to be seen with her:

He took me to the hospital that morning, dropped me off, and didn't bother, you know, didn't *come in*. But then he came back to pick me up and when he *saw* me I think he was *stunned*, as was I when I looked in the mirror, and he said to the nurse, 'You can walk her down to the door, I'll go get the car.' I don't think he wanted to be seen with me!

Like Lisa, Amy had no expectation that her husband would help out during her recovery process. She describes, with no hint of anger, how he didn't "bend over backwards" to care for her. After all, it was her decision and he didn't want her to do it: "You know, he didn't bend over backwards because he said, 'I didn't want you to do this.'"

"He Said, 'It's No Big Deal'"

Like female friends, and unlike husbands, doctors—primarily plastic surgeons and dermatologists—are key players in women's articulation about their aging faces and bodies and in their decision-making narratives about cosmetic anti-aging intervention. Like female friends, doctors confirm that women are right to worry about their eyes looking droopy, or their cheeks looking saggy. Even better, these legitimate concerns can be alleviated and fixed through surgery and medical technologies. Janet, the retired airline ticket agent first introduced in chapter 1, who is sixty-eight, describes the key role her surgeon played in confirming the problem with her eyelids and in advocating surgery as the solution:

And I went there [to the surgeon's office] and I liked right away the whole set up and everything was kind of, you know, gave me confidence, very professional. And so he looked at me and said, "You've got a lot of skin, you know." And I said, "Yes, *I really want to get* [rid of it]" and [he said] "*Of course.*" And so we did it.

Janet's surgeon reassured her not only that she was right to worry about how her eyes looked, but also alleviated her fears about the eyelift surgery itself, describing it as "no big deal." She explains:

I did my research and then I went and had an interview [with the surgeon]. I wanted to find out what they said and what can be done and what they said kind of encouraged me because he said, 'It's no big deal, you just have to take it out and that's all.' And then I finally made the appointment and said, 'Let's get it over with,' and it was really *nothing*. No big deal at all.

Janet trusts her surgeon's assessment as a medical expert—he diagnoses and legitimates her problem and proscribes what to do to fix it. Christina, a fifty-one-year-old recently retired businesswoman-turned-stay-at-home-mom, relies on her dermatologist to help her to navigate the world of ever-expanding cosmetic anti-aging technologies. Christina trusts her dermatologist as the expert on these technologies and draws from her dermatologist's expertise to stay informed. Christina expresses a deep faith and comfort in her dermatologist's recommendations. Even though Christina acknowledges that her dermatologist may promote the use of new technologies to "build clientele," she also appreciates the fact that she is "very low-key" and doesn't push surgery on people. For her fortieth birthday, Christina got her ears pierced, and for her fiftieth birthday, she wanted to do something for herself too. She decided, after seeing and hearing about it, and especially after a conversation with her dermatologist, that her fiftieth birthday present would be Botox. Christina describes the leading part her dermatologist played in her decision:

Then when I was getting to fifty, I was thinking, "Okay, now what would I do?" And I'd been seeing a lot of things and hearing about a lot of things. And my dermatologist had started offering this [Botox]. And so, of course they're trying to build their clientele. And she had actually done some of it [Botox] herself. And so I was like, "Oh, wow." And [I asked] "Is it scary?" and she said, "No, no, no, it's not." And I said, "Okay." So the one thing I thought about was my forehead. She said, "Yeah, we can do that." She said, "It's not a big to-do. You can try it. If you don't like it, fine. But you know, risks are minimal," that kind of thing. So I was, "Okay, I'm turning fifty, this could be it." And that's what I did.

Christina's trust in her dermatologist's advice and opinions is evident from her description above. Christina's dermatologist reassures her that Botox isn't scary or too painful or risky, and she believes her (and her dermatologist's credibility is helped by the fact that she herself uses

Botox). Christina's dermatologist encourages her to try new things without being overly pushy or aggressive: "What I like about her is she would be the first one not to recommend any of the surgery or anything else. She's very low-key about any of that."

Christina's dermatologist is her informant and her liaison to the world of cosmetic anti-aging technologies. She counts on her dermatologist to keep her up to date, and appreciates that her dermatologist shares her knowledge with her:

> Okay, great, now that I did that [Botox], let me consider this, this and that. The dermatologist I go to has expanded the practice and can do everything. You know, now they're doing a lot with lasers too. . . . So those are kind of intriguing. And, you know, yeah, I guess it kind of helps tighten it up without surgery. So, I'm always curious, and my doctor is so open that I can just say, "Okay, so what is this and what is that?"

"He Convinced Me to Have My Eyes Done Too"

Christina portrays her relationship with her dermatologist as a collaborative one, characterized by the sharing of information. Christina's trust in her dermatologist as the expert developed in part because she doesn't push procedures on her. Instead she encourages, reassures, and, at most, gives Christina a gentle nudge to try something out. Janet's plastic surgeon confirmed that her eyes were a "problem," and offered her an efficient surgical solution. However, many women's encounters with plastic surgeons are more suggestive. With the exception of Janet, every woman I interviewed who had cosmetic anti-aging surgical procedures told a story about how their surgeon pointed out additional flaws beyond what they had originally sought to fix, some of which they were not bothered by, or even themselves aware of. Generally speaking, women's narratives appear to reflect a greater degree of emphatic suggestion among plastic surgeons than among dermatologists. All of the plastic surgeons were male, whereas the dermatologists were a more gender-balanced group.

In most cases, plastic surgeons were successful in convincing women to have at least one more procedure than they had originally planned on. Barbara—who, to remind readers, is fifty-nine, a retired mental health facility director, and currently a part-time childcare worker—shares a typical story. Her surgeon convinced her to get her eyes done, when she had originally just planned on having her "jowls taken care of": "So I went in to get my jowls taken care of. [The surgeon] looked at my eyes and, you see, my eyes had a lot of puffs . . . And he convinced me to have my eyes done too."

Before her surgeon brought her attention to this problem, Barbara actually "liked" her eyes and hadn't been aware that anything was wrong with them:

> He was pointing out all the little pockets [around her eyes] and things like that. I mean he's kind of an artist in his way, too. And he was a really good surgeon. And he was just telling me that since I'm having one done, I might want to consider having the eyes done too. And he didn't have to talk long before I said, "Yeah," because you see, I just hadn't thought of it. 'Cause I always liked my eyes.

Barbara followed her surgeon's advice, and got her eyes done in addition to her lower facelift. But, in retrospect, Barbara wishes she hadn't take his advice after all. The pain of recovery from the eyelift was much greater than she had expected: "I will never to that again. That was a nightmare," she says. She was, however, very happy with the results of her lower facelift, so happy that she is planning to have it done again, ten years later: "But the chin part was nothing. So I'm going to have that done again."

"I Knew What I Wanted and That Wasn't It!"

Like most women I spoke to who had cosmetic anti-aging procedures, Lisa agreed to some, but not all, of her surgeon's suggestions for additional intervention. She did concede to having her eyes done in addition to her original plan of a neck lift. But she didn't want to lose all of her wrinkles: "I'm proud of my wrinkles. I've earned every one of them, and I'm proud of them. I don't mind the wrinkles." Therefore, she refused her surgeon's persistent attempts to convince her to have Botox as well:

> The doctor said to me, after saw me, he said, "Now all we have to do is a little Botox and you'll be perfect!" And I said, "I'm not going to get Bo-

tox!" I said, "First of all, I've heard Botox makes you kind of look a little paralyzed." And he said, "No, no, no! There are much better ways now," blah, blah, blah. And I said, "I don't think I look bad," and he said, "We'll get those little wrinkles off your eyes and your mouth," and I said, "No, no, no!"

Part of what motivates Lisa to refuse her surgeon's Botox suggestions is her desire not to look *too much* younger than she really is. Her neck lift and eyelift already make her look significantly younger than her fifty-eight years. As she puts it:

You know, already people have said I look a lot younger. I don't mind *being* fifty-eight. I just don't want to hate the way I look. I mean, this was ugly [*pointing to her chin and neck*]. I don't think the rest of it's ugly. But he was all set to give me a little more.

Both times Wendy went in to have her eyelift surgery—for the original surgery and for the correction—the surgeon urged her to have her eyebrows lifted as well. She decided against it, both times:

One of the things that the surgeon *did* suggest that I do, which I did *not do* was a brow lift. He just pulls up, pulls up [your brows and forehead] and shows you in the mirror. And I didn't feel like it really altered my look except *negatively*, in the direction of 'too overdone.' I didn't want my eyebrows ending up underneath my hairline!

Wendy's surgeon didn't say, "Wendy you *have* to have this done," and he told her to "go home and think about it, let us know, we'll do whatever you wish." But, he *did* say to her: "I think it would be, operatively, the right thing to do." Wendy's husband was concerned about the prospect of brow-lift surgery because it is more involved than an eyelift, and requires an overnight hospital stay. But, like Lisa, who refused Botox because she didn't want to look too young, Wendy rejected the brow lift because she feared she would look *too different* and not like herself. Unlike Wendy's response to the feedback from her friend, wherein she went home afterwards, looked in the mirror, and said to herself "she is absolutely right," Wendy rejected her surgeon as a "human mirror" when it came to her brows. She elaborates:

> I went home and thought about it and I looked in the mirror. I thought, you know what, I'm not going to do that. . . . I'm glad I didn't. I don't think that would have added anything to me. It would have made me look more *unrealistic*. I don't need it. And when I do this to my eyes [*lifting her eyebrows with her fingers*] I look in the mirror, and think, "That looks so *stupid!*"

Anne also rejected her surgeon's suggestions for additional procedures—he wanted to get rid of the wrinkles above her lip and "do something under my eyes"—when she went in to have her second facelift. Anne said to her surgeon, "No, that doesn't bother me." Anne reads her surgeon's additional suggestions as his preoccupation with perfection: "I'm sure he would have done more things to make it perfect." But, she says, "I knew what I wanted and that wasn't it."

Amy's tale of her surgeon's persistence in trying to convince her to have additional liposuction is troubling, particularly because he continued to bring up the possibility, even minutes before her surgery began, when she was already in the operating room, and about to be put under. Amy attributes her surgeon's behavior to the "industry": "This is where the industry, I think, comes in," she says. Amy did agree, reluctantly, to her surgeon's suggestion to have some liposuction in addition to her tummy tuck, "not loving that, but okay." He presented the initial suggestion like this: "I'm sewing you shut, we'll do some lipo, because why not?" However, when he then suggested a much more extensive catalogue of liposuction, Amy refused. As she tells it:

> He said, "Well, you know, we can do your thighs and hips and everything." And I thought, "Well, yeah, part of me would love that, but my husband's gonna flip out and what I *really want* is the stomach skin gone." So that's what I really want. The rest, it is what it is. I can work on it.

Nonetheless, Amy's surgeon made one last attempt at convincing her to have more liposuction, right before her tummy-tuck operation began:

But even the day I was having surgery, he came in for the pre-op consultation, and they were about to put me under, and he said, "Oh well, do you
want me to go down into your vagina and do, you know, lipo there?" And
I said, "*No!* We've talked about *right here! That's all I want.*"

"This Isn't Really a Human Face"

Most women articulate a savvy understanding of how profit drives the
cosmetic anti-aging industry. I heard a lot from women about how
cosmetic procedures are big moneymakers for doctors because most
are not covered by insurance. Julia, like many others, reveals a critical
knowledge of the connection between profit and cosmetic anti-aging
intervention—profit that all kinds of doctors, including her gynecologist, are trying to get in on. Julia explains that gynecologists like her
own, and more and more general practitioners, are offering cosmetic
procedures in their offices "because there is such a demand for it." And,
because they get paid "out of pocket" for most of these procedures, they
are a "cash cow." Julia points to herself as an example. She is going to her
gynecologist for a varicose vein removal treatment, or scelerotherapy,
that afternoon. It will take her gynecologist "fifteen minutes" to do the
procedure and it will probably cost "two-hundred fifty dollars that won't
go through insurance. I have to pay it out of pocket." Julia's gynecologist
told her that "they get so many requests for referrals, like 'where should
I go for a facelift?,' or 'where should I go for hair removal?,'" that they
decided to offer more of those services in-house: "My gynecologist said
to me, 'It does not take a brain surgeon to do these procedures.'" Julia
interprets this move on the part of her gynecologist's office as a smart
business decision: "I'm sure [it's] a business decision for them. . . . Their
clients are asking for this. They can offer it. . . . A lot of patients will
feel more comfortable going to their physician." Julia also expresses a
keen awareness of how smart the marketing campaigns are, including
those she confronts in the posters and brochures at her gynecologist's
office, that equate cosmetic anti-aging intervention with wellness and
self-esteem, and that she, herself, buys into:

> I mean they're saying that, you know, "taking care of women is the total,"
> you know, "feeling good about yourself and self-esteem and confidence

and wholeness and wellness," and I buy that too. We want to feel good about ourselves.

Like Julia, and Amy, who attributes her surgeon's interest in getting her to have more procedures to what she calls "the industry," Caroline also reveals a realist view of the link between cosmetic anti-aging procedures and profit:

> I think it's great that there are less invasive things out there. But, you know, in a way it's sad because somebody else is going to make money off of our insecurities. You know, it's like the food industry with all the stuff making people fatter, then it feeds the diet industry.

Women also equate their surgeons' persistent suggestions to have additional procedures with an obsession for perfection. They describe their surgeons as sculptors who attempt to mold their faces and bodies into perfect works of art. Lisa tells me that her surgeon "seemed very nice and he seemed not to be trying to do things that were really radical." On the other hand, as she puts it:

> Well, for them, it's a *sculpture*, you know. I mean, it's interesting. When you get in to have the surgery, they actually use a marker pen, that's why they tell you not to put any face cream on. And so he's there with the marker pen, and you sort of start feeling like you're—like he's working on a piece of clay.

By refusing their surgeons' additional recommendations, women attempt to maintain their own unique look to some extent. They do not want to become so "perfect" that they no longer look like themselves. After all, the desire to "look like me again" was what motivated many of them to sign up for their cosmetic procedures in the first place. And yet, as Anne puts it, the face her surgeon was after "isn't really a human face, I'm thinking, somehow."

"I Look Pretty Good for a Mom"

Friends, husbands, doctors, and *kids*. Not all the women I interviewed who embrace cosmetic anti-aging intervention have children. But, the women who are moms talked about their kids *a lot*. I listened as women spoke about their influence on their children and, also, their children's influence on them. Women's narratives as moms were filled with ambivalence and contradiction. On the one hand, they are pleased with their children's approval of their youthful appearance, and they stress the importance of appearance among their children. They encourage their children to have various cosmetic surgical and non-surgical procedures—nose jobs, teeth whitening, laser hair removal—and promote the importance of seeking out cosmetic anti-aging procedures later on. On the other hand, they are troubled by their children's preoccupation with appearance. They bemoan the stringent and unforgiving beauty-body ideals their children confront, and they worry about the effect of our media and image-focused culture on their children's self-esteem.

"Mom, Wear Those *Jeans When You Come to School"*

Several women express pleasure in knowing that their children appreciate, and are proud of, their mom's youthful appearance. These women attribute their youthful appearance to "taking care" of themselves by which they mean a healthy diet, exercise, and cosmetic anti-aging intervention. In contrast to some of their friends' mothers who are not as "youthful looking," and who "don't take care of themselves the way I do," Wendy's daughters "realize that they're fortunate" that she looks young and attractive. Wendy tells me that her daughters were "very pleased" with her eyelift surgeries and thought "it was the right thing to have done." She describes their reaction: "They were very behind it afterwards. They say, 'Mommy, you look like you did when you were in your forties.'" Wendy is "very happy" with the result of her surgeries and she tells her daughters: "I think they ought to be planning down the line to do the same."

Claire also recognizes that her kids appreciate her young, hip look. Like Wendy, she equates looking good with being "healthy" and "together," and with "exercise." Like Wendy, she distinguishes herself from some other moms who are not as successful at maintaining their youthful looks. These moms, she tells me, remind her of a recent Oprah episode she watched that featured people who "let themselves go" in middle age. In fact, Claire's kids are "kind of freaking out" about the fact that some of their friends' parents are starting to look old. She elaborates:

> I'll tell you something interesting I've noticed with my kids. And that is that they are proud of the way that I look. And they'll like, say, "Mom, wear *those* jeans when you come to school." Which is nice. They definitely acknowledge that I look okay for being their mom and my age. [They like] that I'm together, and healthy, and exercise. 'Cause they're also seeing this other side, you know. And it's kind of freaking them out. 'Cause it's around this age, like mid-forties and fifties, and they're starting to see that happen. And so they've seen . . . quite some changes in their friends' parents.

Unlike Claire and Wendy, who take pleasure in their children's appreciation of their youthful appearance, Julia finds her daughter's focus on the negative aspects of aging disheartening. Julia tries to teach her daughter that "you gain a lot" and "learn a lot" when you're older. Yet, Julia's daughter continues to express discomfort and anxiety about the age-driven changes she sees in her mom's appearance, and to worry about these changes happening to her eventually, as well:

> My nineteen-year-old daughter will say to me, "Mom, like, is it really depressing when you look in the mirror and you see the wrinkles?" And she's asking me a lot of these questions: "How do you feel that, like, your boobs sag now?" and "Mom, isn't it depressing?" and "I don't really want to get older." And she's watching me and picturing what is this going to be like, and, "isn't it a drag?" and "isn't it sort of all over after twenty?" and "it's all downhill from here."

Julia reflects that some of her daughter's anxiety about aging and appearance probably stems from her own preoccupation with it. Julia seeks out cosmetic anti-aging procedures to treat and fix the age-driven changes in her own appearance and this, in turn, may impact her daughter as well:

> I think she's picturing, "Oh, will I get varicose veins? Am I going to get wrinkles and how am I going to feel about it?" And, if she sees a gray hair, she'll pull it out for me. Because I do that all the time.

Julia's nineteen-year-old daughter is "always bugging" her about using anti-wrinkle cream and her youngest daughter, and her son, are constantly harassing her about what she wears and how she looks. Julia tells me that she is feeling pressure about her appearance from the media, from herself, from her kids—from everywhere and everyone:

> I've got it coming from me. I've got it coming from the media. And I've got it coming from my kids. And my kids love me, we have a great relationship. But my fourteen-year-old, every day, "Oh, Mom, you're wearing tapered pants again, please wear bell-bottoms, you look like such a loser. Mom, how come the waist on your jeans goes so high? Mom, get hip-huggers." So, and then my son: "Oh, Mom, why did you cut your hair? You looked so cute in a ponytail, can't you grow your hair long again?" And I say to them, "I'm forty-seven. I look pretty good for a mom."

"I'm Watching What the Culture Is Saying to Them"

Claire likes that her daughters are "proud" of how she looks and she enjoys, along with them, an interest in fashion. However, she also expresses concern about what she understands as mounting pressure on women and girls to be thin and beautiful. She tells me "it's tragic" how much time women and girls, herself and her daughters included, spend worrying about their bodies. And yet, it's an uphill battle to try and fight against the pressure. As she elaborates:

> It's just tragic, the amount of time that we spend thinking about our bodies and our image. And I continue to struggle with it, and being in the business that I'm in now [as a personal trainer] it's just . . . hardly a day goes by that I'm not just shocked and saddened by the amount of time we

spend on it, and then how hard we are on ourselves. And having raised three daughters, it's such an uphill battle.

Claire tries to teach her kids that they shouldn't compare themselves to the images they are bombarded with minute to minute:

One of the things I tried to do with my kids, from the time they were teeny-tiny, they can tell you what it means, I would use the expression, "That's Madison Avenue." I would explain to them that that picture is not [an achievable or healthy] ideal, that it didn't really matter. I tried.

But, Claire says, "it's very scary," and "I feel like it's just getting worse." Claire has recently witnessed eating disorders in teenagers she knows that she finds "just shocking." Claire wasn't able to fully enjoy her daughter's prom experience because her daughter and her female friends "basically for months starved themselves" in preparation. As she tells it:

I just watched my daughter last spring, about six of her friends, they were seniors in high school, getting ready for their prom. There wasn't one of them that you or I would look at and say needed to lose weight. Six girls basically for months starved themselves. And this was all for what? That's the part that really bothered me. To go to a prom for one night? What is in you to make you want to do that to yourself? I felt sick to my stomach. It was supposed to be such a joyous thing, to go see all the girls dressed up and take pictures. [But] I had such a sinking feeling, 'cause I knew what they had done.

Like Claire, Julia shares her frustration with what she interprets as worsening pressures on young women and girls to be thin and beautiful. And she finds the media images that target young women and girls increasingly sexualized and objectifying. She says:

I'm really pissed off because years ago I read *Reviving Ophelia*, which was the book, you know, on raising daughters, and I feel like the more knowledge we have about the damage that our media does to women, the more it doesn't get fixed. You still stand at the checkout counter at the grocery store and the covers of the magazines are still, oh, you know: "How to make your thighs look thinner, how to make your breasts bigger, how to know if he's cheating, how to bring him to his knees." It's still the same . . . you have to have big boobs, and long lustrous hair, and have sex in sixty-two positions every night, or your life is not fulfilled.

Julia feels discouraged that it keeps getting worse: "It's worse. I think it's worse." And she's really worried about her daughters, and her son, in light of the growing emphasis on physical appearance, and the increasingly stringent beauty-body ideals in our culture: "I'm watching it, you know. I'm going through the aging process, but I'm also raising girls. I have two daughters and a son. So I'm watching what the culture is saying to them."

"If Something Makes You Feel Good, *Do It*"

Claire critiques what she perceives to be a growing cultural emphasis on appearance and beauty-body ideals that are becoming increasingly stringent. Yet, she supported her daughter's decision to get a nose job because she felt it would improve her self-esteem. Claire did not pressure her daughter to have the nose job in any way. However, she did draw her daughter's attention to the option:

> My general view on plastic surgery is that it's a very personal thing. And I am a fan of: if something makes you feel good, *do it*. My eighteen-year-old daughter just had a rhinoplasty. She's a beautiful girl who had, um, you know, not the most beautiful nose. But she had been complaining about it. And I said to her, "Honey, you know, there's something you can do about it."

Several years after Claire first introduced the option of the nose job, her daughter decided to go ahead with it:

> And finally, she did come to us, and she did it. And it's the best thing she's ever done for herself. She's a kid that had some definite self-esteem issues. And [it helped her] to just feel more comfortable in her own skin.

Claire's daughter's rhinoplasty was very difficult and worrying for her, as a mother, in some respects:

As a parent, it was very hard to watch it happen, though. Yeah, I mean, I totally flipped out the day of, you know, when she was going under general anesthesia. Like did I make the wrong [decision]? You know, this is so vain; this is not like, you know, the need for an extreme makeover. This is a beautiful girl who wants to be a little more refined.

Yet, in the end, Claire is "glad" her daughter did it because of "what she got out of it": "It's been huge for her. So that's a good thing." Claire supports her daughter's proactive approach to improving her nose. After all, Claire's Botox shots, and her commitment to "signing right up for a facelift" in future years, demonstrate her own proactive approach to fixing what *she's* unhappy with, too: "When the time comes, and I'm really miserable, I will do something."

"Do They Have to Be Perfect?"

Julia's cannot seem to escape what she calls our culture's "expectations of perfection." She is vulnerable to it and her children are too. She wants to protect her children from these unrealistic expectations, but she's not sure how to do it:

> The expectations of perfection just keep getting ratcheted up and ratcheted up. I mean, I never had braces, my husband never had braces. I think my teeth look great. All of my kids, everybody we know, the orthodontist tells them right from fourth grade, "Well, you're going to have to have braces on your teeth." And I had to question myself, since I never had to suffer it, do I really want to make my kids suffer through braces? Are their teeth good enough? Do they have to be perfect? So I just think it's a very insidious huge problem and dilemma for the whole society and culture.

Julia refuses to indulge her fourteen-year-old daughter's request for whitening strips for her teeth. But now her husband is worried about having a few white hairs and wondering if he should dye his beard:

> My fourteen-year-old wants Crest whitening strips. And I say *absolutely not*. You're fourteen. Now my husband, when the kids pointed out that he had a few white hairs in his beard, he was horrified. And not happy about

it. Very agitated. And he asked me, do I think that when the time comes he could dye his beard? So it's not just women. And I think it's really sad. I think it's really sad and I don't think it's going to change anytime soon.

Julia tells me that she is about to have her "first laser hair bikini line thing" that afternoon, along with her varicose vein treatment, at her gynecologist's office. She says, "I was never was going to do my bikini area," but because she's "a consumer," and because she plans on wearing a bathing suit for the "next twenty years," and doesn't want to have to worry about shaving, she decided to go for it. At the same time, however, she is disturbed by the growing trend among women not only of hair reduction, but hairlessness, in the pubic area. She read an article in the *New York Times* that documents the "different providers and what kinds of services they'll provide for women," each of which center on removing a lot, if not all, of a woman's pubic hair. She finds this trend "amazingly bizarre," and doesn't know "why people would do it." And yet, her nineteen-year-old daughter is worried about it, and it seems to be what more and more women her daughter's age are doing:

> We had a long talk about it, 'cause she asked me, do I think she should be doing that? "Do guys expect that?" "Are you supposed to be all neat and clean down there?" And I said, "I don't really think guys have expectations. They just want to get in there. I don't think they care."

Julia points out that the psychologists and sociologists quoted in the *New York Times* article find this trend "very troubling" and she agrees with them: "Because when a woman, an adult woman, is completely denuded of hair in the pubic area, it's very prepubescent looking. Is this some kind of pedophilia? Are men attracted to little girls?"

Julia wonders out loud about whether all of these new techniques and technologies for hair removal, and women's use of them, are "feeding into and creating expectations then that men will have that are unfair to us. That we are not supposed to have hair?" It's a "slippery, slippery slope," she says. Julia also navigates a "slippery slope," however, when she herself partakes of these technologies. She doesn't want her daughter to have to succumb to these pressures, which, on some level, she feels are out of hand. And yet, Julia's own vulnerability to these pressures means that she worries about fixing "things I wouldn't have thought about before," not only in herself, but also *in her children*. Her son's not-so-white teeth and his unibrow are examples:

> I am so nutty. Every time I look at my seventeen-year-old son, he's so handsome, but he could really use whiter teeth. And I want to get his teeth whitened and he has no interest in it. So, you know, it's boys too now. Like . . . he doesn't have much of a unibrow, but I know that he either shaves it or plucks it or something. And I just said to him recently, "You know, would you like me to take you—you can get laser hair removal, and you will never again, for your whole life, have to worry about that?" And he looked at me, like, what planet was I coming from? He had no interest. But I thought, it's available, why not just do it?

***

Women who embrace intervention speak about their cosmetic anti-aging procedures in a language of individual identity, self-expression, and empowerment: to have cosmetic anti-aging interventions is to fulfill their own needs and wants as *individuals*. They also repeatedly call attention to the youth-saturated, anti-aging environment we live in—inclusive of the marketing and availability of cosmetic anti-aging surgeries and technologies—as they articulate their attitudes about, and their approaches to, their aging exteriors. This chapter illuminated how a woman's decision to have cosmetic anti-aging intervention develops in and through her social interactions with others, and in the context of the social attitudes that permeate her social relationships. The stories of the women in this chapter teach us that female friends and doctors—gynecologists, dermatologists, and plastic surgeons—play a particularly formative role in their decision to have and use cosmetic anti-aging procedures. Female friends and doctors act as "human mirrors," as they reflect back, confirm, and reinforce a woman's need to seek out cosmetic anti-aging intervention. When women see themselves, and their aging faces and bodies, from the perspective of these "social others"—when they incorporate the "social attitudes" of their "social group or community" into their own self-concept, to use George Herbert Mead's language—they also evaluate themselves through a wider cultural lens.[7] To accept the views and attitudes of their female friends and doctors is to accept the broader anti-aging, pro-intervention, cultural message as well. When the women in this chapter, and their female friends, share with one another the view that a woman "should" have cosmetic anti-aging intervention—that it is "no-brainer" to do so—they simultaneously express their own social attitudes *and* the overarching anti-aging cultural imperative.

Not all of the human mirrors, or social others, that are featured in these women's narratives express a pro-intervention perspective. Husbands and male partners can be indifferent, or even opposed to, a woman's decision to have cosmetic anti-aging procedures. Women don't always comply with the feedback they receive from social others. When the women in this chapter go ahead and have procedures done without their husbands' knowledge or support, and when they successfully resist their surgeons' suggestions for additional procedures, they exercise independence and individual agency. Recall Amy's words to her husband: "It's not *your* body."

In their stories about being moms, women express ambivalence, uncertainty, and even outright worry and anger, about the mounting pressures their children feel, and the lengths they will go to, in an attempt to achieve the ever more stringent beauty-body ideals that saturate American culture today. Yet, while many women are sickened by the pressures their children face—and some work to give their children tools to fight back against them—for the most part, they seem resigned to the reality of these pressures and unable to help themselves from encouraging cosmetic technologies and procedures as a solution. By and large, they model a pro-cosmetic intervention approach for their children, encouraging their children to embrace intervention for themselves now, and in the future.

6

"It's Not in My World"

Living as a Natural Ager

The social worlds of women who embrace cosmetic anti-aging interventions generally compliment the celebration of youth, and youth-sustaining surgeries and technologies, in our culture at large. The social worlds of women who refuse cosmetic anti-aging intervention, on the other hand, stand in stark contradiction to the growing cultural prevalence and normalization of cosmetic anti-aging procedures in the United States today. The social relationships that inform the daily lives of the women I interviewed who opt out of intervention are instrumental sources of strength and encouragement in a cultural landscape that offers little in the way of support for the natural aging approach. Recall Elizabeth's plea for some of the powerful women in Hollywood to stand up and age naturally: "If only some of these powerful women, these screen creatures, would stand up!" But hope for this kind of resistance is dim. Instead, like Nina, most of my interview subjects who are aging naturally feel like they are "fighting the culture all the time." And, these feelings of disconnection from the culture at large make their connections with others who share their commitment to aging naturally, and who share in their refusal of cosmetic anti-aging intervention, all the more important.

"It's Really the Context"

Women who refuse cosmetic anti-aging intervention tend to move in social circles wherein a natural approach to aging is the norm. They tell me that they don't bump up against women who have and use cosmetic anti-aging procedures often. As Mia puts it: "I'm surrounded by natural approaches. At least in my immediate family, I mean nobody would dream of it." Over and over again, I listened as women told me that they, and their cosmetically enhanced counterparts, live in two distinctly different worlds. Ellen, the sixty-one-year-old businesswoman who works hard to appreciate her aging exterior, says: "That isn't in my world." Alison, who is fifty-five and, as discussed in chapter 3, finds the prospect of putting her face and body under the knife or needle for cosmetic purposes entirely unappealing, puts it this way:

> It's not in my thoughts. It's not in my world. I think there's a bit [of] separation between us. There's no middle ground here. [It's] either the group that says, "No thank you," or the group that says, "Where do I sign up?" And that's it.

Catherine, the retired career counselor, age sixty-one, who hasn't had any cosmetic anti-aging procedures, nor is planning to, tells me that she actively chooses to live in a world where how you look is not the focus. If for some reason she operated in a different social environment, wherein looking young, was expected, however, she cannot say for sure that she would refuse cosmetic anti-aging intervention. As she explains:

> I have *no idea* what it would be like if I was *in* a world where the external focus was the *thing*. I probably would be in there with the best of them [i.e., having cosmetic anti-aging procedures]. I mean *really*, I have no way of knowing. So I think it's really the *context*. I'm not living in a world, nor have I *chosen* a world—that's not the way I've lived—where the *external* focus has been the key thing. So that also affects the *lens* through which I look. It just isn't what interests me, and what I'm drawn to. It just isn't the focus.

Susan, a sixty-one-year-old college professor, is not interested in having cosmetic anti-aging intervention. Yet, like Catherine, she feels that she might be more likely to consider it if her life circumstances were different. For example, if she were single and competing with other women to find a mate, saying "no" to cosmetic anti-aging procedures would be more difficult:

> I think a lot of it has to do with having a stable life partner. I think if I were single now, trying to find a man out there, I might be a lot more

anxious. Because I know women in their forties who can't, you know—
men in their forties want to go out with women in their twenties. And I
have friends in their fifties who are looking for men and it's very bleak. . . .
But I feel secure now in my relationship and so I don't feel like I need to
attract men.

Susan gives other examples of life contexts and situations, in addition to
the need to "compete with younger women to find a mate," that would,
in her view, increase her likelihood of having cosmetic anti-aging intervention. Imagining women in these alternate contexts makes her more
sympathetic to their choices to have cosmetic anti-aging procedures. As
she explains:

> I can imagine somebody whose whole life has been based on their looks.
> You know, maybe they are an actress, or a model, or a dancer, or some-
> thing, and so to not have that [their youthful looks] really makes them
> think that they're not themselves anymore. I mean, if I was a performer,
> if I was single, if my whole life was based on my beauty, maybe I would
> think, "Of course, you do, *of course* you do that!"

Eva, the fifty-one-year-old psychologist introduced in chapter 2 who is
mourning the loss of no longer getting admiring looks from men on
the street, has no plans for cosmetic anti-aging intervention. However,
like Catherine and Susan, Eva imagines that she would be more likely
to consider intervention if her lived, everyday world was different. For
Eva, it is not an alternate profession, nor the thought of being single,
but a different group of female friends that could potentially shift her
views:

> At this point it's not something that is an active thought. You know, if the
> majority of my friends were saying, "I'm going to do this," "I'm going to
> have my eyelids lifted," it would be harder not to think seriously about
> it. Is everyone going to look younger than I look? I don't know that I'd
> have the sense of self to say, "Fine, you go and do it, and I'll be wrinkled
> and gray and that's okay by me." You know? Because if the majority of
> my close friends are going to do that, then it sort of becomes like, so why
> shouldn't I?

"He Thinks I'm Beautiful"

Women who are married, or in relationships, call attention to these relationships as a crucial source of support in their commitment to growing older without cosmetic anti-aging intervention. Sarah, the fifty-five-year-old writer who feels less anxiety and inadequacy about how she looks with age, feels lucky that her husband finds her beautiful and tells her so: "I'm really blessed to live with a man who thinks I'm beautiful, who tells me that. I mean, he's wonderful that way, you know." Similarly, Margaret, who is seventy-two, appreciates that her husband tells her that she's beautiful and that he likes her body. His expressions "reinforce" her healthy self-image and make her feel better about her body in the context of aging. As she puts it:

> He thinks I'm beautiful. He always has. He's been very proud of the fact that he married me. And he still tells me how beautiful I am, and how much he likes my body. So that really helps, that reinforces it.

Ellen talks about how she enjoyed sharing the experience of growing older with her husband before he passed away two years ago. She and her husband found a kind of comradeship and comfort in experiencing similar age-driven changes in their faces and bodies together:

> I just really love that my husband . . . my husband passed away two years ago . . . and I just *loved* that I didn't have to make excuses, that he just still appreciated and loved what was happening to him, and to me, and that we were at the *same place*. It was *so nice*.

Elizabeth, the sixty-one-year-old artist who embraces a less looks-centered identity with age, hypothesizes that having a husband, being married, probably "protects" her to some degree from the feelings of pain and invisibility of being "over the hill"—and the subsequent pressure to look younger—that her divorced and single female friends encounter. She elaborates:

> I think it is harder for, you know, my friends who are divorced. It is much harder because our society, when they perceive you as somebody who's

over the hill, that's the end of you. You know, you're sort of dismissed. You're not looked at. You're not engaged as a full-fledged woman. But it's been—I mean I guess in that way, it's a lot easier for me because I've been a married person and I've been sort of protected by that.

"My Doctor Wanted Me to Take It and I *Refused*"

I heard a lot of frustration from women about a *lack* of support from their doctors for their natural approach to aging. Overall, women's stories of interactions with doctors were characterized by doctors' proposing different medications to treat "symptoms" of aging that they were not necessarily bothered by, or that they even understood as a negative aspect of aging at all. Some women told me how they were considering taking different medications for bone density loss upon their doctors' recommendations, but that they were skeptical about whether they really needed it, and they were worried about potential side effects of the medication. Some women are taking different hormone replacement therapy (HRT) medications to "treat" menopause, while others are in the process of adjusting or reducing their dosages in response to their concerns about the adverse health effects of the medications. Still others shared their decisions not to take HRT altogether, and relay stories about having to resist their doctors' persistent recommendations to take it. These women do not interpret menopause as a condition in need of medical treatment, but they have to fight against their doctors' insistent promotion of menopause as a condition that requires pharmaceutical intervention.

Elizabeth offers a typical example when she describes how her doctor and her gynecologist encouraged her to take HRT but she refused:

My doctor wanted me to take it, and the gynecologist wanted me to take it, and I *refused* to. I just did not think—I mean those things seem so counter-intuitive to what our bodies are supposed to do. So, I just think, and a lot of people I know of course took it, but I just think it's not much of a hardship [going through menopause]. At least it wasn't for me.

Elizabeth knows that some women experience physical aspects of menopause that are difficult: "I mean, I know people struggle terribly with sleeplessness and sweats and all that stuff, and I'm not saying it's not there." Still, from Elizabeth's perspective, if we are able to understand menopause more holistically, and in the context of what is supposed to happen naturally to the body at that age, it makes it easier to simply accept it: "But I think that if we have an understanding of the whole picture that things are much more acceptable." Elizabeth blames medicine for turning menopause, which she calls "a natural progression of the body," into a negative condition that requires intervention:

> In a way, I mean I do blame medicine for this. But I think that we *have* to pay attention to our own intuition. I mean it doesn't make *sense* to, to get in the way of a natural progression of the body, which has so much *wisdom*. It doesn't make sense to me anyway.

Catherine also recounts having to fight back against her doctor's persistent attempts to get her to take hormone replacement therapy. Catherine didn't feel like she needed to take any medication for menopause. She also had a "gut instinct" that the medication wasn't good for her health. Still, Catherine's doctor persisted to such a degree that she conceded in taking a sample packet of pills home with her, where she promptly threw them out. Here is how she tells it:

> I never took any medication [for menopause]. I had a young doctor who argued with me, and then she said, "I *know* you disagree with this but I want you to *at least* take this package of samples back with you." She was thirty years old and I looked at her and I said, "I'm sorry," I said, "Now I really need to speak as an older woman to you." I said, "You are talking to me, I realize you're just starting off in this profession," but I said, "I'm fifty-five years old," and I said, "I want you to hear this because I think it's important, you are *really selling*, trying to sell this to me. And as one woman to another, and I'm an older woman, and I'm telling you my *gut instinct* is that at some point they're going to find out that this is dangerous." So, she still insisted. She said, "I want you to just think about it." And finally, I just thought there's nothing to do. I took it and when I got here [back home] I threw them out. I never took them.

"Sisters Going through It Together"

Over and over again, women shared with me how important it was to them to talk about the age-driven changes in their faces and bodies with trusted female friends. I heard a lot about how female friendship offered a source of strength and comfort—particularly through shared experiences and laughter. In and through their interactions with female friends, women reinforce their natural approach to aging, and find support for that approach. This support is particularly important in light of their being increasingly bombarded with options for cosmetic anti-aging intervention, and in light of their doctors' typical interpretation of aging as a condition in need of treatment. Some women actually joined together with female friends, and with female family and friends of different generations, to *celebrate* menopause. These celebrations—Nancy calls hers a "jubilee" and Nina refers to hers a "croning ceremony"—mark the transition into a new and exciting phase of life and self-growth. Overall, female friends help women feel better about, and accept, the age-driven changes in their faces and bodies.

Ellen compares the importance of "hanging out" with female friends her own age to the support she enjoyed from friends when they all had young children together:

> I think it's really nice to *hang out* with people your same age. And when you have young babies it's the same thing. I mean you *need* that to—to *be* in that, with people that are going through that.

For Ellen it really "helps" to have women friends to "laugh and talk with" about aging. Sharing her feelings about aging with friends, and witnessing similar changes in her friends' faces and bodies, helps Ellen accept the changes in her own face and body. These changes can be "shocking" at first, but, through her exchanges with friends, Ellen is able to understand that these changes are part of who she is—"I guess that's me!" She explains:

> I sometimes separate [myself from] it [my aging appearance] a little, I think. 'Cause it is *shocking*. You know, and you see it over and over and

over again and you're like, "I guess that's me!" But it *really* helps, as I said, to have women friends to just laugh and talk about it with.

Like Ellen and many others, Eva finds comfort in sharing stories and laughing about her aging appearance with female friends. She and her female friends are like "sisters" going "through it together":

> I think if you only had friends who were younger, it would be hard! I actually have friends of a lot different ages, which is really nice, particularly not having a mother, it is really nice. But you can laugh about it. Alicia [a friend who is Eva's age] and I will show each other our little gray hairs that are emerging. And you laugh about it. That is absolutely the only way to deal with it is to laugh about it and to feel like you do have these sisters that are going through it together.

Catherine and her friends also use humor, both to help them accept age-driven changes, and to deflect the pressures and temptations of having cosmetic anti-aging procedures to "correct" these changes. Catherine laughs with friends about the futility and absurdity of cosmetic anti-aging procedures in light of the inevitability of aging. Humor enables Catherine to confront the aging process with a touch of fatalism, and with humility: aging is just "what happens" and "isn't it too bad." She says:

> Certainly every woman I've talked to my age, we *laugh*, we've *laughed* about it. I know for me one of the things that I think *hugely* has helped me is having humor about these things. My heart *aches* for people who can't access a sense of humor.

Sarah and her friends also laugh a lot together about growing older. She describes:

> There's a lot of joking about aging. We share a lot of our stories about what's transpired. One of my friends has started to eat in a diner by herself and she *loves* this experience. And she'll say, you know, "Well, what do you think they think of me?" And, you know, I'll say, "Well, there's a hungry old lady at the counter," and then we laugh.

Sarah and her friends poke fun of themselves for wearing more "sensible shoes" than they used to—they have fun with, and play with, the label "old ladies." Joking about the age-driven changes in their faces and bodies helps Sarah and her friends accept them. As she tells it:

> We call ourselves "old ladies." It's a very funny thing we do, it's like we're *accepting* it and joking about it. And we just laugh. We *laugh* all the time. We laugh if we go out, a group of us will go out, and we're all wearing sensible shoes. And we just laugh about our shoes, you know, that we don't want our feet to hurt, we want to be able to walk a couple of miles. And just that playfulness of thinking about your look, and how you're getting yourself up, and enjoying the whole *business* of it, the *playfulness* of it.

"What's Happened to *Her*?"

Like Catherine and others, Sarah and her friends also use humor to bond over their disinterest in cosmetic anti-aging procedures. They exchange stories and laugh together about what they see as the absurd and futile aspects of cosmetic anti-aging intervention—the expense, the fact that it doesn't really stop the aging process. Sarah and her friends periodically "check in" with each other, using each other as "sounding boards and reinforcement," reaffirming and reassuring each other about their distance from the cosmetic anti-aging intervention mentality. Sarah tells a story about a friend who met up with an old college classmate she hadn't seen for a while. This classmate "catalogued all the work she'd had done," and said, "'You're looking at fifty or sixty thousand dollars of work.'" Shortly after this interaction, Sarah's friend called her up wanting to talk about what had happened. She sought to connect with Sarah about the alienation she felt from her classmate, and to re-center herself in her own natural aging position, a position she knew Sarah shared. As Sarah puts it: "And my friend was so incredulous, she called . . . and she wanted to tell me all about this. She said, 'Can you imagine,' you know, 'that she has done this to herself?'" When Sarah asked her friend what she thought about how this woman looked, post-procedures, her friend's reaction was mixed. She did admit to thinking she looked good: "'I guess she did look great, yes, she looked terrific.'" But she also told Sarah that interacting with this woman "'was just bizarre, it was really odd,' and

'I kind of felt like I was talking to someone in a different dimension.'" Sarah and her friend continue to bond over the fact that this woman lives in a "different dimension." Together, and through humor, they reinforce and shore up their own shared perspective, one that soundly rejects a cosmetic intervention approach:

> And that's the kind of thing we will check in with each other about. You know, sort of being *amazed* at that. And we'll joke with each other. She went off for a job interview and I said, "Well, have you had your extreme makeover?" You know and she'll laugh. I mean we laugh about these things.

Sarah also tells a story about her own recent, and unexpected, encounter with a female acquaintance who had just had a major cosmetic anti-aging procedure, most likely a facelift. She and her husband, and some of her friends, saw the woman at an event and wondered, "What's *happened* to her?"

> I looked at this woman and I thought, "What's the matter, what's happened to you?" And then Stephen [Sarah's husband] and I walked in to get our coats and he said, "What's *happened* to her?" And I said, "I think she's had cosmetic surgery. She's been enhanced." And a while later someone else came in and said, "Did you see? Has she had something done to her face?" And this has been now this sort of groundswell—at least three other people have said, "Do you think she had something done to her face?"

Sarah uses the word "shocking" to describe the woman's appearance, and to convey her own inability—and the inability of members of her social circle—to relate to the woman's action to have cosmetic anti-aging intervention:

> And we're all kind of amazed that she looks kind of wide eyed, you know, she's now the perennial deer-in-the-headlights kind of look. And it's kind of *shocking* in a way. I mean, I don't know anybody, I don't think I can tell you that I know *anybody* who would go in for *any* cosmetic surgery other than this one person who was kind of a surprise.

"What Did She Do This For?"

Despite repeatedly stressing a strong distinction between themselves and their female friends, and women who have and use cosmetic anti-aging procedures, my naturally aging interview subjects increasingly find themselves in the surprising and upsetting position of having to confront more of their own close friends who *are choosing intervention as well.* Sarah, introduced earlier, said that, other than the woman she saw at the recent event, she doesn't "know *anybody* who would go in for *any* cosmetic surgery." Yet, later on in our interview, Sarah tells me that a friend recently asked for her help in finding out how and where to get a particular cosmetic anti-aging procedure done to her face. Sarah said she couldn't help her friend except to tell her—in partly tongue-and-cheek fashion—that she could go to somewhere in Africa to get it done. According to a program she heard on National Public Radio, Africa is an increasingly popular cosmetic surgery destination for women who hail from the United States. Its geographical distance from home offers them anonymity: "'You go, you check into a hotel, and then no one knows you've done this.'" But Sarah doesn't want to help her friend move forward with surgery and she's not going to. Instead, she honestly expresses her opinion in opposition to it, and she tries to get her friend to see that she doesn't need it, and that she looks "terrific" just as she is. As she tells it:

> I said, "I think it's ridiculous." You know, "I'm not going to aid and abet you in this journey. I think it's stupid." She said, "But it would make me feel so much better." I said, "No it wouldn't." I said, "It won't make you feel any better and you'll hate spending that money." I said, "What's it's going to be, five, ten thousand dollars, that's crazy! You know, you're worrying about money as it is." So I really was quite outspoken. I said, "You're talking to the wrong person here, you know. I think you look terrific and I'm not going to get you names of people because I don't know anybody."

Sarah describes this friend as someone "I just love. I just love everything about her." For Sarah to discover, therefore, that this friend wants to "fix" part of her face, simply because it has changed with age, is troubling.

Sarah doesn't have any close friends who have actually had cosmetic anti-aging intervention. Others, like Ellen and Alison, do. Despite emphasizing that cosmetic anti-aging intervention is "not in my world," it turns out that both Ellen and Alison have friends who have had cosmetic anti-aging procedures. They tell me they find it hard to relate to their friends' decisions, which signify, in their view, too much of an emphasis on appearance and, also, a capitulation to a narrow, exclusively youth-centered understanding of what an attractive appearance is. Ellen describes how she felt when she first learned about a good friend's cosmetic anti-aging intervention: "I guess my first thought was like, 'Why is she so unhappy with herself?' I *didn't know* she was so unhappy with herself." Alison reveals feelings of alienation upon learning about her friend's eyelift surgery: "I don't relate to it. I don't care about it. I have a different world I live in." When she learned about another friend who had a facelift, Alison thought to herself: "Yuck, you know, how can you be friendly with someone like this? And I thought maybe we're just on a different—maybe our ideas and values are different."

Adjusting to friends' post-intervention faces can also be difficult. Diane is currently struggling with accepting her close friend's new appearance, post-eyelift and post-facelift:

> And my friend who did it, I mean she looks sort of ghoulish. I didn't even know that—a lot of times you look different than the way you looked when you were young, so it doesn't even—it's not exactly the way, it's just a little bit different.

When Alison saw her friend for the first time after her facelift, she thought to herself, "'Oh my God, she doesn't look the same. Oh my God, what did she do this for?' Her eye is crooked, definitely." And Alison also misses her other friend's eyes, and the way they looked, before she had her eyelift surgery:

> I have to tell you she had the most gorgeous, *beautiful* eyes. They were her redeeming feature, *big*, no makeup, big blue eyes. They're not the same. The *shape* is different. The bags are gone but the shape is different. It's just different. They're a different shape. She's very pretty. But not the same. There's something different.

Alison tells me that she, herself, would not feel comfortable with a changed appearance like this: "I could never deal with that. Never, *never*." Yet like Diane, who says about her friend's post-facelift and post-eyelift appearance, "I mean I'm sure that soon I'll see her and I'll recognize her. I mean, it'll be who she is," Alison says that she has gotten "used to" her friends' new appearances. Even though Alison doesn't want cosmetic anti-aging intervention for herself—"Who wants that? I don't!"—she has come to realize that she doesn't want to judge her friends who do. It was "wrong" of her to be critical of her friend who had the facelift:

> But you know what? It's wrong, it was wrong, that's *her issue* or whatever, that was her choice and it's nothing to do with me. And it's obviously inside, if it makes her feel better, and that's why—I mean, I should never judge someone.

And Alison tells me that it was wrong of her to criticize her friend who had the eyelift as well: "She was willing to do it. She said it was the best thing she'd ever done. And she said, 'Jack [her husband] loves it!'"

"They're People *Just Like Me* and They're *Doing It*!"

Living in a rural New England town, Diane—the fifty-seven-year-old therapist who, as discussed in chapter 2, is trying to appreciate the changes in her appearance due to aging—tells me that she felt pretty immune to the phenomenon of cosmetic anti-aging intervention until recently. In the last year, however, she has learned that two good friends have had cosmetic anti-aging procedures, and that a third is contemplating having a facelift soon. Diane describes her unease in knowing that her good friends, people she describes as being "a lot like me," are starting to have cosmetic anti-aging interventions. It's no longer a practice she can write off as just a "New York" or "LA thing." She describes how she felt when she first learned that her third friend is considering a facelift: "My third friend, she just said to me that if she could *afford* it she would *have a facelift* and I almost cracked. I mean, it's like, '*Oh my God!*' . . . she's a lot like me. . . . It's just so *scary* to me."

Diane continues to wrestle with the erosion of her protection from the world of cosmetic anti-aging surgeries and technologies: "It has been far away from me but now it's not so far." She's unsettled by the fact that she can no longer assume that her close friends are going to share her natural approach to aging. She would have never thought that her friends would have facelifts, but now, here they are, signing up for them. Diane describes an interaction with her friend who is thinking about a facelift: "I said I thought it was awful, and she said, 'Oh well then I won't do it!' I don't think she would do it anyway. Well, she might. She might. It's just, it's really *scary*." Like Diane, her friend practices yoga and meditation, activities that Diane associates with being philosophically distant from the appearance-based cosmetic intervention mentality. And yet, Diane's friend tells her that she was actually introduced to the prospect of having a facelift by people who share her participation in an eastern philosophy group. Here's how Diane tells it:

> It's like these are *normal people*, they're people *just like me* and they're *doing it!* I mean this is kind of ironic to me because it's this mix. You think there are *yoga people* and the *Botox people*. But this *woman*, who's my friend, she is very active in this group. It's this organization that she's belonged to for about twenty years and they go to all these meetings. And it's basically a meditation group. They go on these weeklong meditations and they do a little yoga and that's a *huge* part of her life. And she knows two people who've had it done and she met them in *that group*! So, you see the mix!

As discussed earlier, Diane elaborated on her critiques and concerns about the increasing trend of cosmetic anti-aging intervention. On a societal level, it "separates the rich from the poor," and on a personal level, she doesn't like the thought of someone "messing with," or "tampering with" her body. And yet, now that her own friends are having cosmetic anti-aging interventions, it is more difficult for her to hold fast to these views. She is starting to make a distinction between what she feels is best for the good of society, and the particular wants and needs of her individual friends. As she puts it:

> It's easy to think one thought in terms of what you think is good for society and then a whole other set of thoughts for your individual friends, right? So you can say what you think is good, or right or wrong, but then

you can always make exceptions and have compassion for anybody who thinks that they ought to have it for various reasons.

Diane can also see the benefit of the option of cosmetic intervention for someone who is really suffering, for example, for someone who has "obsessive-compulsive disorder" and really hates a facial or bodily feature or characteristic that is glaringly outside of what is considered beautiful or normal:

> I mean, if somebody had some kind of obsessive-compulsive disorder, and all they could think about was that their nose was really ugly, if they want to change their nose and then they can live a better life, do I think that's wrong? Well, I guess not.

Diane is also sympathetic to her friend who had breast reduction surgery: "She said her breasts were uncomfortable because they were heavy so, certainly, I can certainly understand that."

Diane demonstrates an increasing capacity for compassion and understanding of her friends' decisions to have intervention. But she continues to be upset and disturbed by it: "But do I like it? You know, *no*, I don't like it. It just gives me the *creeps*." Part of Diane's unease comes from her suspicion that the more people she knows that have it, the more pressure she'll feel to have it too: "If more people have it, then the more—to be normal, obviously—you would feel that you should do it too." Diane tells me that she is hopeful that she will continue to refuse options for cosmetic anti-aging intervention, and age naturally. But, as she points out, if she had "five friends who had facelifts," and who looked "suddenly younger," it would make her feel "old," "bad," and "worse." And, even if it doesn't happen in her lifetime, she worries that by the time her children reach her age, cosmetic anti-aging intervention will be an imperative:

> Well, I look in the mirror and I go like this [*lifting her face with her hands*]. And you see how pretty you would look, you know? But it's just in passing. I'm not doing it *often*. You know, if [I] had *five friends* who had facelifts, I would certainly feel *old*. If I had a number of people who suddenly looked younger, it would make me feel *bad*, it would make me

feel like I looked worse. But hopefully I can just be really happy that that's not going to happen to me. But it might happen to my children. And I don't like the thought, you know, it's like if more and more people do it . . .

Rebecca is the fifty-eight-year-old flute-maker who, as revealed in prior chapters, attributes her newly discovered self-confidence to her older-looking appearance. Yet, Rebecca also tells me that, if everyone around her starts having cosmetic anti-aging interventions, she cannot be sure she wouldn't start having interventions too. Here's how she puts it: "You know, if something happens that I really look old, and everybody else my age is doing that, I don't know, who knows? Who knows what'll happen? But right now I don't have any desire to do that."

Ellen sometimes struggles with seeing age-driven changes in her face and body in the mirror. But overall she feels pretty good about her aging appearance. It's when she spends time with a family member who has had cosmetic anti-aging procedures that she feels most self-conscious about how she looks: "Most of the time, though, I think I look great. I mean, when I leave the house I think I look great. And then [when] I'm with her, I think, 'Oh my God, what did I wear this for?' or 'Oh, I forgot to do this thing.' You know, I don't even notice it until I'm with her."

Ellen, Rebecca, and Diane's articulations leave one to wonder what will happen to women who currently embrace "natural" aging as their exposure to cosmetic anti-aging intervention increases. Being surrounded by others who are also resisting the intervention route helps to reinforce and protect their natural aging stance as one that is both comfortable and normal. Yet, as more and more women choose intervention, and as support for aging naturally erodes, it may become more difficult for natural agers to maintain their position. "Normal" may be reversed from natural to surgical—or, as Diane puts it, "If more people have [cosmetic anti-aging intervention] then the more—to be normal, obviously—you would feel that you should do it too." Ellen is comfortable with her physical appearance—she engages in a daily beauty routine that feels right to her. She doesn't obsess over her appearance, but she takes good care of herself, and she spends a few minutes trying to "look nice" before she leaves the house each day. After spending time with her family member who has had two facelifts, however, Ellen is left to wonder whether she is doing enough. As she puts it: "And then it's like,

'Oh wow, [there's] this whole other level people go to.'" Should Ellen be more focused on her physical appearance? Should she spend more time and money, and endure more pain, to look younger, and therefore, more "beautiful?" These are the questions that women who are aging naturally may begin to ask themselves as the exploding world of cosmetic anti-aging surgeries and technologies encroaches on their own.

* * *

The perspectives expressed by the women in this chapter bespeak the power of social interactions, and the social environment that encapsulates them, and their impact on an individual's understanding of who she is. The self "arises in social experience," to revisit George Herbert Mead's language. The women in this chapter are deeply committed to growing older without cosmetic anti-aging intervention. They subscribe to natural aging strategies that are complex and multi-faceted: for them, to age naturally is to embody an ongoing process of identity reconfiguration, adaptation, and self-discovery over time. Women's commitment to growing older without intervention is increasingly questioned, tested, and challenged as they confront direct-to-consumer advertising for cosmetic anti-aging procedures, and as they navigate our increasingly image-centered, youth-centered culture. Still, they soldier on. But when women in their own social circles, like close female friends and family members, begin to have cosmetic anti-aging interventions, a new vulnerability emerges.

The women in this chapter rely on a "separate worlds" framework to sustain their natural aging approach—they check in with their naturally aging friends and family to remind themselves, and each other, just how different their social worlds are from the worlds of women who choose intervention. The specific social contexts they live in, and the social relationships that inform these contexts, are instrumental sources of support. The women in this chapter are quick to point out that if their life circumstances or social environments were different, their approaches to aging would likely be different, as well.

To be surrounded by "human mirrors" who share a commitment to natural aging, and whose aging faces and bodies resemble one's own, brings comfort and security, and enables a woman to find solid footing, and to re-center herself, within the anti-intervention camp. To come

back to Diane's language, it's about feeling *normal*. For women who resist cosmetic anti-aging procedures, finding normalcy within their own
social circles is crucial, particularly in a cultural climate that offers little support for the natural aging position. Unease grows, however, as
women who embrace intervention enter these circles, and as women
who refuse intervention find it harder to take their natural aging position for granted, even inside their own social worlds.

Conclusion

Taking the Body Back

I don't watch soap operas anymore. The beloved *Guiding Light* of my childhood went off the air in 2009, followed by *As The World Turns*, *One Life to Live*, and *All My Children* shortly thereafter. Confident predictions that all soaps would soon be history, however, have not come to pass. There are only four soaps left, but, apparently, they are thriving.[1] Melody Thomas Scott, who continues to play the character of Nikki on the *Young and the Restless*, just as she has since 1979, is now a grandmother on the show. Despite the passing of well over three decades, her appearance has changed little. Alas, Susan Lucci's ageless face—born in 1946, she played the character of Erica Kane on *All My Children* from 1970 until its end in 2011—is no longer a fixture on daytime TV. But, rest-assured, her face remains frozen in time. Just take a look, for instance, at the recent images of Lucci, alongside her daughter, on *People.com*: Who is the mother? Who is the daughter? It is hard to tell.

The rise of reality television is widely credited with toppling soap operas' supreme reign. But it also overwhelms us with cosmetically altered faces and bodies like never before. Reality shows enable us to follow celebrities and regular folk on their journeys of cosmetic intervention. We listen to doctors, aestheticians, and psychologists talk about the benefits of cosmetic procedures. We watch cosmetic procedures being performed. We are regaled with cheerful and inspiring "before and after" stories from patients and practitioners alike.[2] Even when cosmetic intervention is not the explicit focus of a given show, however, physical appearance, physical prowess, and body display are frequent and central themes in the landscape that is reality television. From *Toddlers and Tiaras* to *The Biggest Loser*, from *Survivor* to *The Amazing Race*, from the many iterations of *The Real Housewives* to *Keeping Up with the Kardashians*, we are bombarded with scantily clothed bodies, sweaty bodies, made-up faces, wrinkle-free faces, implanted breasts, thinned noses, and plumped lips and cheeks.

I don't watch soap operas anymore. But I am addicted to *People.com*. These days, our exposure to cosmetically altered celebrities—not just soap and reality stars, but television stars more broadly, and pop stars, and movie stars, the list goes on—can have little to do with seeing their TV shows, concerts, and movies. New technologies enable more flexibility, individual choice, and instant gratification, when it comes to when, where, and how many times we can watch our favorite celebrities in action. The internet and social media, combined with the near to constant presence of screens in so many of our lives—Androids, iPhones, tablets, laptops, desktop computers, and widescreen televisions—offer us live access to a continuous stream of cosmetically altered faces and bodies. We can watch celebrities' daily comings and goings on *Popsugar.com*, *USWeekly.com*, and *People.com*. We can also observe their cosmetically altered exteriors, and catch intimate glimpses into their personal lives, via their own selfies and posts on social media. I don't watch *Keeping Up with the Kardashians*. But I do, along with millions of others, pour over the photos and video clips taken of the Kardashians by the paparazzi and others—or by the Kardashians themselves—and posted, or reposted, from Instagram, Facebook, and Snapchat, on *People.com*. Kylie's eighteenth birthday party, Kendall's twentieth, Kim's thirty-fifth, or mom Kris's lavish 1920s-themed sixtieth birthday party; Caitlyn, Kendall, and Kylie's "Girls' Night In"; Kendall backstage before her Victoria's Secret fashion show debut—Kris and Caitlyn, sixty and sixty-five years old, respectively, proud parents at Kendall's debut, with matching pumped up breasts, pulled brows, wrinkle-free faces, and plumped up cheeks and lips.

I check out the reposted Instagram images on *People.com* of former *King of Queens* television star Leah Remini, cheek-to-cheek with actress and singer Jennifer Lopez, both in their mid-forties, with arched brows, plumped lips, and not a wrinkle or sag in sight. I watch a repost, on *People.com*, of *No Doubt* bandleader Gwen Stefani—also in her mid-forties—performing her most recent single, "I Used to Love You," for the first time on television, on the Ellen DeGeneres show. Despite the heart-wrenching lyrics and the emotion in Stefani's voice (she herself is calling it a "breakup song" in reference to the end of her marriage to singer and musician Gavin Rossdale), her pulled brows, plumped cheeks and lips, and wrinkle-free forehead hardly move as she sings.

As the year 2016 comes to a close, we are deep into our two-dimensional culture, subsumed into our screens, our near-constant companions. When I watched soap operas in the early 2000s, it was actors and fictionalized story lines. Then came the manufactured celebrities of reality TV—watching the "real" lives of the very rich and well-connected, and even a few ordinary folk. But now, we gaze not only at the intimate images and clips of the faces, bodies, and daily lives of celebrities, but at images and clips of *ourselves*. Just as celebrities more and more willingly offer us minute-by-minute, up-close-and-personal visuals of themselves, we are posting our own selfies on Facebook and Instagram, and video clips of ourselves on YouTube. We democratize the conception of celebrity as we turn the screens onto our own faces and bodies and lives, and aspire to constant and conscious identity-construction and self-documentation via our screens. We share these images and clips of ourselves with infinite others as we post them into the air and space that is the internet—we inform, communicate, and build connections through two-dimensional images and in two-dimensional space. And, as our culture becomes more visual, as more of our days are spent interacting with images of ourselves, and images of others, via two-dimensional screens, more and more of us are having cosmetic interventions.

Three Feminist Icons on Intervention

Actress, social activist, and self-proclaimed feminist Jane Fonda, who, as of this writing is seventy-eight, has offered thoughtful and honest reflections on her own insecurities about her appearance over the years, and continues to speak out about the intense pressure women face in Hollywood, and more generally, to conform to narrow and stringent beauty-body ideals. She celebrates the success of female celebrities who, in her words, are not "conventionally pretty"—like Lena Dunham, creator and star of the HBO show *Girls*, singer-actress Jennifer Lopez, who is not rail thin, and Vanessa Redgrave, whom Fonda describes as one of the "brave" actresses who has "allowed us to see them age."[3]

Some years ago, Fonda co-founded the Women's Media Center with feminist writers Gloria Steinem and Robin Morgan. The Women's Media Center, in her words, "seeks to amplify women's voices in all aspects of the media, from behind the camera to op-eds." And yet, Fonda explains, it is still men who run the show: "Men are very visual, they want young women. So, for us, it's all about trying to stay young."[4] Fonda admits to her own plastic surgeries, explaining that her cosmetic anti-aging procedures have enabled her to keep working: "I wish I were brave enough to not do plastic surgery, but I think I bought myself a decade."[5] Fonda's perspective is practical, with a heavy dose of wistfulness and fatalism thrown in: "Ageism is alive and well," she says. It is not only ageism, but ageism with a gendered twist, however, that Fonda calls our attention to: "It is okay for men to get older, because men become more desirable by being powerful. With women, it's all about how we look," she tells the *Telegraph* in a recent interview.[6]

Even American feminist writer, activist, and founder of *Ms.* magazine, Gloria Steinem herself, now eighty-two, has admitted to having some cosmetic anti-aging work done around her eyes in light of what would be a brief stint on the *Today Show* some years ago. Steinem regrets her own procedure and encourages women to age naturally. Like Fonda, she also concedes, however, that cosmetic intervention is necessary for women in certain fields of work. Steinem shared this view on a recent episode of the television talk show *Mondays with Marlo* titled, "How Does a Feminist Validate Plastic Surgery?" She said: "It's important to evaluate why you're getting surgery done. If you're in the public eye, for instance, a few nips and tucks might add another decade to your career. If not, embrace aging as your body's way of adapting to a different life stage."[7] I must admit, however, that it was hard for me to listen to what Steinem saying, because I was so distracted by the motionless face of her interviewer and host, Marlo Thomas, the award-winning actress, activist, and producer of the beloved 1970s feminist children's album *Free to Be You and Me*. Thomas—who was seventy-six at the time of this episode—had incredibly tight, wrinkle-free skin and plumped lips and I kept wondering when she was going to start talking about her own cosmetic anti-aging procedures. She never did.

Generally speaking—and the women I interviewed for this book articulated this view—we tend to think of Europeans as having more respect for, and interest in, women as they grow older than Americans do. While gendered ageism is certainly alive and well in Great Britain, British actresses like Helen Mirren, Judi Dench, and Maggie Smith are hailed as examples of women who are embodying strong and complex roles in their older years, and whom continue to be admired for their appearance, as well. Take award-winning actress Helen Mirren, now seventy-one. Mirren speaks openly about how her sex life has only gotten better with age. She also regularly speaks out about sexism and ageism in the movie business, and claims she doesn't need to call herself a feminist because "it's just fucking obvious."[8] Mirren, it seems, has nothing against plastic surgery. It has been reported that in the months leading up to her seventieth birthday, the then sixty-nine-year-old Mirren shared her plans to have cosmetic procedures "very, very soon."[9] Quotes attributed to Mirren on the subject invoke sentiments of individual choice and empowerment: "People have the freedom to do what makes them happy," and "If you can look in the mirror and feel good about yourself . . . why not?"[10] When reporter Hannah Betts addressed the matter directly with Mirren in a recent interview, she responded with humor and neither confirmed nor denied having had cosmetic surgery herself, saying only that it was "brilliant if you want it, full stop!"[11] In my own assessment, Mirren has most certainly had work done. Yes, her look is less extreme and less dramatic than many actresses her age who have had cosmetic anti-aging procedures. But in current photos, and in live footage, Mirren sports a noticeably smoother jaw line and a tighter face.

Choosing Intervention: Individual Choice, Empowerment, and Practicality

Between them, Gloria Steinem, Jane Fonda, and Helen Mirren—three strong, famous, accomplished women in their seventies and eighties— illuminate an individual empowerment-individual choice perspective *and* a practical, looks-matter perspective on cosmetic anti-aging intervention. These two, albeit somewhat contradictory, perspectives are also widely shared among the women in this book who embrace intervention. Choosing intervention means fighting back against age-centered invisibility, stereotyping, and stigma. To achieve smoother skin, flatter stomachs, and perkier breasts—in short, a younger-looking appearance—is to feel more attractive and sexually desirable, and to receive increased attention and positive feedback for how you look, thereby unsettling the widely held belief that older women cannot be sexy or physically attractive. Choosing intervention means increasing your chances of finding a new romantic partner after divorce, maintaining success at your job, and simply being visible, respected, and listened to as an individual with worthy ideas and perspectives of your own. Choosing intervention means being practical, and accepting that, as a woman, you cannot look old and expect to be considered physically attractive, much less realize any of these other positive outcomes.

It is what the women in this book perceive and experience as negative aspects of aging—age-driven changes in appearance to be precise—that prompt them to have and use cosmetic anti-aging surgeries and technologies. Yet, these women also present aging as a story of progress: they favorably equate their cosmetic interventions with an increased capacity to act freely *and* to be practical, and they attribute these new and improved capacities to age. The women who embrace intervention draw from what we might call the classic American liberal feminist language of individual empowerment, choice, and self-determination as they speak about being able to make their own decisions, stand up for themselves, and pursue their own wants and needs now that they are older. And they use this same language when they talk about their cosmetic anti-aging procedures: "I'm more comfortable focusing on myself," "I put up with less now," "this isn't about what you want, it's about what *I want.*"

When women couch their interventions in a language of individual agency and choice, however, they apply this language differently, and with a very different meaning, than what the original leaders of the first- and second-wave liberal feminist movements in the United States intended. Take Betty Friedan's 1963 classic, *The Feminine Mystique*, for instance, wherein she encouraged women to realize their capacities as individuals in the workforce outside of what we might read as the traditional feminine roles and expectations of housewife, mother, and sex object.[12] The women in this book who embrace intervention equate their cosmetic procedures with a newfound freedom for themselves as individuals, now that they are less consumed with the physical and emotional demands of nurturing and caring for others. Yet, while they enjoy greater freedom from what can be read as traditional feminine roles and expectations in some respects, they exercise this freedom by choosing to continue to conform to the traditional feminine imperative of a youthful appearance.

For the women in this book who are having and using cosmetic anti-aging procedures, cosmetic intervention is about exerting individual control over an aging appearance with technology. And this, too, is empowering. Just as they use a liberal feminist language of individual choice, albeit with a new twist, to describe their cosmetic anti-aging interventions, when the women in this book talk about their interventions as a technological means to control their aging bodies, they echo the perspectives of some influential American second-wave radical feminist writers, as well. Radical feminist Shulamith Firestone, for example, enthusiastically embraced the libratory potential of technology for women. Technology, she argued, offered women an escape hatch from their own biology.[13] Freed from the constraints of pregnancy, childbirth, and the demands of motherhood, they could become gender-neutral, focus on their minds instead of their bodies, and pursue their unique dreams as individuals. To embrace intervention is to fight back against age-driven changes in appearance—or what we might call the constraints of biology—with technology. Yet, unlike Firestone and other radical feminists who conceived of technology as a tool by which women could move beyond their biological bodies and the limiting cultural expectations of traditional femininity that accompanied them, cosmetic anti-aging intervention means reconnecting to the body and reinforcing its significance. The women in this book credit their cosmetic anti-aging procedures with overcoming alienation from their aging exteriors. Through their surgical and technological transformations they reclaim their bodies away from nature and biology and for themselves. They come to feel their bodies as *their own again*: "I look and feel like *me* again, and not simply *old*."

The younger-looking appearance a woman achieves through her interventions is one that feels more comfortable to her, more familiar, and more like her own. Yet, when the women in this book use technology to challenge the biological process of aging, and to remake their bodies differently from how nature intended, they also disrupt the widely held cultural belief that older women cannot be sexually desirable. It is now possible for women to meet the cultural criteria of a feminine sex object—to look young—at much older ages. And, in this way, too, the women in this book are empowered by their interventions, and by the compliments and favorable attention they receive from others about how they look, as a result of them.

For the women in this book, the decision to have cosmetic anti-aging procedures is one that reflects a kind of knowledge, wisdom, and practicality that comes only with age. This means a new and improved ability to know what you want and how to get it, and a new and improved understanding about how society works and what you need to do to be successful in it. If you are Lisa, for instance, aging translates into being more true to yourself, and more able to admit to yourself, that you do care about what you look like, even if others judge you for being vain or superficial: "It's *okay* for me to say, 'I do care, and it does make a difference to me, and *why not* let myself do this?'" If you are Mary, on the other hand, to be older means accepting that looks matter, and that looking young matters, if you are a woman who hopes to realize her aspirations in today's world, whatever those aspirations may be.

Refusing Intervention: Individual Choice, Empowerment, and New Freedoms

The women in this book who choose to grow older without intervention—like the women who embrace it—are living out what Margaret Morganroth Gullette calls an age-centered "progress narrative" in many respects.[14] Like their pro-intervention counterparts, they equate aging with a welcome shift from caring for others to caring for the self. Like their pro-intervention counterparts, they are happy to be released from the demanding physical and emotional labor of nurturance— the mothering of young children, for instance—that consumed a good amount of their energy and identity in their younger years. However, this newfound individual freedom does not translate into the pursuit of cosmetic anti-aging intervention. Instead, these naturally aging women treat not only the ebbing of their intensive caretaking responsibilities, but also the age-driven changes in their appearance and other age-driven changes their bodies, like menopause, as interconnected parts of a new, more self-determined life phase. They draw from a classic liberal feminist language of individual choice, freedom, and self-determination to narrate their departure not only from what we might describe as the traditional feminine imperative of nurturance—in both its cultural and biological aspects—but also from the traditional feminine imperative of youthful beauty. Age frees them from pregnancy, childbirth, and breastfeeding—from a body given in the service of nurturing others. Age offers new space for individual expression outside of the realm of physical appearance. And age means more time to cultivate new and different parts of themselves outside of the body altogether.

The women in this book who choose to grow older without intervention celebrate the distance from their bodies—and from the traditional and heterosexual feminine roles and expectations that are commonly conflated with their bodies—that age brings. They enjoy being less caught up in their physical appearance, and many experience menopause as a new phase of freedom from the body, as well. That is not to say that they don't ever struggle with uncomfortable feelings of disconnection from their aging exteriors—"who *is* that person in the mirror?"—nor is it to say that they don't find age-centered invisibility painful. Significantly, it is not only the shift in focus away from their bodies with age, but the connection these naturally aging women feel to their bodies, age-driven changes and all, that explains their lack of interest in having cosmetic anti-aging intervention. On the one hand, they articulate a kind of humility, deference, and respect for the natural, bodily process of aging that is beyond their individual control—my body "knows what to do," "it's just what happens," "it's what's supposed to happen." On the other hand, many of these women articulate an increasingly reflexive relationship between the body and the self with age. Age-driven changes in appearance communicate not only a biological process, but also a woman's current and past thoughts, feelings, experiences, and emotions. In this way, for the women in this book who refuse intervention, their aging exteriors reflect and express who they were, who they are, and who they are becoming, over time.

When women who are aging naturally speak about their deference to the inevitability of their changing bodies over time, they echo the strand of American second-wave radical feminist thought that—in contrast to Firestone's emphasis on moving beyond the body altogether via technology—called upon women to celebrate their bodies' natural and

biological capacity for menstruation, pregnancy, childbirth, and menopause. But these naturally aging women read the changes in their bodily
exteriors not only as biological, natural, or inevitable, but also as unique
reflections of their own lived experiences. In this way, they challenge the
"binary opposition between the natural and the cultural," and practice,
in and through their interactive self-body relationship, what feminist
constructivist Elizabeth Grosz calls "embodied subjectivity" as well.[15]

Nonetheless, the natural agers in this book clearly heed the widely
shared call among radical feminists for women to assert autonomy over
their own bodies, and to take their bodies back from under male control. They experience an increased comfort and connection to their bodies, just as their bodies' role as sex object and target of the male gaze
lessens. They enjoy feeling less preoccupied with their physical exteriors,
less beholden to their bodies as vessels for nurturing others, and *more
connected* to their bodies in new and different ways. They explore, as
Adrienne Rich puts it, how their bodies can serve them in infinite ways
beyond "maternal function" and in ways that newly reflect the "corporeal
ground" of their intelligence.[16] For some, this means reclaiming their
bodies for themselves after menopause: "My body is mine now." Others
articulate a shift in focus from how their bodies look to how their bodies feel: they "listen" to their bodies more and take "better care of them."
Still others come to appreciate, not only a new and different beauty in
the aging face and body, but also the way in which these changes in appearance reflect the complexity of an evolving identity and the wisdom
of accumulated experiences over time.

The women's stories of aging that populate this book push us to have
new conversations about women and the body, women and the self,
women and society, and feminism. It is my hope that the women's stories in this book will join the small, but robust and growing, feminist
community calling for the integration of the older woman's body—and
women's perspectives on aging—into current discussions of women's
representation, power, status, and equality in the United States today.[17]
The women in this book draw from, but also creatively reinvent, core
feminist beliefs and practices as they experience, and strive to make
sense of, their aging faces and bodies. By sharing their perspectives,
the women in this book challenge the privileging of the young woman's
body that continues to guide much of the body-centered discussion, ac-

tivism, and scholarship in the United States today and heed the rising call among feminist age studies scholars to chart new terrain.

Beauty Culture and the Limits of Choice

To feel good about how your body looks, to show it off at a party or on Facebook, and to receive face-to-face and virtual compliments and attention as a result, can be an individually empowering experience for women. We can even interpret "selfies"—whether taken by female celebrities or everyday women of all ages—as a means by which we can assert new agency and control over our bodies. We decide what images of our bodies to share, when, and with whom. We choose to take the selfie, and to gaze at ourselves through the camera's lens, as if to say, "I like looking at myself. I have value." We look at ourselves *and* we look back: "Look at me. I am here. Look at me looking at you." Facebook, Instagram, Snapchat, and other visual social media platforms offer women of diverse backgrounds, shapes, and sizes the opportunity to destabilize the unidirectional and heterosexual power dynamics we traditionally associate with the male gaze, and to democratize the images of the female bodies displayed. Actress and producer Lena Dunham's recent Instagram post of her not-so-stick-thin, more rounded self, lounging in a bikini with some underarm hair, proves but one powerful example.

But these visual circuits can also reproduce a beauty culture, or to use Victoria Pitts-Taylor's phrase, a "cosmetic culture," that promises women freedom and empowerment while simultaneously distracting them from what needs to be done to truly achieve it.[18] As journalist Ariel Levy points out in her book, *Female Chauvinist Pigs: Women and the Rise of Raunch Culture*, young women in this country use a language of individual choice, agency, and even sexual empowerment as they talk about their dreams of being in reality TV shows like *Girls Gone Wild* or *The Girls Next Door*, walking the Victoria Secret catwalk, or posing for *Playboy*.[19] Yet, as young woman aspire to look sexy by having hairless, taught bodies with large breasts like Kim Kardashian, and to inspire sexual desire in others, millions of American women—young and old—have yet to feel comfortable expressing and satisfying their own sexual wants and desires.[20] Peggy Orenstein's recent book, *Girls and Sex: Navigating the Complicated New Landscape*, reiterates these glaring contradictions through the lives of primarily heterosexual teenage girls and female college students who are engaging in sexual interactions, but who are struggling to express and fulfill their own sexual pleasure and desire in the context of these interactions.[21]

In the early 1990s, in her book *The Beauty Myth: How Images of Beauty Are Used Against Women*, Naomi Wolf argued that the exploding beauty industry—and American women's anxiety about, and obsession with, physical appearance that it feeds—undermined women's focus on gender equality and gender justice and diverted their energies away from fighting for social and political change.[22] More recently, in *The Rise of Enlightened Sexism: How Pop Culture Took Us from Girl Power to Girls Gone Wild*, feminist media studies scholar Susan Douglas builds from Susan Faludi's classic, *Backlash: The Undeclared War Against American Women*, and extends it—along with the work of Wolf, Bordo, Levy, and others—into the present when she calls attention to a new, post-feminist, girlie-girl popular culture infused with breezy celebrations of traditional hetero-normative ideals of femininity—marriage, motherhood, and beauty-body work—and packaged as the ultimate in female fulfillment.[23] All the while, mind-boggling inequalities between women and men in the United States today, like the gender pay gap and women's glaring underrepresentation in politics, remain.

"Looks are the new feminism, an activism of aesthetics. As vulgar and shallow as it sounds, looks matter more than they ever have—especially for women," writes journalist Alex Kuczynski.[24] In *We Were Feminists Once: From Riot Grrrl to CoverGirl, The Buying and Selling of a Political Movement*, Bitch Media cofounder and editorial/creative director Andi Zeisler makes exactly this point and—like Wolf and others—reveals the profit-seeking beauty industry as a primary culprit. Women continue to be bombarded with what Susan Bordo has called a "rhetoric of choice and self-determination" in advertisements for beauty-body products and cosmetic procedures.[25] This rhetoric is clearly expressed in a revisiting of recent and current Botox advertisements: "It's all about FREEDOM OF EXPRESSION. Don't hold back! Express it all! Express yourself by asking your doctor about Botox Cosmetic!" and "It's really up to you. You can choose to live with wrinkles. Or you can choose to live without them" and "Re-Look, Re-Think, Re-Imagine."[26] But this re-looking, and re-thinking, and re-imagining, is, of course, code for one option, and one option only: a more youthful appearance. As Bordo succinctly puts it: "One cannot have *any* body one wants—for not every body will *do*."[27]

The female body *can* be a source of empowerment, and pleasure, and a site for creative expression, freedom, and exploration in limitless ways. But not, in my view, if a woman's relationship to her body is increasingly centered on how her body looks, and not if that look is increasingly narrowly prescribed. If women's preoccupation with their bodies can be recalibrated away from the time, pain, and money-intensive work of beautifying and channeled into the fight for substantive social, cultural, economic, and political equality in and through their bodies *and* outside of them, then—and only then—will we be moving closer to gender justice in this country. As I write this, I read, with discouragement, that Miley Cyrus is no longer embodying her short-haired, armpit-haired, free-spirited ways—her engagement to Liam Hemsworth is back on, and, according to an exclusive feature on *People.com*, twenty-three-year-old Cyrus is now living a "very secluded life," wherein she has gone from "a wild child to a housewife" who is "doing everything to please and make Liam happy."[28]

Cosmetic Intervention and the Limits of Empowerment

To have cosmetic intervention, as a woman, is to prioritize the body—specifically how the body looks—as fundamental to your sense of self and self-value. But achieving a physical appearance that conforms to current and narrow youth-beauty norms via intervention also brings potential risks like bodily harm, and compromised bodily sensation and function, not to mention a loss of aesthetic diversity. In the summer of 2015, I received a letter from a doctor who practices and resides in the northeastern United States. In it, he expressed his concern about the current and exploding popularity of silicone breast implants in the United States today, and called attention to medical data and research outlining a range of potential health risks for women, particularly over time, if and when the implants rupture and the silicone and platinum contained within the implants escapes into a woman's chest cavity, and, potentially, her body at large. This doctor expressed frustration with what he described as the casual attitude, and lack of attention to potential health risks, with which American plastic surgeons were proceeding with implanting silicone implants into American women's bodies.

Breast implantation is the most popular cosmetic surgery in the United States today and 80% of the breast implants American women now receive are silicone implants.[29] But saline implants are also encased in a silicone shell. Thousands of American women who claimed to be sick from their breast implants protested in the early 1990s, eventually causing Dow Corning, the leading manufacturer of silicone implants at the time, to declare bankruptcy.[30] Still, saline implants first received approval from the Food and Drug Administration (FDA) in 2000, and three silicone implant manufacturers—Allergan, Mentor, and Sientra—received official FDA approval for their implants in 2006 and 2013 rulings, respectively. The FDA's conditions for approval mandated that each of the silicone implant manufacturers conduct follow-up studies to "further characterize the safety and effectiveness of their breast implants."[31] In the FDA's most recent report on the ongoing safety studies conducted by Mentor and Allegan, which reveals a host of troubling data, including implant rupture rates among some groups of women as high as 27%, it summarizes its rationale for approving silicone implants as follows: "Despite frequent local complications and adverse outcomes, the FDA determined that the benefits and risks of breast implants were sufficiently well understood for women to make informed decisions about their use."[32] The FDA's mandate of these longitudinal studies on silicone implants in live human subjects is important, and marks a progressive shift away from a long-standing dearth of such studies in the United States overall. Still, studies on the safety of breast implants are relatively few, and studies conducted by researchers other than those employed by the implant manufacturers themselves are fewer still.

Labiaplasty—a procedure wherein the labia minora or the labia majora (the folds of skin surrounding a woman's vulva) are surgically cut and altered in the name of symmetry and beautification—is growing in popularity in the United States and across the globe.[33] In the United States, labiaplasty increased 49% in 2014 alone. [34] While there is no systematic data on what is driving this trend, some medical experts attribute it to the normalization of pornography, specifically to the hairless and "perfect" vaginas on display in pornography, and to the mirroring and exploding phenomenon of Brazilian waxes and entirely hairless vaginas among everyday women.[35] Now that vaginas are no longer hidden by hair, their "imperfections" are fully exposed and fair game for cosmetic intervention.[36] Women's long-term satisfaction and complication rates from labiaplasty have not been tracked. But the risks and side effects of labiaplasty include bleeding, infection, permanent changes in sensation, ongoing pain, and scarring.[37]

In her film, *Orgasm, Inc.*, documentary filmmaker Liz Canner shares a woman's experience of vaginal rejuvenation surgery wherein, upon returning home from surgery, she began hemorrhaging and nearly died. At a recent live presentation on the growing popularity of vaginal plastic surgery—both labiaplasty and vaginoplasty—Canner recounted how she had accompanied her research assistant on an experiment wherein she went undercover to a number of vaginal plastic surgery clinics that were popping up in a small New England city. This research assistant was perfectly happy with how her vagina looked, but, in each clinic, Canner explained, the plastic surgeon recommended at least one surgical procedure.[38]

The potentially long- and short-term health risks a woman undergoes by having silicone implants, or vaginal plastic surgery, are deeply troubling. But, to think about women's motivations for having these surgeries and procedures and enduring these risks saddens me too. Women are seeking out procedures to fix and improve bodies that, in my view, don't need fixing or improving. Perhaps a woman thinks her breasts are too small, or that her labia are too long, or too short, or not symmetrical enough—but those breasts and those labia are perfectly healthy, and perfectly normal. Just as no two women age in exactly the same way, no two woman's breasts, or labia, are alike—each are unique to her. It makes me sad to think that a woman feels that her body needs improvement when it simply reflects the natural and normal diversity and difference among and between each of us. In this respect, to live in a culture of cosmetic intervention is to live in a depleted culture, a culture of aesthetic homogenization, a culture that promotes what feminist philosopher Kathryn Pauly Morgan has called the "pathological inversion of the normal."[39]

How empowering can cosmetic interventions truly be for women if—even apart from the potential health risks—to have them is to feel good about your body only if it conforms to an incredibly narrow and stringent set of aesthetic standards? And how can cosmetic interventions be empowering for women if they bring with them the risk of reduced sensation in some of the most sensitive and potentially pleasure-producing areas of the woman's body, like the breasts, or the vagina, or the neck, or the face, or the mouth? What is the point of having "perfect" breasts, or a "perfect" vagina, if your capacity to feel pleasure in these bodily areas is compromised? As some of the women in this book expressed, tingling and numbness can continue long after the surgeries have been performed. Reality star Kylie Jenner speaks openly about how her lip-injections have increased her self-confidence and self-esteem. But I can't *help* but wonder: Does she have any feeling left in those incredibly inflated things? And what about speaking itself? In a recent clip from *Keeping Up with the Kardashians*, Kylie's sister and reality star Kim Kardashian's lips were so plumped up, it looked to me like she had trouble moving them as she spoke. I was instantly reminded of a kind of pure female objectification wherein women are to be looked at, and to inspire sexual desire in others, but to have no voice, or physical pleasures, of their own.

Women, Aging, Ageism, and Cosmetic Intervention: Final Reflections

My friends and family make fun of me. But I can't help it. I still get a little down when an actress or female celebrity I admire suddenly looks different than she did and, therefore, less unique and more inevitably in keeping with our reigning beauty-body ideal in the United States today: slim; toned; large breasts; slim nose; big lips; smooth, tight, light, young-looking skin. Like when actress Kate Hudson or, more recently, celebrity and model Gisele Bündchen—both of whom looked refreshingly lovely, I thought, with small breasts—got larger ones. Or, when, several years ago, actress Courtney Cox of *Friends* and, more recently, *Cougar Town* fame, first acquired the inflated lips she has today, or when Nicole Kidman's lips first expanded, or, most recently, Gwen Stefani's. Indeed, Nicole Kidman and Gwen Stefani's faces look pulled and tight and move very little when they speak and express different emotions. Madonna's face is another that resembles marble.

But I do not begrudge any of these women in their decisions to have and use cosmetic interventions. (For the record: to my knowledge, none of these female actors, celebrities, and musicians has publicly admitted to their cosmetic interventions. I think Kidman may have confessed to trying Botox "once." I am making the assumption that they have had interventions based on my own careful observations of their exteriors over time.) It's like what Jane Fonda said: "With women, it's all about how we look." Without her interventions, would Nicole Kidman be able to keep working? Would she be able to keep her musician husband, Keith Urban, who happens to be about her age and not significantly older? Courtney Cox, who is fifty-two, was engaged to a former model in his late thirties until recently—could she have secured him as a romantic partner without her cosmetic anti-aging procedures? Gwen Stefani's former husband of some years, musician Gavin Rossdale, with whom she has three children, apparently had an affair with their nanny around the time their youngest child was born. Were her latest interventions in response to his infidelity and would she now be dating younger musician Blake Shelton without them?

In the last few years, middle-aged and older women's faces and bodies are becoming more visible in popular culture. Actress Jessica Lange was recently in ads for a Marc Jacobs makeup line, and Diane Keaton and Helen Mirren are currently featured in anti-aging cosmetics ads for L'Oreal. Diane Keaton says she hasn't yet had surgery: "I haven't, but that doesn't mean I won't."[40] But does she opt out of Botox too? I'm not sure. Jessica Lange and Helen Mirren, on the other hand, have had more than Botox shots, I *am* sure of it. By contrast, writer Joan Didion, now in her early eighties, and recently in an ad for the designer clothing line Celine, looks lovely and entirely and uniquely unaltered.

In the United States today, film and television continue to be male-dominated and women, particularly middle-aged and older women, are severely underrepresented. There are some notable exceptions in film; Diane Keaton and Meryl Streep have had recent leading movie roles, for instance. The American television landscape is also becoming more promising when it comes to primary roles for actresses in their forties and older. It's exciting to see Viola Davis, who is fifty-one, and Julianna Margulies and Téa Leoni, both fifty, playing a law professor, a lawyer, and the secretary of state, in the ABC show *How to Get Away with Murder*, and the CBS shows *The Good Wife* and *Madam Secretary*, respectively. It's fantastic that Jane Fonda stars in the new Netflix series, *Grace and Frankie*, alongside Lily Tomlin, who, like Fonda, is in her seventies. It's encouraging that Jamie Lee Curtis, who is in her late fifties, plays a leading character in the new Fox series *Scream Queens*, and that Kim Cattrall, now sixty, leads the new HBO series *Sensitive Skin*. Television series in Europe and across the globe that center on compelling and powerful older women are also increasing. *Downton Abbey*, a British BBC series popular among American viewers, featured an inspiring number of interesting and important female characters in their fifties, sixties, seventies, and eighties.

Jane Fonda is one of the few actresses I know of who openly admits to surgical cosmetic anti-aging procedures, and who explicitly states that she is able to keep working—to star in a television show at her age—precisely because of them. Call me cynical, but it looks to me like many of these other actresses have had at least some anti-aging procedures—including Lily Tomlin, Fonda's co-star—as well. In the past, Kim Cattrall has admitted to using Botox and has expressed that, while she feels it's a woman's choice to have surgery—"It's your body, it's your life, do what you want to do"—she doesn't want to have surgery because "I don't want to look in the mirror and not recognize who's looking back."[41] Some years ago, Jamie Lee Curtis spoke about her lack of interest in having cosmetic anti-aging procedures. Julianna Margulies has said that she's not going to "blank out her face" because "I want people to know what I'm feeling."[42] Téa Leoni has proclaimed to have a "fear of Botox because I know it will make me look better and then I'll be addicted."[43]

When watching live interviews with Margulies and Leoni, and watching their shows, I can't be sure whether or not they've had Botox or other interventions. Leoni's face seems to move more than Margulies's does, and both have some signs of aging on their faces, but their foreheads are pretty immobile, and definitely move less than mine does when I express emotion. In a recent interview about her new TV show on *Today*, Jamie Lee Curtis looked pretty unaltered to me: her eyebrows moved and rose along with her emotions but, then again, her jaw line looked awfully tight. I suspect intervention of many of the female stars in *Downton Abbey* too: actress Penelope Wilton, who plays Isobel Crawley, and is seventy, has hardly a wrinkle or sag in sight, and neither does actress Phyllis Logan, who plays Mrs. Hughes, who is sixty. Most upsetting to me, however, was when I recently noticed changes in actress Elizabeth

McGovern, age fifty-five, who stars as Cora Crawley *and* in the beloved Maggie Smith, who stars as Violet Crawley, and is eighty-one. I had always been pleased that Elizabeth McGovern actually had some wrinkles and looked lovely and that Maggie Smith's face bore signs of aging and she looked beautiful. Yet, suddenly, there they were, with smoother, tighter skin, particularly around their eyes and on their foreheads. I blame Botox. This shift in McGovern and Smith's appearances—not inconsequently it seemed to me—corresponded with new story lines for both actresses that involved romantic-sexual interest from men.

Outright and public resistance against cosmetic anti-aging interventions in Hollywood is scarce. The British Anti-Cosmetic Surgery League, formed by British actresses Emma Thompson, Kate Winslet, and Rachel Weisz in 2011, is one of very few examples.[44] However, I haven't been able to find any updates since the original founding of the league was announced over five years ago now. Have these three actresses been able to stick to their commitment to refuse cosmetic intervention of any kind over the intervening years? Emma Thompson continues to look unaltered. Kate Winslet and Rachel Weisz may also still be procedure-free, but it's harder for me to tell. In 2004, *People* magazine reported that actress Téa Leoni, then thirty-eight, and her friend, actress Elisabeth Shue, "refuse to resist wrinkles as they age." Leoni declared to *People*: "We have a pact that we will never do cosmetic surgery. When we feel weak about Botox or surgery, we'll call each other for support and just say, 'No.'" As *People* reported: "The pair think that their stand will eventually pay off." Leoni put it to the magazine this way: "Someday we'll be the only two actresses who will get roles for sixty-five-year-old women, because everyone else will look like they're thirty."[45] I am not sure what happened to Elisabeth Shue. In a 2011 interview with the *New York Times*, Téa Leoni shared her fear of Botox, as noted above. In this same interview, she equates Botox with being too "obsessed" with appearance, and, while she does prioritize taking care of her skin, she reiterates that she will continue to be one of the only female actresses who looks their age: "What I am concerned with is taking care of my skin as well as I can. Giving it the best chance it has to age gracefully. I will be one of the only seventy-five-year-old actors who will look their age."[46] But this interview was conducted several years before filming began for Leoni's new series, *Madame Secretary*.

The thing is, most roles—or should I say the few roles—designed for women in their sixties and older continue to be played either by actresses who are younger than sixty-five, or by actresses who have had cosmetic anti-aging interventions. Actress, writer, and comedian Carrie Fisher, who is fifty-nine, and who recently reprised her role of Princess Leia along with actor Harrison Ford, who is seventy-four, in the *Star Wars* movie series smash hit, *Star Wars: The Force Awakens*, makes clear the no-win situation that aging women face in Hollywood today. I don't think many would disagree with me when I say that Fisher's face clearly betrays cosmetic anti-aging interventions. She has received criticism on social media, and from the likes of conservative talk show host Bill O'Reilly, about having had too much work done *and* about not having aged well. Ford, on the other hand, has endured fewer negative comments about his appearance. Fisher provided her critics with this powerful response on Twitter: "Please stop debating whether or not I aged well. . . . My body hasn't aged as well as I have."[47]

In December 2015, a delegation of three women from Poland, the United Kingdom, and Costa Rica spent ten days touring the United States on behalf of the United Nations working group on discrimination against women.[48] Their assessment of the overall treatment of women in the United States was grim. Women in the U.S. were found to be lagging well behind much of the rest of the world when it comes to the pay gap, maternity leave, affordable childcare, reproductive rights and pre- and post-natal care, violence against women, and in other areas too. The increasing politicalization of some high-profile women in popular culture, on the other hand, is cheering. In her recent speech at the UN marking the launch of the HeforShe campaign, British actress Emma Watson called attention to gender injustice and gender inequality, both nationally and internationally, and the need to fight to overcome it.[49] Jennifer Lawrence and Patricia Arquette have made scathing indictments about the gendered pay gap, and sexism and ageism in Hollywood, more generally.[50] Young female actors and entertainers are beginning to express themselves through their bodies in ways that challenge dominant, stringent, white, hetero-normative beauty-body norms. Mexican-Kenyan actress Lupita Nyong'o currently sports short hair, as does entertainer Miley Cyrus. Lena Dunham is at home in her more rounded body, and with underarm hair, along with Cyrus, and, most recently, Michelle Rodriguez.

Musicians like Beyoncé are proudly calling themselves feminists, and more and more women in the film-television-entertainment business—actress Kristen Stewart among them—are comfortable embodying and expressing multiple sexualities that are not hetero-normative.

While I wonder whether or not Julianna Margulies has had any cosmetic anti-aging interventions, she does share the following advice her mother gave her: "When you look in the mirror and see one more line, do you say, 'Oh God,' or do you say, 'Wow, I've lived?' That's the choice you have."[51] Diane Keaton—like several of the women in this book—puts a positive spin on age-induced invisibility: "As you get older, you're looked at less. The compensation is that you get all this pleasure from being the observer, not just from being observed."[52] It is evident, not just from actress Helen Mirren, but from medical and sociological life-course research, that women continue to experience sexual desire, and to enjoy sexually satisfying relations, in the years after menopause. In fact, the post-menopause phase can be one of sexual discovery, a time during which women—and heterosexual women in particular—freed from fears of pregnancy, are more confident exploring and fulfilling their own sexual desires.[53] As some of the women in this book made clear, however, menopause can mark an exciting shift in focus away from the sexual realm—whether that means having a less constant and less urgent libido, or feeling less beholden to embodying an aesthetic that elicits sexual desire in others. Feminist Gloria Steinem made this same point a couple of years ago in a *New York Times* piece titled "This Is What 80 Looks Like." "Ever the positive thinker," columnist Gail Collins writes, "Steinem composed a list of the good things about starting her ninth decade. A dwindling libido, she theorized, can be a terrific advantage." In Steinem's own words: "The brain cells that used to be obsessed are now free for all kinds of great things."[54]

Gloria Steinem does not judge women who have cosmetic interventions and she readily admits that cosmetic procedures may be necessary, particularly for celebrities, if they want to keep working into their older years. But despite having had some work done on her eyes, albeit quite some time ago, Steinem is now able to appreciate the age-driven changes in her physical appearance. While she is sometimes surprised by these changes, she also respects them as part of a natural and "fascinating" bodily process. Steinem's words, and the words of the women in this book who refuse intervention, echo each other as Steinem describes her relationship to her aging appearance this way:

> Well, I'm shocked. Sometimes, you're passing a store, and you see this person in the window, and you think: "Who is that? Oh, it's me." But I've also realized that aging is a bit like what being pregnant must be like, by which I mean that your body knows how to do something that you don't know how to do—and it's quite interesting. Your body loses what it needs to support someone else, and it keeps what it needs to support you. That's very smart. Just watching the process is somehow fascinating.[55]

Actress Julia Roberts, who, as I write this, is forty-eight, has articulated her own lack of interest in having cosmetic anti-aging interventions. "By Hollywood standards, I guess I've already taken a big risk in not having had a facelift," she recently asserted.[56] I must say, watching a recent television interview with Roberts was an incredibly refreshing experience—and in stark contrast to so many other interviews I've watched lately with actresses Roberts's age and older—as her lovely face animated and emoted her thoughts and feelings as she spoke.[57] Yet, when I was watching Roberts speak about her life and work, and enjoying how her face reflected and expressed her lived experiences, the uniqueness of what I was witnessing called me back to the stubborn truth of feminist philosopher Sandra Bartky's point: "The face of the ideally feminine woman must never display the marks of character, wisdom, and experience we so admire in men." Roberts's face stands out in a popular culture and media scape saturated with the Kardashian-like face: the smooth, unblemished face—the "infantilized face," as Bartky puts it—that carries "the theme of inexperience" and "never ages or furrows its brow in thought."[58]

From my perspective, when a woman has cosmetic anti-aging intervention, she loses the fight against that "almost inescapable" judgment that older women's bodies are unattractive.[59] She reinforces the cultural understanding of the older women's body as the "rejected body" and the cultural assumption that the only attractive female body is a young-looking one.[60] We can understand cosmetic anti-aging intervention as a means for women to push back and resist against the stigmatization, negative stereotyping, and invisibility many experience simply because they look old. But, because cosmetic intervention enables women to look younger, the act of having intervention does little to combat ageism more generally. As more women practice "age avoidance" by taking advantage of an ever-growing stockpile of new cosmetic anti-aging products and procedures, women who are aging naturally are increasingly penalized for looking old *and* for failing to do anything about it.[61]

Julia tells me that cosmetic culture makes her sad because it ignores the beauty she sees in her seventy-one-year-old mother's "happy and twinkly" appearance and persona. Laura expresses similar frustrations when she says of her ninety-one-year-old mother-in-law: "She *is attractive*, just in a *different* way." Julia's mother's beauty, and the attractiveness of Laura's mother-in-law, may be appreciated less as the opportunities for controlling and minimizing age-driven changes in appearance expand. But I also worry about what this opportunity for increased control over aesthetic aging means for confronting and accepting old age and death. As we bear fewer marks of life experience and the passage of time on our faces and bodies, doesn't that make it more difficult to come to terms with things ending? Celebrity and comedian Joan Rivers went into cardiac arrest while under sedation during what was to be a routine medical procedure to treat a hoarse voice.[62] She was eighty-one, and she had nary a wrinkle, sag, or bag, in sight. One minute she was smooth, wrinkle-free Joan, and then, suddenly, she was gone.

Epilogue

I am now forty-six years old. I am struggling—like many of the women in this book—to adjust to my changing appearance. I am not a woman who has aged particularly "well." Translation: I look my age. In fact, I am quite sure that people often think I am older than I am, based on how I look. When I come face-to-face with a friend, acquaintance, or colleague that I haven't seen for a stretch of time, I can sense their unsettlement and surprise, and their distraction from what I am saying to them, because they are adjusting and reorienting to my new and different appearance. I am close to having that upsetting experience that Lisa shares in this book—one experience, albeit one of many, that informed her decision to have her neck lift—wherein friends she hadn't seen in a while would say to her, "I didn't recognize you."

I find my age-induced invisibility difficult to endure and hurtful at times. I certainly know exactly what Claire meant when she told me that she had become "just another middle-aged woman." I, too, have become that "middle-aged woman." From my teenage years until about age thirty, I would get looks and comments from men while I was out in public—on the way to school, at work, on the subway, and on the street. While I enjoyed this attention in some respects, it also made me feel self-conscious and uncomfortable, just as it did for many of the women I interviewed for this book. That attention was an imposition at times, and sometimes even forced me to restrict my movements and change my plans. There was an eyeglasses shop that carried a fantastic and relatively affordable selection of frames. But I decided to stop going there, because one of the male employees made me uncomfortable by persistently commenting on my appearance and asking me out. I altered my favorite walking route in my neighborhood to avoid a man's invasive invitations. When I was in high school, I quit my job because of my boss's sexualized comments and unwelcome physical advances. I felt uncomfortable running on the street because of catcalls and stares.

In what is most likely my last experience of being hit on by a man, I was forty-two, by then married with two kids, and in a café having a lovely time catching up with a good friend and mentor, when a male graduate student—who looked to be in his late twenties or early thirties—came up and interrupted us and asked for my phone number. I was startled, caught off guard, and humiliated. I was so shocked, in fact, that I actually gave him my phone number just because I wanted him to go away and leave us alone. He seemed like a nice person, and it was flattering. He texted, and called and left a voicemail the next day, to which I never responded. I was flattered, but I was also resentful and angry. He had invaded my space, and my treasured time catching up with someone I really respect and care about, but rarely have the pleasure of spending time with.

This graduate student was perfectly polite in his tone and language— and his behavior did not cross lines the way some of these other men's behaviors did. Had I been single, and interested in dating, perhaps I would have felt differently—and even been impressed by—his courage in approaching me cold turkey. Still, I felt he took liberties that were not his to take. And, I must admit, that being older brings me some welcome relief: the age-driven changes in my appearance offer me protective armor against these kinds of uncomfortable and annoying incidents where simply because you are young and female, men invade your time and space with words and worse.

In some ways then, I feel lucky. I am enjoying that age-induced and newfound freedom, as a woman, to take up space in public space—to enjoy public space in the new way that Diane and other women in this book, and that the actress Diane Keaton, too, call attention to. I can go to a café and enjoy the luxury of being in my own world and reading, or working, or simply taking in my surroundings, without having to feel self-conscious about, or annoyed by, being looked at or approached.

Like the women in this book who are aging naturally, I aim to work hard to recognize, and take advantage of, new opportunities for self-growth and self-expression—new sources of agency and empowerment—*outside* of traditional codes of heterosexual femininity, like a youthful-looking appearance. But I also don't think it's right, fair, or in any way just that physical attractiveness is so caught up in being young-looking, particularly for women. The naturally aging women in this book have inspired me to work hard to expand the beauty canon for myself, and for other women my age and older, by finding beauty and physical attractiveness in our aging appearances.

The changes in my appearance communicate a lot about me, who I am, and the life I've lived. My childhood in rural Vermont was spent outdoors—winter, spring, summer, and fall—without a thought of "protecting" my skin with hats or sunscreen. I don't spend much time or money on my appearance. I don't wear makeup or blow-dry my hair. I don't even shower every day. I still love being outside, as I always have, whether in the mountains, the fields, or the woods, or near ponds or the ocean—mostly without a hat, or sunglasses, and almost always without sunscreen. My face communicates the pain and heartache of my parents' divorce, and the loss of loved ones, but lots of happiness felt and laughter, too. My aging appearance not only reflects my lived experiences, but also my biology and my genes—my cellulite and my age-betraying skin run in my family (or in *some* of my family, I should say). My lived experiences interact with my biology—my biology interacts with my lived experiences—and each play out on my aging exterior. My relationship to my aging body is reflexive and changeable—but I aim not to criticize it, or to feel shame about it. After all, why should there be anything wrong with looking old?

I hope to resist the narrative—promoted by the booming cosmetic anti-aging industry in our country today—that aging is a story of "identity stripping" and "losing what we had."[1] I aspire, instead, to heed Margaret Morganroth Gullette's call to treat my aging exterior as a reflection of "changeable and continuous selves together," and to see "multiple identities" and "multiple selves" reflected back at me.[2] I aim to emulate the women in this book who live aging as a challenging and rewarding process that involves building and rebuilding the relationship between the body and the self *and* forging new avenues for self-expression outside of the body altogether.

APPENDIX A

Research Methods

SAMPLING STRATEGY

This book is drawn from forty-four in-depth interviews with women between the ages of forty-seven and seventy-six. My sampling strategy was purposive and strategic.[1] I recruited women who were over the age of forty-five, and I intentionally sought to populate my sample with women who inhabit a diverse range of attitudes about and approaches to aging. My aim was to solicit women who demonstrate an awareness of their bodies and a commitment to taking care of them. To this end, I selected women who participate in physical activity on a regular basis in a variety of forms, including gym workouts, dance classes, walking, running, yoga, and Pilates. In sum, the women I interviewed represent a variety of approaches to aging, yet they also share, albeit to different degrees of intensity, a common concern for the health of their bodies practiced through an array of body movement activities.

I utilized the snowball sampling technique to construct my sample of forty-four women.[2] Sixteen women are having and using cosmetic anti-aging surgeries and technologies, twenty-two women are not having or using cosmetic anti-aging surgeries and technologies (these women often describe themselves as growing older "naturally"), and six women are "on the fence" about whether they will or will not have and use cosmetic anti-aging surgeries and technologies in the future. At the end of each interview, I asked my interview subject to refer me to any female friends or acquaintances who might be interested and willing to talk to me about their thoughts, feelings, and experiences connected to a changing appearance with age.

The snowball sampling technique worked particularly well given the personal and potentially sensitive nature of my research questions. Sharing thoughts, feelings, and experiences about the body and identity in the context of growing older can be difficult. The fact that I had been referred to each interview subject through a friend or acquaintance helped "break the ice" between us and enabled my interview subjects to speak more freely about issues pertaining to aesthetic aging. As I was not coming to them entirely unscreened, comfort levels increased and building rapport became easier.

SAMPLE DEMOGRAPHICS AND CHARACTERISTICS

With the exception of two who live in the Midwest, the majority of the women I interviewed reside in New England. They inhabit a range of lifestyles—some live in urban centers, others in suburbs, still others live in small towns in rural settings. Some are retired; others are stay-at-home moms. They work in a variety of professional fields, from education to business, from social work to psychology, from real estate to journalism. One is a personal trainer and several are yoga instructors. A few are artists or writers; two are musicians and another is an instrument maker. The variety of lifestyles, livelihoods, and professions is fairly evenly distributed across my entire sample (see appendix B for a complete list of interview subjects). Businesswomen, retirees, and stay-at-home moms are represented in slightly higher numbers among women who are having and using anti-aging surgeries and technologies verses women who choose to grow older "naturally." However, for every businesswoman or retiree who is having and using cosmetic anti-aging procedures, there is a musician or a jewelry maker, a childcare provider or a restaurant manager, who is also having and using these procedures.[3] Furthermore, there are businesswomen, stay-at-home moms, and retirees among the women who are not having and using cosmetic anti-aging surgeries and technologies, and who are "on the fence" about such surgeries and technologies, as well.

Approximately three-quarters of my interview subjects enjoy financial security—of this group some are economically privileged, while others can be described as comfortably middle class. Approximately one-quarter of my interview subjects endure more financially precarious positions. These women often articulate worries and anxieties about money, and can be described as inhabiting a range of economic categories, from middle to lower-middle to low income. As with lifestyles, livelihoods, and professions, the distribution of wealth among all of women I interviewed is fairly even distributed across the sub-samples. There are a few more women in economically privileged positions who are having and using cosmetic anti-aging procedures than in the other sub-samples. However, four of the sixteen women who are having and using cosmetic anti-aging procedures express concern about money and are struggling to various degrees financially. Each of these women have and use cosmetic anti-aging procedures at considerable financial sacrifice, utilize payment plans, and identify the expense of cosmetic anti-aging surgeries and technologies as something they are highly cognizant of—in fact, cost is often identified as a barrier to their desires to have more procedures done.

The diversity of my sample is rooted more in the women's wide range of professions, livelihoods, and lifestyles, and more in the different attitudes and approaches to growing older they inhabit, than in race and class-based differences. My sample incorporates enough socioeconomic diversity such that the perspectives of less privileged women are heard. However, all of my interview subjects but one (who is Latina) are white. In the United States today, people of color account for 25% of the total number of recipients of cosmetic procedures.[4] There are no national statistics on class and cosmetic intervention available at this time—yet, we do know that saving up for cosmetic procedures, paying for cosmetic procedures over time on credit cards, and "payment plans" are increasingly common. In these respects, the women in this book represent the most common recipients of cosmetic procedures in the United States today: they are mostly white and middle- and upper-middle-class women, a solid minority of whom live in less privileged socioeconomic circumstances.

GROUNDED METHODOLOGICAL FRAMEWORK

My epistemological approach to data gathering and analysis was largely informed by the grounded theoretical tradition. Several aspects of grounded theory, including simultaneous data collection and analysis, and memo writing throughout the data collection phase, proved an integral part of my own data gathering and writing process. The primary tenet of grounded theory—whereby analytic categories are derived "directly from the data, not from preconceived concepts or hypotheses"—guided my research from its inception.[5] Kathy Charmaz's scholarship on the translation of grounded theory into practice was particularly instructive. Charmaz warns researchers against forcing "preconceived ideas and theories directly upon their data" and reminds researchers to follow their data's lead.[6] In addition to benefiting from Charmaz's expertise on data analysis—from coding to memos—her approach to data collection both influenced, and resonated with, my own data gathering strategies. Charmaz adheres to the early traditions of grounded theory in some respects, yet she also diverges from these traditions. She advocates a more reflexive and collaborative relationship between researchers and respondents than more traditional grounded theoretical approaches allow.

Grounded theorists Barney G. Glaser and Anselm L. Strauss imply that categories "inhere in the data and may even leap out at the researcher" and that "significant issues in the field setting, and therefore the significant data, will be readily apparent to the researcher."[7] By contrast, Charmaz argues that it is the "interaction between the researcher and the researched that *produces* the data, and therefore the meanings that the researcher observes and defines."[8] In order to gather "rich, detailed data" that lends itself well to full or "thick" description, researchers need to "listen closely" to their respondents and attempt to "learn the unstated or assumed meanings" behind their respondents' talk and silences.[9] Charmaz urges us to pay close attention to the dynamics of the researcher-researched relationship and to the intricate and complex art of data gathering. There is a delicate balance, Charmaz argues, between listening and probing, between building rapport and respecting differences, all in the name of collecting deep, thick data. Charmaz inspired my own interviewing techniques and strategies—techniques and strategies that reflect the grounded theoretical tradition, and that make me feminist researcher.

INTERVIEWING TECHNIQUES AND STRATEGIES

Through my interviews, I sought to appreciate and understand human experience *"from the subjective point of view of the person undergoing it."*[10] My interviewing style largely draws from the feminist interviewing techniques outlined by Kathryn Anderson and Dana C. Jack; Marjorie DeVault; and Marjorie DeVault and Glenda Gross.[11] In my interviews, I engaged in a combination of "deep listening," gentle probing, and active "collaboration" with my respondents.[12] Some of my interview subjects found talking about their bodies and their identities in the context of

APPENDIX A | 227

growing older difficult, and, at times, struggled to put their thoughts and feelings into words. These moments of the "messiness of everyday talk," often punctuated by pauses, "ums," and "you knows," can signal a "realm of not-quite articulated experience, where standard vocabulary is inadequate, and where a respondent tries to speak from experience and finds language wanting."[13] When confronted with pauses, hesitations, and halting talk, I tried hard to hear what my interview subjects "implied, suggested, and started to say but didn't" and encouraged them to explain their meanings "in their own terms."[14] When my interview subjects' use of "ums" and "you knows" seemed to indicate a struggle for words, we engaged in what Marjorie DeVault terms the "co-construction of language," collaborating together to find words that lent genuine expression to their thoughts, feelings, and experiences.[15]

My interview subjects and I, as women, are likely to share some common experiences, from encounters with dominant norms of heterosexual femininity, to insecurity or anxiety about our appearance, to the unique biological capabilities and characteristics of the female body. These shared experiences helped me to build rapport and trust with my interview subjects. Certainly, we were not able to bond in all ways; as a feminist researcher, I also must be mindful and respectful of difference. I am significantly younger than many of my interview subjects. I am not retired. I have not yet gone through menopause. Unlike many of the women I interviewed who were mothers, I had not yet had children when I conducted the interviews for this book. Like the discovery of commonalities, however, openly acknowledging difference can be vital to developing trust and rapport between the researcher and her interview subjects.[16] I have not encountered the bodily experience of menopause, yet my interview subjects and I connected over our bodily memories of puberty and the onset of menstruation, that transition from girlhood to "womanhood," and all of the social and cultural imperatives that accompany it. Finally, the universality of aging made it easier and more comfortable for my interview subjects and me to discuss these issues, despite my own lack of experience, or different experience, of them. I have a mother who I'm very close to and I had two grandmothers whom I adored. I am starting to experience aesthetic, age-driven changes in my appearance, like wrinkles and gray hair, and I, too, will experience menopause in the coming years. My interview subjects and I are simply at different phases of the same trajectory; as I grow older, our common experiences will expand and deepen.

As a feminist researcher, I acknowledge that I am "intertwined" with what I study and how I study it.[17] My earlier research on media portrayals of cosmetic surgery informed several of my research questions and sensitized me to look for potential interconnections between prevalent media frames and individual women's attitudes and lived experiences. Further, my own lived biography, feminist positionality, and worldview influence how I collect, interpret, and make sense of my data. In accordance with several strands of feminist epistemological thought, I treat my situatedness as a researcher, not as a hindrance or a contaminant, but as a *tool for knowledge building*.[18] Drawing from Joyce McCarl Nielsen's description of "maps," and Donna Haraway's conceptualization of "vision," my situated location shifts from a barrier to achieving truth or knowledge, to a *focusing device*.[19] Each of our unique biographies enable us to catch, see, and understand phenomena in ways that others cannot; they can serve as "cognitive resources" that direct our attention to features that we would "otherwise overlook."[20]

My feminist positionality and my prior research on cosmetic surgery proved useful resources in several respects—from topic selection and research focus to developing interview questions and building rapport. On the other hand, I sought to practice "holistic reflexivity" throughout the research process.[21] My situated perspective functioned as a set of "sensitizing concepts."[22] I was careful to treat these concepts as "points of departure" for "*developing, rather than limiting*" my ideas about my data.[23] For example, my feminist concerns about women undergoing painful and invasive cosmetic procedures to achieve and comply with dominant youth-beauty norms contributed to my choice of topic. However, my conversations with women who were having these procedures inspired me to reevaluate and rework my original perspective. As I came to understand that my interview subjects experienced these cosmetic procedures as self-empowering, as a source of confidence and independence, I shifted and expanded my feminist lens to accommodate these new points of view. Actively recognizing our standpoints and starting points, and taking a "reflexive stance towards them," is part of what it means to be a feminist researcher.[24] According to Helen Longino, good feminist research is at once "*honest and value-laden*."[25] Honesty and feminist values merged in my own research as I worked to deconstruct and reconstruct my own standpoints and starting points in the service of accurately representing my interview subjects' thoughts, feelings, and experiences.

TRANSCRIPTION, ANALYSIS, AND WRITING

I started transcribing my interviews and writing reflective memos about them, after completing my first several interviews. Simultaneously interviewing, transcribing, and memo writing enabled me to remain close to, and grounded in, my data throughout the research process. By using an integrated approach to data collection and analysis, I "avoided the pitfalls of amassing volumes of general, unfocused data." Instead, my emerging analysis "shaped" my data collection procedures: I followed up on topics and themes that were "explicit" in one interview and "implicit" in others.[26] I transcribed twenty (nearly half) of my interviews myself, noting the "ums" and "you knows" and the pauses, sighs, and laughter as well. I was careful to select two transcribers who were willing and able to follow my own transcription style—they too paid close attention to the "ums" and "you knows," and noted the "extra-linguistic" aspects such as pauses, laughter, and sighs. The thoroughness of these transcription techniques anchored and strengthened my analysis. Preserving the "messiness" of my respondents' "everyday talk" increased my ability to accurately and authentically communicate my respondents' voices.[27]

My coding process mirrored the coding stages outlined by Kathy Charmaz.[28] I started with line-by-line coding of each transcript. From my line-by-line codes, I developed code categories.[29] My memos consisted of reflection on—and explication of—the code categories, as they provided the "intermediate step" between coding and the first draft of my completed analysis.[30] The first drafts of my data chapters evolved from my completed memos. My memos offered not only starting points and outlines for my chapters but also fairly developed themes and analyses as well. My writing began not with my chapters, but with my memos. In this respect, my project consisted of three integrated components: data collection, analysis, and writing phases, which were simultaneous and continuous throughout.

ETHICAL REFLECTIONS

Feminist researchers are increasingly open about their own positionalities, perspectives, and worldviews and engage in collaboration with their respondents throughout all phases of the research process—from data gathering to analysis.[31] Many of my interviews contained lively and collaborative conversations between my interview subjects and myself. I shared my interview guide with each interview subject and encouraged them to contact me with any additional thoughts, critiques, concerns, or questions following the interview. Sharing interview guides increased transparency; for my subjects, having their own copy of the interview guide also made it easier for them to identify, reflect on, digest, and process their thoughts and feelings after the interview had ended. Copies of interview transcripts were offered to each interview subject. Sharing interview transcripts served as another medium for interview subject participation; interview transcripts became a vehicle for soliciting their input and feedback. Along with each transcript, I included a thank-you note and a reminder of my openness to any additional comments. Interview transcripts offered a concrete record of the time, energy, knowledge, and emotion that my interview subjects shared with me. In this respect, sharing interview transcripts was also about giving back to my interview subjects. The transcripts served as a small token of recognition and appreciation for their efforts and contributions.

Several of my interview subjects encountered new realizations and insights about themselves as a result of the interview itself, or from reading their interview transcripts; others experienced elements of self-transformation. One woman let me know that after our interview she decided to let her hair "go gray" and that she felt "liberated" by this decision. Another explained that, as a result of our interview and reading her interview transcript, she developed a greater awareness of her own self-confidence and how it had grown with age. Some also expressed concern with how many "you knows," "ums," and "ahs" they used—comments like "oh, I sounded so inarticulate" or "so stupid" or "I didn't make much sense" or "I hope you were able decipher what I was getting at" were common. Several women requested that their language be "cleaned up" a bit before I quoted them in any subsequent publications. These articulated anxieties led me to begin to include a reassuring explanation in the thank-you note I sent along with each transcript. I explained that the "ums," "ahs," and "you knows" were included as part of my methodological strategy and with the intention of representing each of my interview subjects as fully and thoroughly as possible. I also explained, however, that interview excerpts would be streamlined to some degree, in part to increase reading ease and clarity, before being included in any subsequent publications.

My interview subjects' concerns about sounding inarticulate raised a quandary for me as a feminist researcher: on the one hand, I sought to preserve the fullness and messiness of their speech to achieve as authentic a representation as possible. Some of those pauses, "ums," and "you knows" signaled feelings, emotions, and even hidden meanings that might otherwise have been overlooked. On the other hand, I wanted to be respectful of my interview subjects' worries about sounding "bumbling" and "unclear," and responsive to their wishes to clarify and clean up their speech. Judith Preissle's framework for a "situated feminist ethics" guided me out of this dilemma.[32] Drawing from Carol Gilligan's innovative work on female morality, and feminist philosopher Nell Noddings's "ethics of care," Preissle advocates a feminist ethics that centers on the relationship between researcher and participant.[33] Integrating this feminist ethics into the research process—taking seriously the "situation-specific quality of human relationships and interactions"—can be a complex and challenging task.[34] There is no one answer, or universal principle, that teaches us how to cultivate the researcher-researched relationship or how to attend to the wellbeing, goals, and needs of participants. Different approaches, methods, questions, and decisions may be required in different contexts and with different communities of participants. Researchers much evaluate each case based on its particularity and situated location—an approach to building respectful relationships between the researcher and her participants may succeed in one community but alienate another. Upon reflection (prompted by Preissle's feminist ethics), I came to realize that being respectful of my relationships with my interview subjects meant striking a balance between authentic representation and deference to their wishes. Through removing most, but not all, of the "ums," "ahs," and "you knows," I preserved the integrity of my interview subjects' original meanings. At the same time, through editing and streamlining some of the "messiness" of my interview subjects' talk, I demonstrated my responsiveness to their concerns.

My interactions with one interview subject in particular highlight some of the complexities and intricacies that can characterize researcher-researched relationships. Following our interview, this particular interview subject had referred me to two friends that might also be interested in talking to me. After receiving her interview transcript in the mail, however, she sent some highlighted passages of her transcript back to me, along with a note explaining her concerns. The highlighted passages included her thoughts and reflections on cosmetic anti-aging intervention, some of which were somewhat critical in nature. As both of the friends that she had referred me to had undergone cosmetic anti-aging interventions, she was concerned that, should they read and recognize her words in any subsequent published material, they might be offended.[35] She felt comfortable sharing her thoughts and feelings about cosmetic intervention with me as a neutral recipient; she did not necessarily want to share her views with her friends and risk hurting their feelings or appearing overly critical. This interview subject requested that I delete the highlighted passages in question, should I proceed with interviewing her two friends. After a lengthy and collaborative phone conversation, we decided that I would leave her interview transcript in tact, but refrain from contacting and interviewing her friends.

My feminist sensibilities were less than comfortable with leaving out parts of my respondent's interview transcript—editing out her views on cosmetic anti-aging intervention would make her narrative less complete and reduce my capacity to authentically and accurately represent the full range of her thoughts, feelings, and experiences. On the other hand, I hated to give up the possibility of interviewing women who were having cosmetic anti-aging intervention—these two women presented particularly interesting cases given their lived contexts. Further, my interview subject and these women were close friends, despite the fact that she was aging "naturally" and choosing not to go the intervention route. Given that most of my interview subjects who were having, and refusing, cosmetic anti-aging surgeries and technologies operated in fairly distinct social worlds, the crossover aspect made the case for interviewing these women even more intriguing. In the end, however, it was most important to me to (1) respect my interview subject's wishes, and (2) represent her thoughts, feelings, and experiences as authentically and accurately at possible. These goals are both feminist ones—and the decision my interview subject and I reached together rang true to each of them.

APPENDIX B

Interview Subjects

PRO-COSMETIC INTERVENTION GROUP (16 WOMEN)

Anne: age 65; retired social worker, currently an artist (jewelry maker); married; two facelifts[1]

Anne lives in a midwestern city and explains that she cannot rule out the possibility of another facelift in roughly ten years, when she is in her seventies.

Lisa: age 58; retired business woman (finance), currently volunteering and involved in philanthropic work; married; a neck lift and an eyelift

Lisa lives in a New England city. She has not ruled out future surgeries and is considering the possibility of a tummy tuck.

Janet: age 68; retired airline ticket agent; single (divorced); eyelift

Janet lives in a New England city. She explains that she may have a "mini-facelift" in a few years.

Caroline: age 47; radio producer; married; ongoing collagen and Botox shots

Caroline lives in a New England town, not far from the city. She articulates the likelihood of having an eyelift in the future, in addition to possible other cosmetic anti-aging surgeries.

Debra: age 56; musician; single; two eyelifts and laser resurfacing

Debra lives in a New England town, not far from the city. She has not ruled out future cosmetic anti-aging surgeries and technologies, though she did not offer any specific plans for what procedures she might have done in the future.

Barbara: age 59; retired mental heath facility director, currently a part-time child care worker; single; lower facelift and eyelift

Barbara lives in a small town in rural New England. At the time of our interview, she was planning for a second facelift, and possibly a neck lift, as part of her sixtieth birthday present.

Nora: age 62; restaurant manager; married; eyelift

Nora lives in a New England city. At the time of our interview, Nora had no future cosmetic anti-aging surgeries planned.

Melissa: age 53; currently unemployed; single; facelift, chemical peels, collagen
    injections
Melissa lives in a New England town, not far from the city. At the time of our
interview, she was preparing her plans for a second facelift. She was lean-
ing towards having the procedure done in Latin America, where it would be
cheaper than in the United States.
Wendy: age 53; retired nurse; married; two eyelifts, ongoing Botox shots
Wendy lives in a New England town, not far from the city. She articulated the
likelihood of having more surgery (for instance, a mini-facelift) in the future.
Sadie: age 53; retired businesswoman (telecommunications); married; Botox
    shots
Sadie lives in a small New England city. She articulated mixed feelings and no
definitive answers about whether or not she would use more cosmetic anti-
aging technologies or surgeries in the future.
Claire: age 49; personal trainer; married; ongoing Botox shots
Claire lives in a New England town near the city. She articulated the likeli-
hood of having more cosmetic anti-aging procedures in the future, particu-
larly an eyelift or a facelift.
Mary: age 72; semi-retired commercial real estate agent; married; facelift
Mary lives in a city on the West Coast. She explained that she probably would
not have more cosmetic surgical procedures in the future.
Christina: age 51; retired businesswoman (finance); married; Botox shots
Christina lives in a small New England city. She indicated that she probably
would experiment with more cosmetic anti-aging technologies, like other
injectables, in the future. She was less sure, however, about whether or not she
would have cosmetic anti-aging surgeries.
Amy: age 48; retired businesswoman (finance); married; tummy tuck
Amy lives in a New England city. She explained that she probably will have
more cosmetic anti-aging surgery and is seriously considering having an
eyelift in the near future.
Julia: age 47; stay-at-home mom; married; scelerotherapy (varicose vein re-
    moval), laser age-spot removal
Julia lives in a New England town close to the city. She explains that she probably will use more cosmetic anti-aging technologies, like Botox and collagen,
in the near future. She also indicated that she probably will choose to have
cosmetic anti-aging surgeries—like an eyelift, for example—in the future, as
well.

Natalie: age 52; musician; married; microdermabrasion, velasmooth
Natalie lives in a New England town, about forty-five minutes from the city.
She expresses her willingness and openness to using more cosmetic anti-aging
technologies in the future, and to having cosmetic anti-aging surgeries, like an
eyelift or a neck lift, in the future, as well.

"NATURALLY" AGING GROUP (22 WOMEN)

Alison: age 55; homemaker; married
Alison lives in a New England town, about forty-five minutes from the
city. She colors her hair. She uses "cheap" moisturizer—even Vaseline on
occasion—and wears some makeup on a daily basis.
Ellen: age 61; a businesswoman; single (widowed)
Ellen lives in a midwestern city. She colors her hair. She uses moisturizer and
doesn't wear makeup very often.
Elizabeth: age 61; an artist; married
Elizabeth lives in a small New England city. She does not color her hair. She
uses moisturizer and wears makeup occasionally, when she gets dressed up to
"go out."
Catherine: age 61; a retired career counselor; single (divorced)
Catherine lives in a small New England city. She colored her hair for many
years, but followed up with me to tell me that she stopped coloring her hair as
a result of our interview. She uses olive oil and lemon water to moisturize and
wears some makeup, not every day, but usually when she goes out.
Sarah: age 55; a writer; married
Sarah lives in a small New England city. She uses moisturizer. She does not
color her hair or wear makeup very often.
Diane: age 57; a therapist; married
Diane lives in a New England town in a rural area. She colors her hair. She
uses moisturizer and wears some makeup on a regular basis.
Nancy: age 59; a clinical social worker; married
Nancy lives in a New England town in a rural area. She colors her hair. She
uses moisturizer and wears makeup occasionally.
Margaret: age 72; a retired nurse, currently a part-time hospital administrator;
   married
Margaret lives in a small New England city. She does not color her hair. She
uses moisturizer and wears makeup only very occasionally.
Sonya: age 57; an artist; single

Sonya lives in a small New England city. She does not color her hair. She uses moisturizer and wears some makeup every day.

Nina: age 57; a psychotherapist; married

Nina lives in a New England town in a rural area. She does not color her hair. She uses moisturizer and wears makeup occasionally, when she is going out, or getting dressed up for a special occasion.

Rebecca: age 58; a flute-maker; single (divorced)

Rebecca lives in a small New England city. She colors her hair. She uses moisturizer and very rarely wears makeup.

Helen: age 59; a homemaker; married

Helen lives in a New England city. She does not color her hair. She uses moisturizer and wears some makeup every day.

Lucy: age 62; a retired shop owner; married

Lucy lives in a New England town close to the city. She does not color her hair. She uses moisturizer and wears makeup only very occasionally.

Joan: age 76; an artist; married

Joan lives in a New England town close to the city. She does not color her hair. She uses moisturizer and toner, and wears makeup everyday.

Mia: age 59; a real estate agent; married

Mia lives in a New England town about 30 minutes from the city. She colors her hair. She uses moisturizer and wears some makeup every day.

Teresa: age 62; a yoga instructor; single

Teresa lives in small New England city. She does not color her hair. She does not use moisturizer and usually does not wear makeup, except for lipstick, which she wears only very occasionally.

Eileen: age 53; a movement instructor in the public school system; single

Eileen lives in a small New England town in a rural area. She does not color her hair. She uses moisturizer but does not wear makeup.

Sophia: age 65; an education advisor; married

Sophie lives in a New England city. She colors her hair. She uses moisturizer and wears some makeup everyday.

Cara: age 55; a yoga instructor; married

Cara lives in a New England town near an urban center. She colors her hair. She uses moisturizer and wears some makeup everyday.

Lydia: age 55; a stay-at-home mom; married

Lydia lives in a New England town in a rural area. She does not color her hair. She uses moisturizer but does not wear makeup.

Adriana: age 49; a dance and yoga instructor; single (divorced)

Adriana lives in a New England town in a rural area. She colors her hair. She uses moisturizer and wears some makeup every day.

UNDECIDED GROUP (6 WOMEN)

Maya: age 49, stay-at-home mom; married

Maya lives in a New England town close to the city. She does not color her hair. She uses moisturizer but wears makeup only occasionally.

Maya explains that in the future, she "may" use cosmetic anti-aging technologies, like Botox or collagen, or have cosmetic anti-aging surgery, like a neck lift, but she cannot, at this point, be sure.

Evelyn: age 54; a pre-school teacher; married

Evelyn lives in a New England town close to the city. She colors her hair. She uses moisturizer with some anti-aging ingredients and wears makeup everyday. Evelyn has had scelerotherapy (varicose vein treatment) and says she may use other cosmetic anti-aging technologies in the future, like Botox or collagen shots, or even have anti-aging surgery. One the one hand, she cannot rule it out. On the other, she thinks that it is more unlikely (than likely) that she will have any full-blown surgical procedures.

Rachel: age 64; an adjunct college professor; married

Rachel lives in a New England town about forty-five minutes from the city. She colors her hair. She uses moisturizer and wears makeup everyday. She has had a chemical peel and is considering having Botox and collagen injections in the future.

Eva: age 51; a psychologist; married

Eva lives in a small New England city. She does not color her hair. She uses moisturizer and wears makeup everyday. She cannot rule out using cosmetic anti-aging technologies, like Botox or collagen, or having cosmetic anti-aging surgery, like an eyelift, in the future. She "hopes" she chooses not to take the cosmetic anti-aging surgery/technology route, but she is not sure she will be able to resist, especially if more and more people around her start having and using cosmetic anti-aging surgeries and technologies.

Laura: age 51; an education advisor; married

Laura lives in a small New England city. She does not color her hair. She uses moisturizer and wears makeup everyday. She cannot rule out the possibility of having/using cosmetic anti-aging surgeries and technologies in the future, especially if a part of her face drastically "changes shape" (e.g., if her "neck suddenly goes"). On the other hand, Laura, like Eva, really hopes to be able to resist the surgery/technology route and instead "embrace" the natural aging process. Laura did break down and purchase a home microdermabrasion kit at her local CVS drugstore because it was on sale, but then, she said, it was "too much trouble" to actually use it—she has only used it once.

Susan: age 61; a full-time college professor; married

Susan lives in a New England coastal town. She colors her hair and wears moisturizer. She has had laser spot removal. She doubts that she will have or use any other kinds of cosmetic anti-aging surgeries and technologies in the future (such as Botox, collagen, or eyelifts, neck lifts, etc.), but she can't "honestly" rule them out for herself in the future either.

NOTES

PREFACE

1 In their heyday—and even today—American soap operas stand out as an
   entertainment genre that provides plentiful roles and opportunities for female
   actors, of all ages. Most female roles in soap operas, however, continue to be
   constructed for, and in embodied by, white actors, though there is data to
   suggest that American soap operas historically, and even today, feature more
   African American roles, for both female and male actors, than other entertainment genres, like film and prime time television. See Aaron Foley, "The Unsung
   Legacy of Black Characters on Soap Operas," *Atlantic*, March 31, 2015; and Errol
   Lewis, "The Diversity Issue: TV Guide Grades the Soaps," *Soap Opera Network*,
   December 31, 2015. The viewership of American soap operas, while primarily
   female, also stands out in its strong representation of women of color, and of
   women of all income levels. Despite greater diversity in viewership and in roles,
   however, the vast majority of characters in soap operas today continue to be
   white, and, equally troubling, are the ways in which too many characters and
   story lines perpetuate racist, sexist, empirically false, and demeaning stereotypes
   about women, and men too. While female actors of a diversity of backgrounds
   may find comparatively more role opportunities on soap operas—these roles often perpetuate traditional and limited understandings of women's value (or lack
   thereof) and behavior, by emphasizing physical appearance as a primary source
   of female power, negatively framing female sexual activity, glorifying stay-at-
   home motherhood among white female characters, pathologizing stay-at-home
   motherhood among women of color, and demonizing women who wield power
   outside the home more generally.

2 In 1981, roughly 12 million American viewers tuned in to watch the wedding of
   characters Luke and Laura on *General Hospital*. Jake Tapper, "Soap Operas Back
   from the Dead, Get a New Life Online," *CNN.com*, June 17, 2013.

3 Daytime soap operas have lost more than three-quarters of their audience over
   the past twenty years in the United States. There were 78 million viewers of
   soap operas in the United States in 1990, compared with 17 million in 2009. See
   "Perspective: Scholars Barbara Irwin and Mary Cassata on the State of U.S. Soap
   Operas" (based on an interview by C. Lee Harrington), in *The Survival of Soap
   Opera: Transformations for a New Media Era*, eds. Sam Ford, Abigail De Kosnik,
   and C. Lee Harrington (Jackson: University of Mississippi Press, 2011), 23.

INTRODUCTION

1 This slogan ran in Botox advertisements in the 2010s in the United States, including in popular celebrity-centered and women-centered magazines like *People*, *Harper's Bazaar*, and *Vogue*, and on television.

2 The top five nonsurgical procedures in the United States in 2015 were Botox, hyaluronic acid, hair removal, chemical peel, and microdermabrasion. Each of these procedures are not exclusively, but commonly, used to minimize aesthetic signs of aging on the face and body—to make the face and body younger-looking: Botox, by minimizing wrinkles; hyaluronic acid (branded products include Juvaderm, among several others) by plumping lips and cheeks; chemical peels and microdermabrasion by removing blemishes, including wrinkles and age spots, and smoothing and "re-vitalizing" skin; and hair removal by removing facial hair that can increase with age. The top five surgical procedures performed on women in the United States in 2015 were liposuction, breast augmentation, tummy tuck, breast lift, and eyelid surgery. Eyelid surgery is commonly centered on removing sags, bags, and excess skin on the upper or lower eyelids to make the eyes look younger, but liposuction and breast lifts also often reflect cosmetic anti-aging motivations on the part of patient-consumers, as do tummy tucks, and even breast implants. For more on the most popular procedures, see American Society for Aesthetic Plastic Surgery (hereafter cited as ASAPS), "Statistics 2015," http://www.surgery.org/.

3 Brazil is first, then the United States, followed by Mexico, Germany, Columbia, Venezuela, Spain, Italy, Argentina, and Iran as the ten countries with the highest number of plastic surgeries performed in 2013. See Joel Stein, "Nip, Tuck, or Else. Now Everyone Gets Work Done. Will You?," *Time*, June 29, 2015.

4 See Wei Luo, "Aching for the Altered Body: Beauty Economy and Chinese Women's Consumption of Cosmetic Surgery," *Women's Studies International Forum* 38 (May–June 2013): 1–10; and Jacqueline Sanchez Taylor, "Fake Breasts and Power: Gender, Class, and Cosmetic Surgery," *Women's Studies International Forum* 35 (November–December 2012): 1–10.

5 See Margaret L. Hunter, "Buying Racial Capital: Skin-Bleaching and Cosmetic Surgery in a Globalized World," *Journal of Pan African Studies* 4, no. 4 (June 2011): 142–164; Evelyn Nakano Glenn, "Yearning for Lightness: Transnational Circuits in the Marketing and Consumption of Skin-Lighteners," *Gender and Society* 22, no. 3 (June 2008): 281–302; Eric P.H. Li, Hyun Jeong Min, and Russell W. Belk, "Skin Lightening and Beauty in Four Asian Cultures," *Association for Consumer Research* 35 (2008): 444–449; and Lauren E. Gulbas, "Embodying Racism: Rhinoplasty in Venezuela," *Qualitative Health Research* (March 2013): 326–335.

6 See Erynn Masi de Casanova and Barbara Sutton, "Transnational Body Projects: Media Representations of Cosmetic Surgery Tourism in Argentina and the United States," *Journal of World-Systems Research* (2013): 57–81.

7 To learn about the history of rhinoplasty in the United States is to learn about the intersection of racism and aesthetics. The Jewish nose, the African American

nose, the Asian nose—all required "fixing" to more closely conform to what was considered an acceptable-looking (read: Anglo or European) nose. See Virginia Blum, *Flesh Wounds: The Culture of Cosmetic Surgery* (Berkeley: University of California Press, 2003); Elizabeth Haiken, *Venus Envy: A History of Plastic Surgery* (Baltimore: John Hopkins University Press, 1997); and Eugenia Kaw, "Medicalization of Racial Features: Asian American Women and Cosmetic Surgery," *Medical Anthropology Quarterly* 7, no. 1 (March 1993): 74–89.

8 Racial and ethnic minorities account for 25% of the total number of recipients of surgical and nonsurgical cosmetic procedures performed in the United States today: African Americans (7.7%), Asians (6.2%), Hispanics (9.7%) and other non-Caucasians (1.3%). ASAPS, "Statistics 2015."

9 See Sam Dolnick, "Plastic Surgery Among Ethnic Groups Mirrors Beauty Ideals," *New York Times*, February 18, 2011; and Maureen O'Connor, "Is Race Plastic? My Trip into the 'Ethnic Plastic Surgery' Minefield," *New York*, July 27, 2014.

10 In the scholarship of Eugenia Kaw ("Medicalization of Racial Features"), and in Regina Park's documentary film, *Never Perfect* (2007), Asian American women talk about their double eyelid and nose bridge surgeries as a vehicle for empowerment and individual expression—a means to move beyond being reduced to a racial category by others. In her dissertation, "Body Objectification, Ethnic Identity, and Cosmetic Surgery in African American Women" (Loma Linda University, School of Behavioral Health, 2013), Allycin Powell-Hicks illuminates how African American women can experience their cosmetic procedures as an act of autonomy and control over their bodies. Powell-Hicks also found, somewhat contradictorily, that her research subjects' feelings of racial and ethnic pride, security, and belonging in their African American communities actually empowered them to have cosmetic intervention to "align their bodies with cultural standards."

11 Americans spent more than $13.5 billion on cosmetic procedures in 2015 alone, and women had more than 11.5 million cosmetic procedures, or 90.5% of the more than 12.5 million procedures performed. People age thirty-five to fifty had the most procedures, accounting for over 40% of the total, followed by people ages fifty-one to sixty-four years of age. Racial and ethnic minorities had approximately 25% of all procedures performed. It can be inferred from this data, then, that white women, ages thirty-five and older, are a particularly lucrative group of cosmetic procedure consumers. See ASAPS, "Statistics 2015."

12 These statistics are drawn from a survey commissioned by the American Society for Aesthetic Plastic Surgery (ASAPS) and conducted by independent research firm Synovate. In the United States, cosmetic procedures have increased by 39% over the last five years. Since 2011, surgical procedures have increased by 17%, and non-surgical procedures by 44%. The number of cosmetic procedures for women in the United States has increased by 471% since 1997; the number of cosmetic procedures for men has increased by 273% since 1997. See ASAPS, "Survey Shows More Than Half of Americans Approve of Cosmetic Plastic Surgery," *Statistics, Surveys, and Trends*, April 4, 2011; "Statistics 2015"; "The American Society for

Aesthetic Plastic Surgery Reports Americans Spent the Largest Amount on Cosmetic Surgery since the Great Recession of 2008," *Statistics, Surveys, and Trends*,
March 20, 2014, http://www.surgery.org/.

13 While there are certainly parallels between and among different nation-states
when it comes to the hows and whys of the expanding cosmetic surgery industry,
patterns of difference in cultural and individual patient rationales for having cosmetic interventions are also evident. In her cross-cultural, interview-based investigation of cosmetic surgery in the United States and Great Britain, for instance,
Debra Gimlin uncovered similarities, but also differences, in patients' meaning
making around their cosmetic interventions that reflected nation state-specific
ideologies, economies, and health care systems. See Gimlin, *Cosmetic Surgery
Narratives: A Cross-Cultural Analysis of Women's Accounts* (New York: Palgrave
Macmillan, 2012).

14 The United States is one of only three countries, along with New Zealand and
Brazil, that allows direct-to-consumer advertising of pharmaceuticals. For a de-
tailed account of the de-regulation and commercialization of American medicine,
particularly as it pertains to the growth of the cosmetic surgery and pharmaceuti-
cal drug industries, see Deborah Sullivan, *Cosmetic Surgery: The Cutting Edge of
Commercial Medicine* (New Brunswick, NJ: Rutgers University Press, 2001); Jay
Cohen, *Overdose: The Case Against the Drug Companies; Prescription Drugs, Side
Effects, and Your Health* (New York: Tarcher, [2001] 2004).

15 Drawn from six issues of *People* magazine randomly sampled from the months of
March through June 2014.

16 Disturbingly, examples abound. I will mention only two—pertaining to the pharmaceutical drugs Vioxx and Fosamax—here. Developed by drug manufacturer
Merck to treat osteoarthritis and acute pain conditions, Vioxx was on the market
for over five years (from 1999 to 2004) before it was recalled for being linked to
nearly thirty thousand heart attacks or sudden cardiac deaths—and before studies showed Vioxx users had a rate of heart disease 3.7 times higher than those of
non-users. Vioxx was prescribed to more than 20 million people and featured
advertisements with famous athletes like Dorothy Hamill and Bruce [now Caitlin]
Jenner. See Alex Berenson, Gardiner Harris, Barry Meier, and Andrew Pollack,
"Despite Warnings, Drug Giant Took Long Path to Vioxx Recall," *New York Times*,
November 14, 2004, http://www.nytimes.com; Gina Kolata, "A Widely Used
Arthritis Drug is Withdrawn," *New York Times*, October 1, 2004; Reuters, "A Time
Line of Vioxx," *New York Times*, August 19, 2005; and Duff Wilson, "Merck to Pay
950 Million Over Vioxx," *New York Times*, November 22, 2011. Fosamax (alen-
dronate), another drug developed and aggressively marketed by Merck, in this
case to treat osteoporosis, using actresses like Lauren Hutton, among others, has
now been shown to risk bone weakening and crumbling. In addition to permanent jawbone damage and crippling bone fractures, other serious side effects can
include esophageal cancer, painful eye disorders, debilitating muscle and joint
pain, and an irregular heartbeat. Merck also engaged in a successful campaign of

diagnostic expansion pertaining to Fosamax, wherein the company was able to reach not only the osteoporosis market, but also women who were diagnosed with osteopenia, which is a slight thinning of the bones. (In fact, by opening its non-profit, the Bone Research Institute, Merck played a significant role in developing osteopenia as a condition in need of medical treatment. My mother, and several of her friends, were among those patients prescribed Foxamax for osteopenia. Before Fosamax came to market in the 1990s, osteopenia was rarely treated. Treatment for osteopenia continues to be controversial today). Over the years, the FDA repeatedly reprimanded Merck for falsely advertising the benefits of Fosamax, and for failing to adequately warn consumers about its side effects. In response, Merck has added more warnings in its marketing and labeling of the drug. Yet, as of 2016, Fosamax remains on the market. See Tara Parker-Pope, "WELL: FDA Is Wary of Lengthy Use of Bone Drugs," *New York Times*, May 9, 2012; Jane E. Brody, "Revisiting Bone Drugs and Femur Fractures," *New York Times*, March 16, 2011; Duff Wilson, "FDA to Review Safety of Popular Bone Drugs," *New York Times*, September 5, 2011; Natasha Singer, "Drug Suits Raise Questions for Doctors, and Juries," *New York Times*, November 10, 2010; and "High Stakes for Merck in Litigation on Fosamax," *New York Times*, September 2, 2009. New iterations of pharmaceutical drugs to treat osteoporosis also continue to come to market. Boniva (ibandronate) features advertisements with actress Sally Field, and Prolia (denosumab) features ads with actress Blythe Danner; the potential side effects for each of these drugs include jawbone damage, eye inflammation, thigh-bone fractures, and serious infections. See Tara Parker-Pope, "New Cautions about Long-Term Use of Bone Drugs," *New York Times*, May 9, 2012.

17 This is up from 51% of U.S. adults reporting the use of prescription drugs in 1999 to 2000. See Elizabeth D. Kantor et al., "Trends in Prescription Drug Use among Adults in the United States from 1999–2012," *Journal of the American Medical Association* 314, no. 17 (2015), http://jama.jamanetwork.com; Brady Dennis, "Nearly 60% of Americans—the highest ever—are taking prescription drugs," *Washington Post*, November 3, 2015. The Mayo Clinic and Olmsted Medical Center study revealed that nearly seven in ten Americans now take at least one prescription drug, more than half take two, and 20% take five or more prescription medications. Mayo Clinic News Network, "Nearly 7 in 10 Americans Take Prescription Drugs, Mayo Clinic, Olmsted Medical Center Finds," (2013), http://newsnetwork.mayoclinic.org.

18 According to the National Council on Alcoholism and Drug Dependence, "Prescription drugs are the third most commonly abused category of drugs behind alcohol and marijuana and ahead of cocaine, heroine, and methamphetamine. . . . Overall, an estimated 48 million people have abused prescription drugs, representing nearly 20% of the U.S. population." See https://ncadd.org/.

19 Centers for Disease Control and Prevention, National Center for Injury Prevention and Control, *Prescription Drug Overdose: What You Need to Know*, http://www.cdc.gov/.

20 According to the Centers for Disease Control and Prevention, "The United States is in the midst of a prescription painkiller overdose epidemic. Since 1999, the amount of prescription painkillers prescribed and sold in the U.S. has nearly quadrupled, yet there has not been an overall change in the amount of pain that Americans report. Overprescribing leads to more abuse and more overdose deaths." See Centers for Disease Control and Prevention, *Prescription Drug Overdose*. According to another recent report, prescription opioids, or pain medications, along with prescription stimulants and prescription central nervous system depressants, are the three main broad categories of pharmaceuticals that present abuse liability in the United States today. The report also outlines that, in the U.S. today, death certificates list deaths due to prescription pain medication overdoses—or opioid analgesic poisoning—more commonly than heroin or cocaine. Strikingly, the report attributes the "severity of the current prescription drug abuse problem" in the United States today to the following factors: "drastic increases in the number of prescriptions written and dispensed, greater social acceptability for using medications for different purposes, and aggressive marketing by pharmaceutical companies." These factors "together have helped create the broad 'environmental availability' of prescription medications in general and opioid analgesics in particular." The report also outlines growing evidence that suggests a relationship between the increased non-medical use of opioid analgesics and heroin abuse in the U.S. See Nora D. Volkow, M.D., "America's Addiction to Opioids: Heroin and Prescription Drug Abuse," National Institute on Drug Abuse, National Institutes of Health, delivered to the Senate Caucus on International Narcotics Control, May 14, 2014, http://www.drugabuse.gov/.

21 Ray Monniyan, "Selling Sickness: The Pharmaceutical Industry and Disease Mongering," *British Medical Journal* 324, no. 7342 (April 13, 2002): 886–891. For more on the medicalization of routine bodily processes in the United States and for an analysis of some of the troubling implications of this trend, see Peter Conrad, *The Medicalization of Society: On The Transformation of Human Conditions into Treatable Disorders* (Baltimore, MD: John Hopkins University Press, 2007); Carl Elliot, *Better Than Well: American Medicine Meets the American Dream* (New York: W.W. Norton and Company, 2004); and Meika Loe's *The Rise of Viagra: How the Little Blue Pill Changed Sex in America* (New York: New York University Press, 2004).

22 See Pia C. Kontos, "Local Biology: Bodies of Difference in Ageing Studies," *Ageing and Society* 19 (1999): 677–689; Margaret M. Lock, "Menopause in Cultural Context," *Experimental Gerontology* 29, no. 3–4 (1994): 307–17; and Margaret M. Lock, "Anomalous Aging: Managing the Postmenopausal Body," *Body and Society* 4, no. 1 (1998): 35–61.

23 See Margaret Morganroth Gullette, "Hormone Nostalgia: Estrogen, Not Menopause, Is the Public Health Menace," in *Agewise: Fighting the New Ageism in America* (Chicago: University of Chicago Press, 2011); Abby Hyde, Jean Nee, Etaoine Howlett, Michelle Butler, and Jonathan Drennan, "The Ending of Menstrua-

tion: Perspectives and Experiences of Lesbian and Heterosexual Women," *Journal of Women and Aging* 23, no. 2 (April 2011): 160–176; and Sonja J. McKinlay, Donald J. Brambilla, and Jennifer G. Posner, "The Normal Menopause Transition," *American Journal of Human Biology* 4, no. 1 (May [1992] 2005): 37–46.

24 See Heather Dillaway, "Menopause is the 'Good Old': Women's Thoughts About Reproductive Aging," *Gender and Society* 19, no. 3 (June 2005): 398–417; Miriam Bernard, Pat Chambers, and Gilliam Granville, "Women Ageing: Changing Identities, Challenging Myths," in *Women Ageing: Changing Identities, Challenging Myths*, eds. Miriam Bernard, Judith Phillips, Linda Machin, and Val Harding Davies (London: Routledge, 2000), 1–22; Linda Gannon, *Women and Aging: Transcending the Myths* (New York: Routledge, 1999); Linda Gannon and Jill Stevens, "Portraits of Menopause in the Mass Media," *Women and Health* 27, no. 3 (1998): 1–15; and Margaret M. Lock, *Encounters with Aging: Mythologies of Menopause in Japan and North America* (Berkeley: University of California Press, 1993).

25 Medical advertisements for hormone replacement therapy (HRT), in the form of synthetic estrogen therapies, like Osphena, Premarin, Duavee, and Estring, have been running in *People* magazine from April 2014 through April 2016. The largest and most comprehensive study on HRT in the U.S. today was conducted by the Women's Health Initiative, or WHI. Launched in 1991, the WHI study followed over 160 thousand healthy, post-menopausal, American women, over many years. The first set of findings was published in 2002, and follow-up studies ended in 2010. The WHI study entirely contradicted commonly held perspectives among the American medical community that HRT protected older women from heart disease and breast cancer. The WHI study showed, instead, that women taking combination HRT therapy (both estrogen and progestin) had an increased risk of heart attack, stroke, blood clots, and breast cancer, and that women taking estrogen alone had an increased risk of heart attack, stroke, and blood clots. See Women's Health Initiative (WHI), "Questions and Answers about the WHI Postmenopausal Hormone Therapy Trials," *National Heart, Lung, and Blood Institute*, https://www.nhlbi.nih.gov/whi. The WHI study showed that the overall risks of taking HRT outweighed the benefits. The study was terminated after fifteen years, and earlier than originally planned, because of the clear evidence of health risks for the women in the study taking HRT. (See WHI, "Findings from the WHI Postmenopausal Hormone Therapy Trials," "Questions and Answers about the WHI Postmenopausal Hormone Therapy Trials," "The Estrogen-Alone Study," and "The Estrogen-plus-Progestin Study," specifically). Since then, several other studies have shown that women taking HRT have a higher risk of breast cancer, heart disease, stroke, and blood clots. On the other hand, data released from the WHI follow-up studies (with over twenty-seven thousand women) demonstrate that for younger menopausal women, the health risks of HRT may not be as severe as for women who are ten years or more after menopause—and, in some cases, the benefits of taking HRT may outweigh the risks. Still, lead WHI researcher, Dr. Joanne Manson asserts that, even with new findings that indicate

that for younger menopausal women, the benefits may outweigh the risks, HRT really should not be a long-term use medication for women because of the increased risk of blood clots and stroke. See "The Last Word on Hormone Therapy from the Women's Health Initiative," *National Pubic Radio*, October 4, 2013. See also Dennis Grady, "Study of Hormone Use in Menopause Reaffirms Complex Mix of Risks and Benefits," *New York Times*, October 1, 2013; Cynthia Gorney and Denise Grady, "Earlier Hormone Therapy Elevates Risks of Breast Cancer, Researchers Say," *New York Times*, January 28, 2011; and "The Estrogen Dilemma," *New York Times*, April 14, 2010.

26 See Loe, *Rise of Viagra*; and Conrad, *Medicalization of Society*.

27 For empirical research, discussion, analysis, and documentation of the growing phenomenon of the medicalization of aesthetics in the United States and globally, see Ashley L. Merianos, Rebecca A. Vidourek, and Keith A. King, "Medicalization of Female Beauty: A Content Analysis of Cosmetic Procedures," *Qualitative Report* 18, no 91 (2013): 1–14; Alexander Edmonds, "Can Medicine Be Aesthetic? Disentangling Beauty and Health in Elective Surgeries," *Medical Anthropology Quarterly* 27, no. 2 (2013): 233–252; and Kaw, "Medicalization of Racial Features," 74–89. Labiaplasty—a procedure wherein the labia minora or the labia majora (the folds of skin surrounding a woman's vulva) are surgically cut and altered in the name of symmetry and beautification—is but one increasingly popular surgical manifestation of the medicalization of aesthetics in the cosmetic surgery industry, both in the United States, and globally. In the United States, for instance, labiaplasty increased 49% in 2014 alone. I return to the matter of labiaplasty in the conclusion of this book.

28 By in large, cosmetic procedures in the United States are considered "elective," and, therefore, they are not covered by medical insurance. There are a few exceptions—patients in the United States can, depending on their particular type of medical insurance, get coverage for breast reduction surgery, for instance, because of physical discomfort related to large breasts. For the most part, however, because cosmetic procedures are not "medically necessary," patients must pay out of pocket for them, and, therefore, these procedures are particularly profitable for the doctors who perform them. In her book, *Beauty Junkies: Inside Our $15 Billion Obsession with Cosmetic Surgery* (New York: Doubleday, 2006), Alex Kuczynski describes this as the "beauty" of cosmetic procedures for doctors (98). See also Kate Murphy, "Ear Doctors Performing Face-Lifts? It Happens," *New York Times*, January 30, 2012, http://www.nytimes.com; Elizabeth Lazarowitz, "Doctors Branch Out into Lucrative Cosmetic Procedures," *New York Daily News*, July 26, 2008, http://www.nydailynews.com; and Natasha Singer, "Doctors Turning to the Business of Beauty," *New York Times*, November 30, 2006. Further, doctors who perform cosmetic procedures also benefit from our system of de-regulated medicine in the United States in another way. If you are a practitioner of medicine in the United States today who performs procedures that are not beholden to oversight by medical insurance companies (and most cosmetic procedures are

not), you are free to practice these procedures with little to no regulation and accountability. As Kuczynski (*Beauty Junkies*, 98) puts it, "Anyone with a medical degree can hang a shingle on the door that says he or she practices cosmetic surgery." While American insurance companies, and the federal government, fail to regulate the cosmetic surgery industry overall, a few states have, or are working on, legislation that requires more regulation and accountability for medical practitioners of cosmetic procedures (ibid., 99–101). At the same time, however, the administration of less invasive cosmetic procedures by physicians' assistants and nurse injectors—and by aestheticians in beauty spas outside of medical settings and the purview of medical regulation altogether—is exploding.

29 It is ironic that the medicalization of aesthetics brings profit and legitimacy to the practice of cosmetic intervention and, yet, as a general rule, patients' procedures are *not* covered by medical insurance. In fact, it is precisely because patients' procedures are not covered by health insurance that these procedures are so profitable for doctors. The medicalization of aesthetics in popular discourse, in marketing and advertising campaigns for cosmetic procedures, and in the language of the doctors who perform cosmetic procedures, brilliantly transforms cosmetic procedures into serious and *needed* procedures for patients that they must pay for themselves.

30 In her book *Surgery Junkies: Wellness and Pathology in Cosmetic Culture* (Piscataway, NJ: Rutgers University Press, 2007), Victoria Pitts-Taylor illuminates and problematizes the increasing tendency in the United States among practitioners and patients of cosmetic intervention, and in our shared cultural understandings of cosmetic intervention more generally, to frame and understand intervention as indicative of health and wellness, both physically and mentally.

31 Abigail T. Brooks, "Under the Knife and Proud of It: An Analysis of the Normalization of Cosmetic Surgery," in *Culture, Power, and History: Studies in Critical Sociology*, eds. Stephen Pfohl, Aimee Van Wagenen, Patricia Arend, Abigail T. Brooks, and Denise Leckenby (Boston: Brill, 2006), 34–36.

32 Haiken, *Venus Envy.*

33 Alfred Adler (1870–1937) is author of *The Practice and Theory of Individual Psychology* (1927) and *Understanding Human Nature* (1927). Adler is best known as the founder of individual psychology and is sometimes credited as a key influence—along with the likes of Carl Jung and Sigmund Freud—on modern practices of psychology more generally, particularly in the United States and Europe. For more on Adler, and for an informative history of how surgeons in the United States took up Adler's concept of the "inferiority complex" as a lucrative means to promote cosmetic intervention in the 1930s, see chap. 3, "Consumer Culture and the Inferiority Complex," in Haiken, *Venus Envy.*

34 Haiken, *Venus Envy*, 15.

35 These are quotes featured in *People* magazine articles on cosmetic intervention in three different issues, October 28, 2001, February 18, 2002, and January 15, 2001, and drawn from a businessman, country singer Carnie Wilson, and Greta Van

Susteren, host of the Fox nightly news program *On the Record*, respectively, each of whom are describing their reasons for choosing to have cosmetic intervention. Cited in Brooks, "Under the Knife and Proud of It," 39–40.

36 For examples of this Dysport advertisement, see *People*, March 7, 2016, 68–70; and *People*, February 22, 2016, 32.

37 American Advertising Slogan for Botox in Print, Television, and Online Advertisements for Botox—and in marketing posters and pamphlets in doctors' offices—in 2008.

38 American Advertising Slogan for Botox in Print and Online Advertisements—and in marketing posters and pamphlets in doctors' offices—in 2015. See, for example, *People*, March 9, 2015, 121.

39 Brooks, "Under the Knife and Proud of It," 32.

40 Ibid., 46. The trend of celebrating Botox as a miracle technology continues with current advertising slogans like, "This Is Not Photo-Shopped, This Is Botox Cosmetic" and "It's Not Heavy Make Up, It's Not Tricky Lighting, It's Botox Cosmetic" (found in *People*, August 25, 2013, 30).

41 Slogan in Botox advertisements that ran in the United States in 2000—see issues of *People* magazine in 2000.

42 Brooks, "Under the Knife and Proud of It," 33.

43 "Rush Hour: Laser Facials, Light Therapy—And Even Botox—In A Flash. L.A.'s New Speed Spas Are the Latest in In-And-Out Beauty," *Vogue*, July 2014.

44 The "somatic society" is Bryan S. Turner's term. See Bryan S. Turner, *The Body and Society* (London, Thousand Oaks, New Delhi: Sage [1984] 1996), 1.

45 Chris Shilling, *The Body and Social Theory* (London, New Delhi: Sage, [1993] 2013), 2, 4–5, 7.

46 Haiken, *Venus Envy*, 17.

47 Anthony Giddens, *Modernity and Self Identity: Self and Society in the Late Modern Age* (Cambridge: Polity Press, 1991), 5.

48 Blum, *Flesh Wounds*, 49.

49 See Thomas Diprete and Claudia Buchmann, *The Rise of Women: The Growing Gender Gap in Education and What it Means for American Schools* (New York: Russell Sage, 2013).

50 See "Underpaid and Overloaded: Women in Low-Wage Jobs," *National Women's Law Center Report* (July 30, 2014).

51 The United States is one of only three countries—the other two are Papua New Guinea and Oman—that offers no guarantee of paid maternity leave. See "U.S Ranks Last in Government-Supported Time Off for New Parents," *Pew Research Center and OECD* (2014); Brigid Schulte, "The U.S. Ranks Last in Every Measure When It Comes to Family Policy, in 10 Charts," *Washington Post*, June 23, 2014; Margaret Talbot, "America's Family-Leave Disgrace," *New Yorker*, January 22, 2015; and Jessica Valenti, "The U.S. Is Still the Only Developed Country that Doesn't Guarantee Paid Maternity Leave," *Guardian*, December 3, 2014. The United States also stands out with no universal provision of childcare, and lags well behind

many other countries when it comes to providing affordable, quality childcare, as well. See Bernie D. Jones, ed., *Women Who Opt Out: The Debate Over Working Mothers and Work-Family Balance* (New York: New York University Press, 2012); Kathleen Gerson, *The Unfinished Revolution: Coming of Age in a New Era of Gender, Work, and Family* (New York: Oxford University Press, 2011); Jonathan Cohn, "The Hell of American Daycare," *New Republic*, April 15, 2013; and Brad Plumer, "Five Shocking Facts about Child Care in the U.S.," *Washington Post*, April 15, 2013.

52 See Bureau of Labor Statistics, "American Time Use Survey," May 8, 2008, http://www.bls.gov/tus/—specifically, "Married Parents' Use of Time Summary."

53 Long stagnation, and exceedingly low percentages of women in business, particularly in upper-level and top positions, inspired Facebook's Chief Operating Officer Sheryl Sandberg's instant bestseller, *Lean In: Women, Work, and the Will to Lead* (New York: Alfred A. Knopf, 2013).

54 See Women's Media Center, "Divided 2015: The Media Gender Gap," http://www.womensmediacenter.com.

55 See Steven Hill, "Why Does the U.S. Still Have So Few Women in Office?," *Nation*, March 7, 2014.

56 See Office of Violence Against Women, U.S. Department of Justice, www.justice.gov/ovw; Centers for Disease Control and Prevention, Injury Prevention and Control: Division of Violence Prevention, "Sexual Violence: Data Sources," http://www.cdc.gov; National Organization for Women, "Violence Against Women in the United States: Statistics," *NOW.org*, http://now.org; Lisa Schechtman, "Violence Against Women Is a U.S. Problem Too," *Amnesty International Human Rights Blog*, June 11, 2011, http://blog.amnestyusa.org; Shannon Catalano, Erica Smith, Howard Synder, and Michael Rand, "Bureau of Justice Statistics, Selected Findings: Female Victims of Violence," U.S. Department of Justice, Office of Justice Programs (October 23, 2009). For violence against women in the U.S. military specifically, see Patricia Kime, "Incidents of Rape in Military Much Higher than Previously Reported," *Military Times*, December 5, 2014; "Military Sexual Violence: Rape, Sexual Assault, and Sexual Harassment," SWAN: Service Women's Action Network, http://servicewomen.org; and Jenna McLaughlin, "The U.S. Military's Sexual Assault Problem is So Bad the UN is Getting Involved," *Mother Jones*, May 14, 2015, http://www.motherjones.com.

57 Susan Bordo, *Unbearable Weight: Feminism, Western Culture, and the Body* (Berkeley: University of California Press, [1993] 2003).

58 Stacy L. Smith, Marc Choueiti, Elizabeth Scofield, and Katherine Pieper, "Gender Inequality in 500 Popular Films: Examining On Screen Portrayals and Behind the Scenes Employment Patterns in Motion Pictures Released between 2007–2012," Annenberg School for Communication and Journalism, University of Southern California (2013).

59 Gail Dines, *Pornland: How Porn Has Hijacked Our Sexuality* (Boston: Beacon Press, 2011).

60 Ariel Levy, *Female Chauvinist Pigs: Women and the Rise of Raunch Culture* (New York: Free Press, 2005).

61 M. Gigi Durham, *The Lolita Effect: The Media Sexualization of Young Girls and What We Can Do About It* (Woodstock, NY: Overlook Press, 2008).

62 Diane Levin and Jean Kilbourne, *So Sexy So Soon: The New Sexualized Childhood and What Parents Can Do To Protect Their Kids* (New York: Ballentine Books, 2008).

63 Stacy L. Smith and Marc Choueiti, "Gender Disparity On-Screen and Behind the Camera in Family Films," Geena Davis Institute on Gender in Media (2010), http://seejane.org; and Stacy L. Smith, Marc Choueiti, Elizabeth Scofield, and Katherine Pieper, "Gender Stereotypes: An Analysis of Popular Films and TV," Geena Davis Institute on Gender in Media (2008), http://seejane.org.

64 Peggy Orenstein, *Cinderella Ate My Daughter: Dispatches from the Front Lines of the New Girlie-Girl Culture* (New York: HarperCollins, 2011).

65 Stacy L. Smith, Marc Choueiti, and Jessica Stern, "Occupational Aspirations: What are G-Rated Films Teaching Children About the World of Work?," Geena Davis Institute on Gender in Media (2013), http://seejane.org.

66 Stacy L. Smith, Marc Choueiti, Ashley Prescott, and Katherine Pieper, "Gender Roles and Occupations: A Look At Character Attributes and Job-Related Aspirations in Film and Television," Geena Davis Institute on Gender in Media (2012), http://seejane.org; and Smith et al., "Gender Inequality in 500 Popular Films."

67 Jennifer Aniston Interviews Gloria Steinem, *The Makers Conference: The Largest Video Collection of Women's Stories* (February 10, 2014).

68 See Jessica Luther, "Painting Wendy Davis as a Bad Mother is Political Sexism at its Worst," *Guardian*, January 26, 2014; Laura Bassett, "Sexism Against Wendy Davis," *Huffington Post*; and "Sexist Digs Against Wendy Davis Ramp Up After a Big Fundraising Report," *Huffington Post*, January 21, 2014.

69 For more on Hillary Clinton and sexism in the 2008 presidential campaign, see Ellen Goodman, "Hillary's Fine Line," *Boston Globe*, January 11, 2008; and Gloria Steinem, "Women Are Never Front-Runners," *New York Times*, January 8, 2008.

70 For more on Hillary Clinton, Sarah Palin, and gender and sexism in the 2008 election more generally, see Rebecca Traister, *Big Girls Don't Cry: The Election That Changed Everything for American Women* (New York: Free Press, 2011). See also the website of Group UltraViolet (www.weareultraviolet.org) for ongoing documentation of sexist coverage of American women politicians and political candidates, including in the *New York Times* and *Politico*.

71 Susan Sontag, "The Double Standard of Aging," *Saturday Review*, September 23, 1972.

   This essay was later re-published in Marilyn Pearsall, ed., *The Other Within Us: Feminist Explorations of Women and Aging* (Boulder, CO: Westview Press, 1997).

72 See Lynn Luciano, *Looking Good: Male Body Image in Modern America* (New York: Hill and Wang, 2001); Harrison G. Pope, Katharine A. Phillips, and Roberto

Olivardia, *The Rise of the Adonis Complex: The Secret Crisis of Male Body Obsession* (New York: Touchstone, 2000); and Susan Bordo, *The Male Body: A New Look at Men in Public and Private* (New York: Farrar, Straus, and Giroux, 1999).

73 See Jamie Santa Cruz, "Body-Image Pressure Increasingly Affects Boys," *Atlantic*, March 10, 2014; and Dougless Quenqua, "Muscular Body Image Lures Men into Gym, and Obsession," *New York Times*, November 19, 2012.

74 See Alessandra Codinha, "Makeup for Men on the Rise—and No Longer a Taboo," *Daily Beast*, May 14, 2013.

75 See Rebecca Adams, "This Is Why It's More Expensive to be a Woman," *Huffington Post*, September 23, 2013.

76 For an overview of the growing prevalence of the "successful aging" paradigm, both in the United States and globally, see Sarah Lamb, "Permanent Personhood or Meaningful Decline? Towards a Critical Anthropology of Successful Aging," *Journal of Aging Studies* 49 (2014): 41–52.

77 There is growing evidence that middle-aged and older men, particularly gay men, experience concern and anxiety about changes in their appearance due to age. For more on middle-aged and older men's views on and feelings about their aging bodies and middle-aged and older men's bodies in popular culture, see Amy C. Lodge and Debra Umberson, "Age and Embodied Masculinities: Mid-Life Gay and Heterosexual Men Talk About Their Bodies," *Journal of Aging Studies* 27, no. 3 (2013): 225–232; Ellexis Boyle and Sean Brayton, "Aging Masculinities and 'Muscle Work' in Hollywood Action Film: An Analysis of the Expendables," *Men and Masculinities* 15, no. 5 (December 2012): 468–485; and Kathleen Slevin, "'If I Had Lots of Money . . . I'd Have a Body Makeover': Managing the Aging Body," *Social Forces* 88, no. 3 (2010): 1003–1020.

78 Susan Sontag, "The Double Standard of Aging," in *The Other Within Us: Feminist Explorations of Women and Aging*, ed. Marilyn Pearsall (Boulder, CO: Westview Press, 1997), 19–24.

79 Ibid., 23.

80 See Matthew Gray, David de Vaus, Lixia Qu, and David Stanton, "Divorce and Well-Being of Older Australians," *Australian Institute of Family Studies* 46 (April 2010). See also Deborah Carr and Kathrin Boerner, "Dating After Late-Life Spousal Loss: Does It Compromise Relationships with Adult Children?," *Journal of Aging Studies* 27, no. 4 (December 2013).

81 See Winifred Robinson, "Why Is It Such a Struggle for a Single Woman over 45 to Meet a Soulmate?," *Daily Mail*, August, 4, 2011; "The Case for an Older Woman," *OKTrends* February 16, 2010; and Latoya Peterson, "Why No Love for Mrs. Robinson?," *Jezebel* February 18, 2010.

82 See Ros Altman, "A New Vision for Older Workers: Retain, Retrain, Recruit," *Report to Government* (March 11, 2015), https://www.gov.uk; Helen Walmsley-Johnson, "Ageism and Sexism in the Workplace? They're as Ubiquitous as Ever," *Guardian*, March 14, 2014; and Rosalind Chait Barnett, "Ageism and Sexism in the Workplace," *Generations* (Fall 2005).

83 Martha M. Lauzen and David M. Dozier, "Maintaining the Double Standard in Film: Portrayals of Age and Gender in Popular Films," *Sex Roles* 52, no. 7/8 (April 2005).

84 See Chris Wilson, "This Chart Shows Hollywood's Glaring Gender Gap," *Time*, October 6, 2015, http://time.com.

85 See Barbara Herman and Hannah Sender, "Hollywood Couples: Age Difference in Movies, Visualized," *International Business Times*, March 25, 2015; "The Hollywood Gender Age Gap, Part 1: The Band of Brothers," *GraphJoy.com*, August 16, 2015; and Kyle Buchanan, "Leading Men Age, But Their Love Interests Don't," *Vulture*, April 18, 2013.

86 See Rose Weitz, "Changing the Scripts: Midlife Women's Sexuality in Contemporary U.S. Film," *Sexuality and Culture* 14 (2010): 17–32; and Dafna Lemish and Varda Muhlbauer, "Can't Have It All: Representations of Older Women in Popular Culture," *Women and Therapy* 35, no. 3–4 (June 2012): 165–180.

87 See Martha M. Lauzen and David M. Dozier, "Recognition and Respect Revisited: Portrayals of Age and Gender in Prime Time Television," *Mass Communication and Society* 8, no. 3 (2005): 241–256; and Lemish and Muhlbauer, "Can't Have It All."

88 See Beth Montemurro and Jenna Marie Siefken, "Cougars on the Prowl? New Perceptions of Older Women's Sexuality," *Journal of Aging Studies* 28 (2014): 35–43.

89 It should be noted that here, and throughout the book, the ages of all public figures and celebrities are up to date as of this writing—September 15, 2016. The same goes for references to current empirical and statistical data: wherever possible, I draw from the most current data available as of September 15, 2016.

90 Cindi Leive, "Career Advice from Hillary Rodham Clinton: You *Don't* Have to be Perfect, Most Men Never Think Like That," *Glamour*, September 2014.

91 Aliyah Frumin, "The Ageist, Sexist Reaction to 'Grandmother Hillary,'" *MSNBC.com*, April 22, 2014.

92 More examples of the gendered age gap between male actors and their romantic partners include Bradley Cooper (now forty), who was seventeen years older than former girlfriend Suki Waterhouse, and whose current girlfriend of the moment, Irina Shayk, is only twenty-nine. Michael Douglas and Catherine Zeta Jones, Harrison Ford and Calista Flockhart, and Leonardo DiCaprio and his recent girlfriends, offer more evidence of this age and gender gap in heterosexual romantic couplings among celebrities.

93 "Slow Anti-Aging: The New Secret to Looking Your Best," *More* (November 2015): 92–97.

94 Ibid., 94.

95 Nora Ephron, *I Feel Bad About My Neck and Other Thoughts on Being a Woman* (New York: Vintage Books, 2006).

96 Kuczynski, *Beauty Junkies*.

97 See Laura Hurd Clarke, "Anti-Aging Medicine, Wrinkles, and the Moral Imperative to Modify the Aging Face," chap. 4 in *Facing Age: Women Growing Older in Anti-Aging Culture* (Lanham, MD: Rowman and Littlefield, 2011), 69–101.

98 For the purposes of this book, cosmetic anti-aging interventions include surgical procedures (e.g., facelifts, eyelifts, neck lifts, jaw lifts among other surgical
procedures), the non-surgical procedures known as "fillers" or "injectables" (such
as Juvaderm, Botox, and Perlane), and chemical peels, microderm abrasion, and
sclerotherapy.
99 See appendix A for a detailed overview of my sampling strategy and research methods.
100 See appendix B for a complete list of my interview subjects and their biographical descriptors. Throughout the book, interview subject identifiers include name
(pseudonym), age, and occupation only—for all additional biographical information, including whether my interview subjects are single, married, or in a relationship, please see appendix B.
101 See Paige Averett, Intae Yoon, and Carol L. Jenkins, "Older Lesbians: Experiences
of Aging, Discrimination and Resilience," *Journal of Women and Aging* 23, no. 3
(2011): 216–232; Imani Woody, "Aging Out: A Qualitative Exploration of Ageism
and Heterosexism Among Aging African American Lesbians and Gay Men," *Journal of Homosexuality* 61, no. 1 (2014): 145–165; Natalie Jane Sabik, "An Exploration
of Body Image and Psychological Well-Being Among Aging African American
and European American Women," (diss., University of Michigan, 2012); Arline T.
Geronimus, Margaret T. Hicken, Jay A. Pearson, Sarah J. Seashols, Kelly L. Brown,
and Tracey Dawson Cruz, "Do U.S. Black Women Experience Stress-Related
Accelerated Biological Aging? Novel Theory and First Population-Based Test of
Black-White Differences in Telomere Length," *Human Nature* 10 no. 21 (March
2010): 1; S.L. Dibble, M.J. Eliason, and B. Crawford, "Correlates of Well-Being
Among African American Lesbians," *Journal of Homosexuality* 59, no. 6 (2012):
820–838; Krystal Rae Kittle, "The Seasoning of Aging, The Ripening of Culture: A
Study of Heterosexual and Lesbian Women in Their Later Years," (diss., California
State University, Long Beach, 2012).

CHAPTER 1. "I WANTED TO LOOK LIKE ME AGAIN"
1 This is Chris Shilling's (*The Body and Social Theory*, 7) phrase.
2 Blum, *Flesh Wounds*, 49.
3 Ibid., 107.
4 I take this term from Margaret Morganroth Gullette, who writes of this phenomenon in her book *Aged by Culture* (Chicago: University of Chicago Press, 2004).
5 Sandra Lee Bartky, "Unplanned Obsolescence: Some Reflections on Aging," in
Mother Time: Women, Aging, and Ethics, ed. Margaret Urban Walker (Lanham,
MD: Rowman and Littlefield Publishers, 1999), 61–74.
6 Ibid.
7 Gullette, *Aged by Culture*, 130.
8 See Mike Featherstone and Mike Hepworth, "The Mask of Aging and the Life
Course," in *The Body: Social Process and Cultural Theory*, eds. Mike Featherstone,
Mike Hepworth, and Bryan S. Turner (London: Sage, 1991), 371–389; Eileen
Fairhurst, "'Growing Old Gracefully,' as opposed to 'Mutton Dressed as a Lamb,'"

in *The Body in Everyday Life*, eds. Sarah Nettleson and Jonathan Watson (London: Routledge, 1998), 258–275; Peter Oberg, "Life as Narrative: On Biography and Aging," (diss., Uppsala University, 1997); and Sharon Kaufman, *The Ageless Self: Sources of Meaning in Late Life* (Madison: University of Wisconsin Press, 1986).

9 Feminist sociologist Dorothy E. Smith introduces the concept of "doing femininity"—or the daily body work a woman engages in to achieve feminine appearance. *Texts, Facts, and Femininity: Exploring the Relations of the Ruling* (London: Routledge, 1990), 189.

10 Sandra Lee Bartky, "Foucault, Femininity, and the Modernization of Patriarchal Power," in *The Politics of Women's Bodies: Sexuality, Appearance, and Behavior*, ed. Rose Weitz (New York: Oxford University Press, 1998), 27.

11 Blum, *Flesh Wounds*, 183.

12 Ibid., 184.

13 Drawn from interviews with women who have had cosmetic surgery in the United States and Great Britain, Debra Gimlin's *Cosmetic Surgery Narratives* illuminates the phenomenon whereby women draw boundaries between themselves and "surgical others" to attempt to lend legitimacy to their own surgical decisions and procedures (see, in particular, chap. 5, "The Symbolic Boundaries of Surgical Otherness"). My interview subjects certainly employ this normalizing and legitimating tactic of "surgical othering" as they build supportive rationales for their own surgical interventions in and through their critiques of "others" who are having procedures that are "too extreme," whose expectations are "too high," and who are having "too many" interventions."

14 There are troubling contradictions at play here. As discussed in the introduction, journalist Alex Kuczynski cheerfully subscribes to the "maintenance" model of cosmetic intervention—or continued tweaking and interventions over time—and this maintenance model is promoted heavily among practitioners of cosmetic intervention, as well. Yet, if the maintenance model is the healthful model, how can critiques be leveled at so called "surgery junkies" who have "too many" procedures? The women in this chapter critique patients who have low self-esteem and unrealistic expectations—yet they too want to look significantly different—via intervention—than they did before. They too speak about having more confidence, and feeling better about themselves, post-intervention. In her book, *Surgery Junkies: Wellness and Pathology in Cosmetic Culture* (Piscataway, New Jersey: Rutgers University Press, 2007), Pitts-Taylor illuminates these contradictions and the unsettling ethical questions they raise. Patients undergoing cosmetic interventions are increasingly framed as healthy individuals making healthful decisions—but where does that leave individuals who do not have interventions? And where does that leave patients who have had "too many" procedures? Finally, where is the accountability of the cosmetic industry in all of this? As Pitts-Taylor articulates: "When pathologizing comes too easily, we put the burden of the industry's problems disproportionately on the psyches of individuals" (ibid., 126).

15 See Rebecca Wepsic Ancheta, "Saving Face: Women's Experiences with Cosmetic Surgery," (diss., University of California, San Francisco, 2000); Debra Gimlin, *Body Work: Beauty and Self Image in American Culture* (Berkeley: University of California Press, 2002), 107; "Cosmetic Surgery: Beauty as Commodity," *Qualitative Sociology* 23 (2000): 94.

16 Blum, *Flesh Wounds*, 49.

17 Susan Sontag, *On Photography* (New York: Anchor, [1977] 1989), 85, as cited in Blum, *Flesh Wounds*, 201.

18 Ibid., 200.

19 Pitts-Taylor, *Surgery Junkies*, 25.

CHAPTER 2. "I AM WHAT I AM!"

1 Susan Sontag, "The Double Standard of Aging," in *The Other Within Us*, ed. Marilyn Pearsall (Boulder, CO: Westview Press, 1997), 24.

2 Please note that in this chapter, and throughout the book, the phrase "natural agers," and "aging naturally," and similar phrase variations are taken directly from the women I interviewed for this book who refuse cosmetic anti-aging procedures, and who describe themselves, and the aging process, as such. That is not to deny the ways in which these same women experience aging as a social and cultural process and experience (these matters are taken up in chapter 4), nor to deny the aesthetic-centered body practices some of these same "naturally aging" women engage in, like wearing makeup.

3 The title of this section is Susan Wendell's phrase. See Wendell, "Old Women Out of Control: Some Thoughts on Aging, Ethics, and Psychosomatic Medicine," in *Mother Time: Women, Aging, and Ethics*, ed. Margaret Urban Walker (Lanham, MD: Rowman and Littlefield, 1999), 146. For further discussion of women's feelings of surprise, alienation, and disconnection from their aging bodies, see Karen Ballard, Mary Ann Elston, and Jonathan Gabe, "Beyond the Mask: Women's Experiences of Public and Private Ageing During Midlife and Their Use of Age-Resisting Activities," *Health: An Interdisciplinary Journal for the Social Study of Health, Illness, and Medicine* 9, no. 2 (2005): 169–187. See also Valerie Barnes Lipscomb, "'We Need a Theoretical Base': Cynthia Rich, Women's Studies, and Ageism," *NWSA Journal* 18, no. 1 (2006): 3–12, wherein interviewer Barnes Lipscomb articulates the common sensation among aging women that they "cannot believe that their bodies are so different from how they feel"—the sensation of "distancing from their bodies" and that "their bodies are betraying them" (ibid., 4).

4 See Kathleen Woodward, *Aging and its Discontents: Freud and Other Fictions (Theories of Contemporary Culture)* (1991). Woodward builds from Jacques Lacan's mirror stage of infancy as she articulates what she terms the "mirror stage of old age." Jacques Lacan, *Ecrits*, trans. Bruce Fink (New York: W.W. Norton, 2002). See also "Introduction," Kathleen Woodward, ed., *Figuring Age: Women, Bodies, and Generations* (Bloomington: Indiana University Press, 1999), ix–xxix; Kathleen Woodward, "Against Wisdom: The Social Politics of Anger and Aging," *Journal*

of Aging Studies 17 (2003): 55–67; and Kathleen Woodward, "Performing Age, Performing Gender," *NWSA Journal* 18 (Spring 2006): 162–189.

5 Simon Biggs, "Age, Gender, Narratives and Masquerades," *Journal of Aging Studies* 18 (2004): 57.

6 Wendell, "Old Women Out of Control," 146.

7 Margaret Cruikshank, *Learning to Be Old: Gender, Culture, and Aging* (Lanham, MD: Rowman and Littlefield, 2013, 2009, 2003), 147.

8 Diane, Helen, and Ellen's ability to understand their older, heavier, bodies as attractive, despite the fact that such heaviness contradicts current female beauty-body norm of thinness, resonates with other studies that demonstrate a similar capacity in middle-age and older women. See, for example, Laura C. Hurd, "Older Women's Bodies and the Self: The Construction of Identity in later Life," *Canadian Review of Sociology and Anthropology* 38, no. 4 (2002): 429–442; Laura C. Hurd, "Beauty in Later Life: Older Women's Perceptions of Physical Attractiveness," *Journal of Women and Aging* 12, no. 3–4 (2002): 77–97; and Jillian R. Tunaley, Susan Walsh, and Paula Nicolson, "'I'm Not Bad for My Age': The Meaning of Body Size and Eating in the Lives of Older Women," *Ageing and Society* 19, no. 6 (1999): 741–759.

9 Laura Mulvey, "Visual Pleasure and Narrative Cinema," *Screen* 16, no. 3 (1974): 47.

10 Frida Kerner Furman, "There are No Older Venuses: Older Women's Responses to Their Aging Bodies," in *Mother Time: Women, Aging, and Ethics*, ed. Margaret Urban Walker (Oxford: Rowman and Littlefield, 1999), 17. See also Laura C. Hurd, "Older Women's Body Image and Embodied Experience: An Exploration," *Journal of Women and Aging* 12 (2000): 6, wherein she calls attention to how older women strive to focus less on physical appearance and more "on what a person looks like on the inside."

11 Rich, quoted in Barnes Lipscomb, "'We Need a Theoretical Base,'" 4.

12 Bartky, "Unplanned Obsolescence," 72.

13 Wendell, "Old Women Out of Control," 146.

14 John Berger, *Ways of Seeing* (London: Penguin, 1972), 45, 47. It is important to note, too, that John Berger's conceptualization of the male gaze, and Laura Mulvey's related conceptualization of female hypervisibility and "to-be-looked-at-ness," have been critiqued for being white-centric and for failing to acknowledge the power, pleasure, and agency that women can and do experience in being seen. See, for example, Michelle Meagher, "Against the Invisibility of Old Age: Cindy Sherman, Suzy Lake, and Martha Wilson," *Feminist Studies* 40, no. 1 (2014): 101–143—with special attention to pages 129 to 131.

15 By newly practicing of the art of observation with age, Diane is heeding feminist age studies scholar Martha Holstein's call to practice what bell hooks calls "the oppositional gaze" as a transgressive strategy—a strategy which flips the script and the lens—the woman actively *looks at others* as opposed to being passively *looked at*. See Holstein, "On Being an Aging Woman," in *Age Matters: Realign-*

ing Feminist Thinking, eds. Toni M. Calasanti and Kathleen F. Slevin (New York: Routledge, 2006), 330.

CHAPTER 3. "AGE CHANGES YOU, BUT NOT LIKE SURGERY"

1 Furman, "There are No Older Venuses," 18.
2 Peter Oberg and Lars Tornstam, "Body Images Among Men and Women of Different Ages," *Ageing and Society* 19, no. 5 (1999): 639.
3 Holstein, "On Being an Aging Woman," 320.

CHAPTER 4. "CAN WE JUST STOP THE CLOCK HERE?"

1 Zygmunt Bauman, as cited in Shilling, *The Body and Social Theory*, 11.
2 Holstein, "On Being an Aging Woman," 316.
3 Martha Holstein, *Women in Late Life: Critical Perspectives on Gender and Age* (Lanham, MD: Rowman and Littlefield, 2015), 101.
4 Martha Holstein, "A Feminist Perspective on Anti-Aging Medicine," *Generations* 25, no 4, (2001–2002): 38.
5 Peter Oberg, "Image versus Experience of the Aging Body," in *Aging Bodies: Images and Everyday Experiences*, ed. Christopher A. Faircloth (Walnut Creek, CA: Alta Mira Press, 2003); Carolyn Morell, "Empowerment and Long-Living Women: Return to the Rejected Body," *Journal of Aging Studies* 17 (2003): 69–85; Wendell, "Old Women Out of Control," 133–149; and Susan Wendell, *The Rejected Body: Feminist Philosophical Reflections on Disability* (New York: Routledge, 1996).

CHAPTER 5. "WHY SHOULD I BE THE UGLY ONE?"

1 Holstein, "On Being an Aging Woman," 316; Julia Twigg, "The Body, Gender, and Age: Feminist Insights in Social Gerontology," *Journal of Aging Studies* 18 (2004): 59–73.
2 Gullette, *Aged by Culture*.
3 George Herbert Mead, *Mind, Self, and Society: The Definitive Edition* (Chicago: University of Chicago Press, [1934] 2015), 204.
4 Ibid., 154, 156, 213, 218.
5 Mike Hepworth, cited in Biggs, "Age, Gender, Narratives and Masquerades," 51.
6 Ancheta, "Saving Face," 114, 118.
7 Mead, *Mind, Self, and Society*, 156.

CONCLUSION

1 See Andrea Morabito, "Soap Operas Back Away from the Edge, Thriving Again," *New York Post*, January 27, 2014; and Taffy Brodesser-Akner, "Days of Some Shows' Lives Continue," *New York Times*, February 19, 2012.
2 *Atlanta Plastic* (Lifetime), and *Dr. 90210*, *Bridalplasty*, and *Botched* (all on E!), are current reality shows centered on cosmetic intervention. Other cosmetic

intervention reality shows that ran in the 2000s include *The Swan* and *Extreme Makeover*.

3 Liz McNeil, "Jane Fonda: 'I Didn't Feel That I Was Pretty,'" *People*, April 7, 2015, http://www.people.com.

4 Jane Mulkerrins, "Jane Fonda: Men Want Young Women. For Us, It's about Trying to Stay Young," *Telegraph*, May 22, 2015.

5 Catherine Shoard, "Jane Fonda: Plastic Surgery Bought Me a Decade," *Guardian*, May 21, 2015.

6 Mulkerrins, "Jane Fonda."

7 Marlo Thomas, "How Does a Feminist Validate Plastic Surgery?," *Mondays with Marlo*, February 25, 2013, http://www.huffingtonpost.com.

8 Sali Hughes, "Helen Mirren: Do I Feel Beautiful? I Hate that Word," *Guardian*, September 26, 2015, http://www.theguardian.com.

9 These words are attributed to Mirren in Mark Reynolds and Dominique Hines, "Dame Helen Mirren Ready to Go under the Surgeon's Knife 'Very Soon,'" *Sunday Express*, September 6, 2014, http://www.express.co.uk; and Hannah Betts, "So Helen, What is the Truth about You and Cosmetic Surgery? She Looks Sensational at 70, Here She Reveals Exactly How," *Daily Mail*, May 22, 2016, http://www.dailymail.co.uk. In the *Sunday Express* article, Mirren's words are described as sourced from "an interview," and a slightly longer phrase attributed to Mirren is included: "Very soon, I think. Very, very soon. Watch out!" In the *Daily Mail* article, the shortened phrase, "very, very soon," is provided, and attributed to a 2014 interview with Mirren in the *Times*.

10 These are excerpts from longer quotes attributed to an interview with Mirren in *Women's Own*, and cited in Reynolds and Hines, "Dame Helen Mirren."

11 Betts, "So Helen, What is the Truth?."

12 Betty Friedan, *The Feminine Mystique* (New York and London: W.W. Norton and Company, [1963] 2013).

13 See Shulamith Firestone, *The Dialectic of Sex: The Case for Feminist Revolution* (New York: Farrar, Straus, and Giroux, 1970).

14 See Gullette, *Agewise*; and *Aged by Culture*.

15 Elizabeth Grosz, *Volatile Bodies: Towards a Corporeal Feminism* (Bloomington: Indiana University Press, 1994), 21–22.

16 Adrienne Rich, *Of Women Born: Motherhood as Experience and Institution* (New York and London: W.W. Norton and Company, [1986] 1995), 39.

17 This book—and the voices and experiences of the women that inform it— build from, and are inspired by, a vibrant and expanding pool of feminist age and ageism-centered, writing and scholarship, including, but not limited to, the work of (in alphabetical order): Sandra Bartky, Simone de Beauvoir, Toni Calasanti, Laura Hurd Clarke, Margaret Cruikshank, Betty Friedan, Frida Kurner Furman, Linda Gannon, Gillian Granville, Margaret Morganroth Gullette, Carolyn Heilbrun, Martha Holstein, Barbara McDonald, Carolyn Morell, Ruth E. Ray, Shulamit Reinharz, Cynthia Rich, Kathleen Slevin, Susan Sontag,

Julia Twigg, Margaret Urban Walker, Susan Wendell, Kathleen Woodward, and Sharon Wray.

18 See Victoria Pitts-Taylor, *Surgery Junkies: Wellness and Pathology in Cosmetic Culture* (Piscataway, NJ: Rutgers University Press, 2007).

19 See Levy, *Female Chauvinist Pigs*.

20 In the September 2010 cover story in *Allure*, titled "Kim Kardashian: A Head for Business and a Bod for Sin," Kim Kardashian states, "Arms, bikini, legs, underarms . . . my entire body is hairless." In *Female Chauvinist Pigs*, Levy's conversations with young women across the United States uncovered the common theme of "sexy, but not sexual," and "the appearance of sexiness, but not the existence of sexual pleasure" (30). This theme echoes the earlier findings of qualitative researcher Deborah Tolman whose rigorous in-depth interviews with a diverse sample of adolescent girls revealed patterns of fear, alienation, discomfort, and a lack of recognition and ability to express their own sexual pleasure and desires. See Tolman, *Dilemmas of Desire: Teenage Girls Talk About Sexuality* (Cambridge, MA: Harvard University Press, 2002). Finally, Levy also importantly highlights the troubling contradiction wherein adolescent girls in the United States are "blitzed with cultural pressure to be hot, to seem sexy" and yet "have a very difficult time learning to recognize their own sexual desire, which would seem a critical component of *feeling* sexy" (168), and calls attention to the dissonance and contrast between a lack of access to universal and comprehensive sex education in public schools in the United States today and our hypersexualized culture (167, 198–200).

21 Peggy Orenstein, *Girls and Sex: Navigating the Complicated New Landscape* (New York: HarperCollins, 2016). In *Girls and Sex*, Orenstein also calls attention to the incredibly disturbing and all too frequent reality of college-age women's lack of agency and power—potentially culminating in sexual assault and sexual violence—in the context of sexual relations with men on college campuses. Finally, Orenstein, like Levy, highlights our overwhelming lack of comprehensive sex education in the United States, the rising prevalence of pornography, and the ways in which the intersection of these two phenomena does not bode well for gender-equal, mutually satisfying, sexual relationships between young women and men in America today.

22 Naomi Wolf, *The Beauty Myth: How Images of Beauty Are Used Against Women* (New York: HarperCollins, [1991] 2002).

23 See Susan Douglas, *The Rise of Enlightened Sexism: How Pop Culture Took Us from Girl Power to Girls Gone Wild* (New York: St. Martin's Press, 2010); and Susan Faludi, *Backlash: The Undeclared War Against American Women* (New York: Three Rivers Press, [1991] 2006).

24 Kuczynski, *Beauty Junkies*, 5.

25 Bordo, *Unbearable Weight*, 247.

26 Botox advertising slogans in U.S. print and television in 2004, 2008, and 2015, respectively.

27 Bordo, *Unbearable Weight*, 250.

28 "People Exclusive: How Miley Cyrus is Changing for Liam Hemsworth: 'She is Doing Everything to Make Him Happy,'" *People.com*, March 7, 2016.

29 ASAPS, "Statistics 2014."

30 See Barnaby J. Feder, "Dow Corning In Bankruptcy Over Lawsuits," *New York Times*, May 16, 1995. See also Carol Ciancutti-Leyva's 2007 documentary, *Absolutely Safe*. Today, however, Dow Corning is a thriving chemical company again—its chemical giant status fully restored.

31 See U.S. Food and Drug Administration, "Regulatory History of Breast Implants in the U.S.," September 25, 2013, http://www.fda.gov; and "FDA Approves a New Silicone Implant," June 14, 2013, http://www.fda.gov.

32 "FDA Update on the Safety of Silicone Gel-Filled Breast Implants," Center for Devices and Radiological Health, U.S. Food and Drug Administration (June 2011), 5, 10.

33 Labiaplasty is sometimes included under the umbrella term, vaginal rejuvenation surgery. Vaginal rejuvenation surgery can include labiaplasty and vaginoplasty, wherein the vagina itself is tightened by removing parts of the vaginal lining and tightening the surrounding soft tissue and muscles. Vaginal rejuvenation surgery can also be used interchangeably with vaginoplasty alone.

34 ASAPS, "Statistics 2014," *Statistics, Surveys, and Trends*, March 11, 2015.

35 The Manhattan Center for Vaginal Surgery ("What is Labiaplasty?," http://manhattancenterforvaginalsurgery.com) offers the following explanations for why women choose to have labiaplasty: "Many women are born with large or irregular labia. Others develop this condition after childbirth or with aging. The appearance of the enlarged labia can cause embarrassment with a sexual partner or loss of self-esteem. Some women just want to look 'prettier' like the women they see in magazines or in films."

36 The female college students I teach in my women's studies classes can attest to this trend and many ascribe to it themselves. Some even express incredulousness that having "hair down there" was ever acceptable.

37 In our system of largely unregulated medicine in the United States, there is no centralized information system, nor any centralized database of statistics, that prospective patients can access to learn about the potential risks and side effects of labiaplasty, or vaginoplasty, or any other cosmetic procedures. (For some examples of the risks of cosmetic procedures, including death, in the United States in the recent past, see Kuczynski, "The Fatal Quest for Beauty," chap. 12 in *Beauty Junkies*, 232–245). The National Health Service of the United Kingdom, by contrast, provides easily accessible information about the potential risks of labiaplasty: bleeding, infection, scarring of tissue, pain during sex, and reduced sensitivity, (http://www.nhs.uk), and vaginoplasty: scarring, infection, blood loss, blood clots, vaginal collapse, incorrect vaginal shape, nerve damage, unbalanced lubrication, and bowel puncture, (http://www.healthcentre.org.uk).

38 Liz Canner, "*Orgasm, Inc.*," (discussion, presentation, and screening, Providence College, June 6, 2014).

39 Kathryn Pauly Morgan, "Women and the Knife: Cosmetic Surgery and the Colonization of Women's Bodies," *Hypatia* 6 (1991): 26–53.

40 Judith Newman, "Diane Keaton on Airbrushing, Plastic Surgery, and What Her Daughter Taught Her About Beauty," *Allure*, May 21, 2014, http://www.allure.com.

41 Paul Thompson, "'I Want to Embrace Aging': Why Kim Cattrall, 54, Refuses to Have Plastic Surgery," *Daily Mail*, April 14, 2011, http://www.dailymail.co.uk.

42 Quoted in "Julianna Margulies: Before and After Photos," *Celeb Lens*, September 22, 2014, http://celeblens.com

43 Quoted in Tina Turnbow, "Face Time: Téa Leoni," *New York Times*, November 3, 2011, http://tmagazine.blogs.nytimes.com/.

44 See, among other coverage, Charlotte Nathan, "Will Kate Winslet's Anti-Cosmetic Surgery League Catch On?," *Guardian*, August 23, 2011, http://www.theguardian.com; Jenna Sauers, "Kate Winslet, Rachel Weisz, and Emma Thompson Form Anti-Plastic Surgery Alliance," *Jezebel*, August 17, 2011, http://jezebel.com; Vivian Diller, "The Anti-Cosmetic Surgery League: Does It Have Unexpected Consequences?," *Psychology Today*, November 29, 2011, https://www.psychologytoday.com; Vivian Diller, "Kate Winslet, Emma Thompson, and Rachel Weisz Don't Want Cosmetic Surgery—And They Don't Want You Getting It, Either," *Huffington Post*, January 16, 2012, http://www.huffingtonpost.com.

45 *People*, December 20, 2004.

46 Quoted in Turnbow, "Face Time."

47 Carrie Fisher, @carrieffisher (2:26 AM, December 29, 2015). See also Ben Child, "Carrie Fisher Blasts Star Wars Body Shamers on Twitter," *Guardian*, December 30, 2015.

48 "Women in U.S. Lagging Behind in Human Rights, U.N. Experts Report after 'Myth-Shattering' Visit," *UN News Centre*, December 11, 2015, http://www.un.org; Laura Bassett, "The U.N. Sent 3 Foreign Women to the U.S. to Assess Gender Equality. They Were Horrified," *Huffington Post*, December 15, 2015, www.huffingtonpost.com.

49 "Emma Watson: Gender Equality Is Your Issue Too," *UN Women*, September 20, 2014.

50 See Katie Rogers, "Jennifer Lawrence Speaks Out Against Gender Pay Inequality," *New York Times*, October 13, 2015, http://www.nytimes.com. In her February 2015 Oscar speech (upon receiving the Best Supporting Actress trophy for *Boyhood*), Patricia Arquette called for the need to fight for wage and gender equality for women in the United States today. Unfortunately, in her speech, Arquette also implied the falsehood that gay Americans, and Americans of color, have already achieved equality, ahead of women, in the United States today. Her spotlight on gender inequality is notable. Also notable, however, is that for the second year in a row (in 2015 and now in 2016) not one person of color was nominated for an Oscar in any of the four acting categories. See "Another Year, Another Oscar White Out," *Los Angeles Times*, January 14, 2016. See Emily Yahr, "Patricia Arquette Calls for Wage, Gender Equality in Show-Stealing Oscar Speech," *Washington Post*, February 22, 2015, https://www.washingtonpost.com; Alex Needham and Rory

Carroll, "Patricia Arquette uses Oscars speech to call for equal pay for women," *Guardian*, February 22, 2015, http://www.theguardian.com; Amanda Marcotte, "Patricia Arquette's Feminism: Only for White Women," *Slate*, February 23, 2015, http://www.slate.com.

51 "Julianna Margulies: Before and After Photos," *Celeb Lens*, September 22, 2014, http://celeblens.com.

52 Judith Newman, "Diane Keaton on Airbrushing, Plastic Surgery, and What Her Daughter Taught Her About Beauty," *Allure*, May 21, 2014, http://www.allure.com.

53 See Iris Krasnow, *Sex After . . . Women Share How Intimacy Changes as Life Changes* (New York: Gotham Books, 2014); Susan E. Trompeter, Ricki Bettencourt, and Elizabeth Barrett-Connor, "Sexual Activity and Satisfaction in Healthy Community-Dwelling Older Women," *American Journal of Medicine* 125, no. 1 (January, 2012); Laura M. Carpenter and John DeLamater, eds., *Sex for Life: From Virginity to Viagra: How Sexuality Changes Throughout Our Lives* (New York: New York University Press, 2012); Laura M. Carpenter, "Gendered Sexuality over the Life Course: A Conceptual Framework," *Sociological Perspectives* 53, no. 2 (June, 2010): 155–177; Deirdre Fishel, "Still Doing It: The Intimate Lives of Women Over the Age of 65," (New Day Films); and Deirdre Fishel and Diana Holtzberg, *Still Doing It: The Intimate Lives of Women Over Sixty* (New York: Penguin Group, 2008).

54 Gail Collins, "This Is What 80 Looks Like," *New York Times*, March 22, 2014, http://www.nytimes.com.

55 Rachel Cooke, "Gloria Steinem: 'I Think We Need to Get Much Angrier,'" *Guardian*, November 12, 2011, http://www.theguardian.com.

56 Ben Child, "Julia Roberts: I've Risked My Career by Not Having Cosmetic Surgery," *Guardian*, October 27, 2014, http://www.theguardian.com; Charlotte Alter, "Julia Roberts: In Hollywood Not Getting Plastic Surgery Is a 'Big Risk,'" *Time*, October 29, 2014, http://time.com.

57 See "Julia Roberts, Uncut Interview For 'Secret in Their Eyes,'" *MadeInHollywood.TV*, November 12, 2015, https://www.youtube.com; and "Julia Roberts Gives Advice for a Successful Marriage," Interview with Mario Lopez, *Extra*, November 7, 2015, http://extratv.com.

58 Bartky, "Foucault, Femininity, and Modernization," 35.

59 Margaret Cruikshank, *Learning to Be Old: Gender, Culture, and Aging* (Lanham, MD: Rowman and Littlefield Publishers, [2003] 2009), 147. Cruikshank's phrase and concept of "almost inescapable judgment" was also referenced in chapter 2.

60 I take this phrase the "rejected body" from Morell, "Empowerment and Long-Living Women."

61 Holstein, *Women in Late Life*, 101. Holstein's concept of age-avoidance was also referenced in chapter 4.

62 See Jacob Bernstein, "For Joan River's Doctor, Fame Delivers Its Bill," *New York Times*, November 5, 2014, http://www.nytimes.com; and Jessica Glenza, "Joan Rivers' Daughter 'Outraged' Over Mistakes that Led to Comedian's Death," *Guardian*, November 11, 2014, http://www.theguardian.com.

EPILOGUE
1 Gullette, *Aged by Culture*, 130.
2 Ibid., 124–125, 127.

APPENDIX A
1 William Neuman, *Social Research Methods: Qualitative and Quantitative Approaches* (Needham Heights, MA: Allyn and Bacon, 2000); William A. Gamson, *Talking Politics* (New York: Cambridge University Press, 1992); Lillian Rubin, *Families on the Fault Line: America's Working Class Speaks about Family, the Economy, Race, and Ethnicity* (New York: HarperCollins, 1992).
2 Neuman, *Social Research Methods*; Susan Ostrander, *Women of the Upper Class* (Philadelphia: Temple University Press, 1984).
3 The breakdown of professions among interview subjects who are having and using cosmetic anti-aging surgeries and technologies is as follows: four retired businesswomen; one retired social worker, currently an artist (jewelry maker); one retired airline ticket agent; one retired nurse; one musician; one semi-retired commercial real estate broker; one retired mental health facility director, currently a child care provider; one unemployed worker, one restaurant manager; one radio producer.
4 As I discuss in this book's introduction, cosmetic intervention is becoming an increasingly global, multi-racial, multi-ethnic practice. In many nation states outside of the United States, people of color are the majority consumers of cosmetic intervention. The cosmetic surgery industry is booming in nation states in Latin America, Asia, and in the Middle East, and cosmetic surgery tourism, wherein individuals cross nation states borders to have cosmetic intervention, is on the rise. In the United States in 2015, however, people of color account for only 25% of the total number of recipients of cosmetic procedures, which is, albeit, a 3% increase from 2014. Please see the introduction for a more in-depth discussion of the complexities and intersections of cosmetic intervention, race, and racism in both in the United States, and globally.
5 Kathy Charmaz, "Grounded Theory," in *Rethinking Methods in Psychology*, eds. Jonathan A. Smith, Rom Harre, and Luk van Langenhove (Thousands Oaks, CA: Sage, 1995), 9.
6 Ibid., 6–7.
7 Glaser and Strauss, *The Discovery of Grounded Theory* (Chicago: Aldine, 1967), as cited in Charmaz, "Grounded Theory," 6, 8.
8 Charmaz, "Grounded Theory," 8 (emphasis in the original).
9 Ibid., 8–9. Here Charmaz uses Clifford Geertz's (1973) term, "thick description," as well.
10 David Karp, *Speaking of Sadness: Depression, Disconnection, and the Meanings of Illness* (New York: Oxford University Press, 1996), 11 (emphasis in the original).
11 Kathryn Anderson and Dana C. Jack, "Learning to Listen: Interview Techniques and Analyses," in *Women's Words: The Feminist Practice of Oral History*, eds. Sherna Berger Gluck and Daphne Patai (New York and London: Routledge,

1991), 1–26; Marjorie DeVault, "Talking and Listening from Women's Stand-point: Feminist Strategies for Interviewing and Analysis," *Social Problems* 37, no. 2 (1990): 96–116; Marjorie DeVault and Glenda Gross, "Feminist Interviewing: Experience, Talk, and Knowledge," in *The Handbook of Feminist Research: Theory and Praxis*, ed. Sharlene Nagy Hesse-Biber (Thousand Oaks, CA: Sage, 2007), 173–197. My interviewing style also finds its roots in the feminist epistemological frameworks and the accompanying methodological strategies first developed by feminist researchers in the 1960s and 1970s. As participants in second wave feminism and feminist consciousness-raising groups both inside and outside of academia, feminist researchers began to construct new models of research and knowledge building with the goal of granting authentic expression and representation to women's lives. Women's lives and experiences had remained "muted" (Anderson and Jack, "Learning to Listen," 11), "underground and invisible," and relegated to the "underside" of men's lives (Joyce McCarl Nielsen, *Feminist Research Methods: Exemplary Readings in the Social Sciences*, Boulder: CO: Westview Press, 10). Further, because women, as an oppressed group, had internalized the dominant group's (or men's) conception of social reality, they encountered alienation from their own experiences and lacked the language to fully articulate those experiences. See Dorothy Smith, *The Everyday World as Problematic: A Feminist Sociology* (Northeastern University Press, 1987). New, unique, and innovative research methods, particularly interviewing strategies, were needed such that women's voices and experiences could find expression. Feminist researchers continue to develop new strategies and techniques today, and the field of feminist research methodologies continues to thrive. Feminist methods are used by a wide range of qualitative researchers, regardless of whether they, or their subjects of study, are women or not.

12 DeVault and Gross, "Feminist Interviewing," 182; DeVault, "Talking and Listening from Women's Standpoint," 100.

13 DeVault, "Talking and Listening from Women's Standpoint," 103, 109.

14 Anderson and Jack, "Learning to Listen," 17.

15 DeVault, "Talking and Listening from Women's Standpoint," 96–116.

16 Sharlene Nagy Hesse-Biber and Deborah Piatelli, "Holistic Reflexivity: The Feminist Practice of Reflexivity," in *The Handbook of Feminist Research: Theory and Praxis*, ed. Sharlene Nagy Hesse-Biber (Thousands Oaks, CA: Sage, 2007), 493–514.

17 Kathy Charmaz, "What's Good Writing in Feminist Research? What Can Feminist Researchers Learn about Good Writing?" in *The Handbook of Feminist Research: Theory and Praxis*, ed. Sharlene Nagy Hesse-Biber (Thousand Oaks, CA: Sage, 2007), 447.

18 Dorothy Smith, *The Everyday World as Problematic: A Feminist Sociology* (Boston: Northeastern University Press, 1987); *The Conceptual Practices of Power: A Feminist Sociology of Knowledge* (Boston: Northeastern University Press, 1990); Donna Haraway, *Simians, Cyborgs, and Women* (New York: Routledge, 1991); Alison Jaggar, "Love and Knowledge: Emotion in Feminist Epistemology," in *Feminisms*, eds. Sandra Kemp and Judith Squires (Oxford: Oxford University Press, 1997).

19   See Joyce McCarl Nielsen, *Feminist Research Methods: Exemplary Readings in the Social Sciences* (Boulder, CO: Westview Press, 1990); and Donna Haraway, *Simians, Cyborgs, and Women: The Reinvention of Nature* (New York: Routledge, 1990).

20   Helen E. Longino, "Feminist Epistemology," in *The Blackwell Guide to Epistemology*, eds. John Grecco and Ernest Sosa (Malden, MA: Blackwell Publishing, 1999), 335.

21   Nagy Hesse-Biber and Piatelli, "Holistic Reflexivity," 493–514.

22   Herbert Blumer, *Symbolic Interactionism: Perspective and Method* (Berkeley: University of California Press, [1967] 1986).

23   Charmaz, "Grounded Theory," 6 (italics added).

24   Charmaz, "What's Good Writing in Feminist Research?," 445.

25   Longino, "Feminist Epistemology," 349 (italics in the original).

26   Charmaz, "Grounded Theory," 5.

27   DeVault, "Talking and Listening from Women's Standpoint," 109.

28   Charmaz, "Grounded Theory," 11–21.

29   Ibid., 14. Charmaz describes this stage as "focused coding."

30   Ibid., 16.

31   DeVault, "Talking and Listening from Women's Standpoint," 96–116; Katherine Borland, "'That's Not What I Said': Interpretative Conflict in Oral Narrative Research," in *Women's Words: The Feminist Practice of Oral History*, eds. Sherna Berger Gluck and Daphne Patai (New York and London: Routledge, 1991); Esther Burnett Horne and Sally McBeth, *Essie's Story: The Life and Legacy of a Shoshone Teacher* (Lincoln: University of Nebraska Press, 1998).

32   Judith Preissle, "Feminist Research Ethics," in *The Handbook of Feminist Research: Theory and Praxis*, ed. Sharlene Nagy Hesse-Biber (Thousands Oaks, CA: Sage, 2007), 515–532.

33   Carol Gilligan, *In a Different Voice: Psychological Theory and Women's Development* (1982); and Nell Noddings, as cited in Preissle, "Feminist Research Ethics."

34   Preissle, "Feminist Research Ethics," 525.

35   This interview subject's concerns also demonstrate some of the sticky situations and ethical dilemmas inspired by the snowball sampling technique. In general, and in my view, the snowball technique reduces the range of potentially ethically uncomfortable aspects of data collection—the fact that I was referred to each woman by a friend or acquaintance helped them feel more comfortable with me and made it easier for them to speak freely. It is this same aspect of the snowball technique however—the familiarity and connectedness between interview subjects—that can lead to potential dilemmas and concerns, like the one that this interview subject raises above.

APPENDIX B

1   Please note that here, and in each case hereafter, when an interview subject is described as "married," she is married to a man.

INDEX

Abilify, 5

acceptance of aging, 108, 134–35, 233–35. *See also* natural-aging ethic; refusing cosmetic interventions

acceptance of cosmetic interventions, 3–4, 61–63, 140–43, 153–54, 154–55, 189–93

accessibility of cosmetic interventions, 122–24. *See also* variety of cosmetic intervention options

Adler, Alfred, 9, 247n33

adolescence, 110–12, 116, 259n20

advertising: and American consumerism, 9–10; and beauty culture, 206; celebrities utilized by, 240n1; and changing cultural attitudes, 1; and commercialized medicine, 4–6; and demand for cosmetic interventions, 136–39; and hormone replacement therapy, 245n25; and interview subjects, 28; and "maintenance" marketing strategy, 25–26; and malleability of the body, 13; and medicalization of aging, 6–8, 247n29; and modern gender inequalities, 16–17; and natural-aging ethic, 193; and positive views of cosmetic interventions, 14; and prescription drugs, 242n14, 242n16; and pressures to accept cosmetic interventions, 136–37; and refusal of cosmetic interventions, 96; and social support for cosmetic interventions, 150; and technology of cosmetic interventions, 10–11; and variety of cosmetic interventions, 120–21; and youth-centric culture, 119

advocacy for cosmetic interventions, 162–63, 163–66

aestheticians, 150–51, 195, 246n28

aesthetics of cosmetic interventions, 128

Africa, 2, 187

African American women, 2–3, 15, 239n1, 239n3

"age avoidance," 139, 217

ageism: and celebrity culture, 210–17; and current cosmetic interventions practices, 2; and feminist perspective on cosmetic intervention, 198–99, 258n17; and gendered double standard of aging, 22–23; and identity struggles of aging, 34; and modern gender inequalities, 20; and motivations for cosmetic interventions, 30; and social norms of beauty, 55

"aging well," 20–21. *See also* natural-aging ethic

alienation, 201

Allergan, 208

American culture, 8–10, 12, 14, 19, 134

American Medical Association (AMA), 4

American Society for Aesthetic Plastic Surgery (ASAPS), 1–2, 241n12

Ancheta, Rebecca Wepsic, 66, 140–41

Anderson, Kathryn, 226

anesthesia, 107, 125, 173

Aniston, Jennifer, 18

anonymity for cosmetic interventions, 187

Arquette, Patricia, 214, 261n50

Asia, 2–3, 263n4

Asian American women, 3, 241n10

93–94; and post-intervention identity struggles, 58; and social support for cosmetic interventions, 156
choice, 132–35, 205–7. *See also* autonomy
Cinderella Ate My Daughter (Orenstein), 17–18
Clarke, Laura Hurd, 26
classism, 2, 190–91
Clinton, Hillary, 15, 18, 23, 24
Clooney, George, 22, 24
Close, Glenn, 22–23
clothing, 66–67, 81, 83
collagen injections, 26, 32, 36, 49, 65, 106, 122, 137
Collins, Gail, 215
commercialized medicine, 4–6, 7, 10–11, 14
competition among women, 155, 178–79
consumerism, 1, 8–10, 11–12, 14, 29
contradictions of cosmetic interventions, 57–65
Cooper, Bradley, 252n92
cosmetic culture: and American cultural influences, 8–10; and body image, 11–13; and commercial medicine and medical marketing, 4–6; and double standard of aging, 19–24; and female aging interventions, 24–26; and gender roles, 14–19; and medicalization of aging, 6–8; and normalization of cosmetic intervention, 2–13; and popularization of science and technology, 10–11; and visual technologies, 13
Cosmetic Surgery Narratives (Gimlin), 254n13
Couric, Katie, 24
Cox, Courtney, 23, 210, 211
Craig, Daniel, 24
Crawley, Isobel, 212
Cruikshank, Margaret, 75
Cruise, Tom, 22
cultural standards and influences: and acceptance of cosmetic procedures, 3–4,

61–63, 140–43, 152–55; and adjustment to aging, 72; American culture and aging, 8–10; and anti-aging sentiment, 140; beauty standards and aging, 77–81, 104–6; and children, 168–75; and choice of cosmetic interventions, 44–45; and devaluation of old age, 139; and empowerment role of cosmetic interventions, 201; and feminine beauty standards, 28; and gender roles, 51; and interviewing techniques, 242n13; looks-based culture, 30; and natural-aging ethic, 82, 135; and pressures to accept cosmetic interventions, 133–35; and refusal of cosmetic interventions, 104–6; and youth-centric culture, 119, 130–33
Curtis, Jamie Lee, 212
Cyrus, Miley, 207, 214–15

Damages (television), 22–23
data collection, 225–26, 226–29
Davis, Viola, 22, 211
Davis, Wendy, 18
death, 35, 41
defects and deviations paradigm, 7
DeGeneres, Ellen, 196
democratic aesthetics of the body, 94–95
demographics of study group, 224–25
Dench, Judi, 199
Depp, Johnny, 22, 24
deregulation of media, 17
dermaplaning, 8
dermatologists: and innovation in anti-aging industry, 123; and "maintenance" marketing strategy, 25; and medicalization of aging, 7; and post-intervention identity struggles, 57–58; and promotion of cosmetic interventions, 175; and refusal of cosmetic interventions, 104; and social support for cosmetic interventions, 149, 156, 160–62
devaluation of old age, 139

ABOUT THE AUTHOR

Abigail T. Brooks is Director of the Women's Studies Program and Assistant Professor of Sociology at Providence College.